WRITINGS OF FRANK MARSHALL DAVIS

WRITINGS OF

FRANK MARSHALL DAVIS

A Voice of the Black Press

By Frank Marshall Davis

Edited with an introduction by John Edgar Tidwell

University Press of Mississippi / Jackson

www.upress.state.ms.us

The University Press of Mississippi is a member of the Association
of American University Presses.

Frontis: Frank Marshall Davis, ca. 1940.
Used with permission of Beth Charlton for the Davis Estate.

First edition 2007

∞

Library of Congress Cataloging-in-Publication Data

Davis, Frank Marshall, 1905–
    Writings of Frank Marshall Davis : a voice of the black press / by
Frank Marshall Davis ; edited with an introduction by John Edgar
Tidwell. — 1st ed.
        p. cm.
    A collection of the author's writings on race relations, music,
literature, etc.
    Includes index.
    ISBN-13: 978-1-57806-921-7 (cloth : alk. paper)
    ISBN-10: 1-57806-921-1 (cloth : alk. paper)
    I. Tidwell, John Edgar. II. Title.
    PS3507.A727Z46   2006
    818'.5209—dc22   2006010994

British Library Cataloging-in-Publication Data available

This book is dedicated to the children of
Frank Marshall and Helen Canfield Davis:

Lynn M. Smith
Mark K. Davis
Beth Charlton
Jeanne M. Hyde
Jill M. Prive

CONTENTS

ACKNOWLEDGMENTS

To keep alive the work and life of Frank Marshall Davis has been no small undertaking. But thanks to a great many friends, family members, scholars, libraries, and more, we now have the opportunity to explore yet another significant dimension of Davis. This cooperative effort has contributed mightily to the recovery and restoration of Davis to his rightful place in the African American and even the American canons of art and culture. For permission to publish the articles in this collection, selected from Davis's nearly forty years old career as writer, I am grateful to Davis's literary executor Beth Charlton and the Chicago Historical Society.

The thematic focus of this text on Davis's subversive vision self-consciously calls attention to his social activism and the news sources through which he expressed it. For their assistance, provided in numerous ways, I wish to thank Teresa Bill and the Center for Labor Education and Research (CLEAR) at the University of Hawaii, West Oahu; Eugene Dennis Vrana of International Longshore and Warehouse Union in San Francisco; Mel Chang, Communications Director of ILWU 142 in Hawaii; Shannon Sheppard of Holt Labor Library in San Francisco; and Alquon McElrath, who graciously consented to being interviewed about the early days of the *Honolulu Record*.

Collegial support, a necessity in any scholarly undertaking, means offering words of advice, encouragement, time, and other kinds of assistance. I am sorry I cannot mention everyone by name, but I do want to thank especially at the University of Kansas, the English Department, Barbara L. Watkins, Deborah Dandridge, Dorthy Pennington, and Victor Bailey of the Hall Center for the Humanities; Linda Evans and the late Archie Motley of the Chicago Historical Society; Harry Jackson of the *St. Louis Post-Dispatch*; William L. Andrews from the University of North Carolina at Chapel Hill;

Pat Patton of the Morse Department of Special Collections at Kansas State University; Ron Welburn of the University of Massachusetts; the Center for the Study of History and Memory at Indiana University; and Carol Oukrup of Kansas State University.

Funding for this project came from a number of sources: NEH Summer Stipend, NEH Travel to Collections Grant, Kansas University's General Research Funds, and the Office of the Chancellor at Kansas University.

I am greatly indebted to the Word Processing Center at the University of Kansas. Without Paula Courtney, Pam LeRow, the late Lynn Porter, and Gwen Claassen, the task of preparing the manuscript for publication would have been Herculean. Part of this preparation owes to a stellar group of student assistants, some of whom are now scholars in their own right. Thank you Cara Van Nice, Rachel Bateman, Nathan Poell, Liz Montag, Vibha Shetiya, Zeta C. Hall, and Carmiele Wilkerson. Collectively, your excellent work made possible a great collaboration with the University Press of Mississippi, under the expert direction of Seetha Srinivasan and her capable staff.

Finally, Beth Charlton, Frank Davis's daughter, deserves more appreciation than can be expressed in these few lines. She selflessly participated in the process by photocopying hard to access materials. Her greatest act of generosity, again, was the permission she gave to reprint her father's writings. Thank you, Beth. My mother, Mrs. Verlean Tidwell, has also been generous, in that she kept her son and this project in her prayers. Words are simply inadequate when it comes to thanking her. Dr. Carmaletta M. Williams has been another who was very generous with her time and talent. Please know that gratitude expressed from the heart is the sincerest, most sublime feeling of appreciation. It is from the heart I speak.

THE SUBVERSIVE VISION OF FRANK MARSHALL DAVIS

An Introduction

The black press redefined class, restaged race and nationhood, and reset the terms of public conversation. Moving past a narrow definition of the press also opens a trove of materials and challenges traditional scholarly methods. And we gain a fuller understanding of not just African American culture but also the varied cultural battles fought throughout our country's history.

—**TODD VOGEL,** *The Black Press*

By the middle of the twentieth century, the pressure to force America to fulfill its constitutional promise of equal rights for all its citizens intensified dramatically. Determined members of racial and ethnic minorities became even more vociferous in decrying the Supreme Court's 1896 decision that rendered the concept of "separate but equal" the law of the land. As a result, the threat of nuclear warfare and the McCarthy paranoia over Communist incursion slowly gave way to a stark reality: America was on the verge of a very different social and political interracial dynamic. Before television nightly brought the struggle for civil rights into the homes of Americans, the black press was the second highest venue—next to the black church—for disseminating the narrative of this struggle about people of color. Among its several functions, the press made determinations about black literary, cultural, racial, and labor matters. In so doing, it attempted to unify the masses of its readers, in preparation for collective action. At the vortex of this rapidly changing world was Frank Marshall Davis, a print journalist whose reportage helped to reframe political and cultural issues into an analytical critique for black social and political change. An analysis of his news writing reveals the black press's once powerful capacity to shape a people's vision of their identity, to provide contemporary cultural commentary unrecorded by other sources, and to testify to the richness of African American culture and the efforts of one man to define it.

Frank Marshall Davis (1905–1987) was born on the eve of a new year in Arkansas City, Kansas, a place he described as "a yawn town fifty miles south of Wichita, five miles north of Oklahoma, and east and west of nowhere worth remembering" (*Blues* 3). His mother and father divorced before Frank was a year old. When she remarried, to James Monroe Boganey in 1909, Davis gained the only man in his young life he could call "father." Arkansas City, like nearly all other Kansas towns, was quite comfortable in its racial attitudes. Racial discrimination was so pervasive that it seemed normal. In this social context, Davis came to accept what he later described as a sense of inferiority instilled in him by this peculiar community construct.

A number of social institutions fought against the inferiority forced on Davis. The annual Emancipation Day celebrations, called Juneteenth in other parts of the country, were reminders of the hard-won freedom African Americans snatched from the clutches of slavery. The residual effects of post-Reconstruction life were made tolerable each week by a Methodist and a Baptist church that provided faith, hope, and spiritual sustenance. Though he was "fanatically religious," Davis found refuge in his discovery of the blues when he was eight years old. The blues, he said, "talked my language. The blues were basic, vital black music; the rapport was natural" (*Blues* 27). Later, he would reveal that the blues subtly inculcated in him an ability to confront lived experience, transcend obstacles to his achieving full self-actualization, and culminate in triumph over the barriers to his success.

After graduating from high school in 1923, Davis moved to Wichita, where he worked as a busboy at the prestigious Wichita Club and attended, without much enthusiasm, Friends University. He was more highly motivated to learn when he transferred to Kansas State College (1924–1926). While the city of Manhattan lived out many of the larger, systemic racial issues inherent in the state, Davis found a haven in Kansas State and embarked upon an experiential journey that inspired him to develop a transformative vision.

The school of journalism fostered in him a confidence and self-assurance that he felt was a shield against the discriminatory racial practices of the town. Selecting industrial journalism as his major required him to make some important decisions. The course of study he undertook was actually designed to educate future news people into one of two careers: either writing occasionally for newspapers and other periodicals of special interests or writing for farm journals, newspapers, and other publications that focused on agricultural and industrial subjects. The rather limited vocational choices of this curriculum hardly portended the journalist who would later demand the cessation of all racial inequity and discrimination. To Davis's credit, he adapted the extant theoretical underpinnings of this very practical course of study into a journalistic practice that became an important weapon in his arsenal in the war against racism and fascism and a vehicle for promoting black cultural matters. In addition to Davis developing a major in journalism, the freedom he enjoyed in a composition class led to his discovery of another expressive mode: the art of poetry. This venue, as he said later, gave him a subjective alternative to the objective expression demanded of the news writer.

With all the confidence of a thoroughly experienced newsman, Davis departed Kansas State in the middle of his junior year, December 1926. At age twenty-one years, he decided that the academic preparation he had received thus far was sufficient to ensure a successful career. Mindful of the fact that white daily newspapers had no positions for African Americans and that no successful black dailies existed, he decided his academic preparation would more than qualify him for a position on a black weekly newspaper. Encouraged by his aunt and uncle, he moved to Chicago in January 1927, an arrival, incidentally, that fortuitously coincided with Richard Wright's—a writer with whom he formed a cordial relationship that eventually deteriorated into contentiousness.

The two years Davis spent in Chicago hardly fulfilled the dream he had for success. He managed to find hack work writing popular fiction, first at *National Magazine* and then at the *Chicago Evening Bulletin*. The *Chicago Whip* offered little more economic security. His greatest achievement was as a reporter, editor, editorial writer, and regular columnist for the *Gary American* in 1928. An expose he wrote on graft in East Chicago's city government had a deleterious effect. The FBI interviewed Davis and wanted him to present his findings in testimony before a grand jury. The mob, deeply enmeshed in the illegal transactions, strongly suggested the consequences of appearing before the court when it sent him a bullet in an unmarked envelop. Sensing that neither the FBI or the mob would respect his constitutional right to freedom of the press, he sneaked out of Gary and returned to Kansas State in August 1929.

Kansas State once again became his refuge, this time from legal and physical reprisals. The stay was brief but filled with special treatment because of the practical wisdom he gained as a working journalist and a published poet. From these experiences, Davis developed a self that differed considerably from that of the earlier, naïve student. This more mature Davis, invited to write a column for the *Kansas State Collegian*, drew heavily from his "real world" work to confront issues he was formerly ill-equipped to address. Titled "A Diplomat in Black," Davis's column became his forum to attack racial inequity. True, much of the writing he did for the *Collegian* was concerned with college topics: the plight of first-year students, fashion trends, etc. These topics he wrote with a humorous touch, often satirizing the naiveté of new students and the fickleness of style changes. He even devoted a few of his columns to reprinting some of his poems, including "To You" and "Gary, Indiana." But he reserved his most forceful commentary for the policy that permitted only white athletes to compete in the Big Six conference. On this subject he abandoned lighthearted banter for the bitter, sharper, more pointed humor that matched the gravity of racism. Losing the role of "diplomat," Davis spoke with uncharacteristic candor about the "gentlemen's agreement" that sustained this "whites-only" policy. As he wrote in his November 19, 1929, column: "'Gentleman's agreements are, apparently, a last resort to keep a regular eleven from looking bad because of the ability of darker stars on the opposing teams . . . . and the color superiority myth seems even more far-fetched when you have to legislate to keep it" (2). Emerging from this column was a voice of necessity, one that pointed to the need to change the status quo. There is no evidence to confirm whether his outspoken position initiated a revision of the policy. Still, his unflinching address of an entrenched social policy portended the approach that would characterize his postcollegiate work.

Forced by the deepening Depression to leave college one semester short of graduation, Davis, after a brief sojourn at the *Gary American* in the fall of 1930, headed to the Deep South for the first time in his life. The news syndicate owner W. A. Scott recruited him to Atlanta in January 1931. What awaited Davis was not just his fear prompted by the tales of racial terror he had heard but also an opportunity to overcome them and blossom into a more socially conscious newsman, unafraid to defy injustice. For the first time, he was forced to confront the persistence of unmitigated *overt* racism, something profoundly unlike the *covert* racism that had defined his life in Kansas. His terror was not without foundation. The many terrifying stories of lynching and other horrific events African Americans were subjected to, simply because they were black, seemed to make black life expendable. Once there, he must have undergone a metamorphosis. Writing thirty-five years later, he claimed to have developed a courage and confidence that actually made him more daring than most of the black southerners, whom he called "black defeatists." In *Livin' the Blues*, he writes: "I believed that those of us in a position to be heard and act should do all within our power to smash the rigid color barriers. And I am convinced that the *Atlanta World*, the *Black Dispatch* in Oklahoma City, and the *Informer* in Houston, by intelligently blasting away at racism, at least split much of the kindling which was ignited a quarter of a century later by the Reverend Martin Luther King, Jr., and turned into a roaring fire that burned down legal segregation in Dixie" (*Blues* 189–90). A detailed examination of the merits of this claim is beyond the scope of this present analysis, but there is more than enough evidence to prove that the *World*, under Davis's editorship, was unafraid to address current events.

Davis's self-proclaimed lack of fear accounts for his practice of "swinging at the racists." The *World* often reported the atrocities many black people experienced at the hands of whites. One especially heinous instance was the case of a fourteen-year-old black youth who was caught burglarizing the home of a white couple. In his delinquency, this juvenile did not succeed in stealing anything, nor did he harm the couple. Yet, to make his punishment serve as a deterrent, the courts found the boy guilty and mercilessly electrocuted him. And there were other, equally abominable practices. When white policemen played judge, jury, and executioner, southern white justice routinely exonerated those charged with upholding the law, by rendering verdicts of "justifiable homicide." Davis's response, in the form of editorial comment, was often swift and courageous. He took strong, contentious positions in defense of the Scottsboro Boys, whose crime of raping two white prostitutes proved to be a false accusation. He also responded to the spectacular trial of Angelo Herndon, whose only "crime" was to lead a poor peoples' march on the state capitol. For his deed, the courts sentenced him to death also. Because Davis placed these especially volatile editorials on the front page and signed his name, there was no mistaking the authorship. Even though some threats followed his editorializing, Davis was undeterred by the potential for personal danger. It appears he never held back from "speaking truth to power." Perhaps that's why some of his white colleagues in the press often admired his bravery but also considered him a bit foolhardy.

Davis's bold commentary did not focus solely on crimes committed against or even by African Americans; he also directed his anger at the white press for persistently using negative images in representing black people. The three white daily newspapers had little regard for accuracy or authenticity in the portrayal of black life. Each of them fostered the various stereotypes commonly held by whites. On one occasion, when the white papers belittled blacks in a story by saying the majority of people at an important black gathering were in pain because this was the only time of the year they wore shoes, Davis wrote a front page editorial and rhetorically asked if black readers were pleased with such stories about themselves. Instead of attacking the white news for poorly representing blacks, he turned their negative into the potential for a racial positive. He convinced black readers that they needed a paper that would depict them as the beautiful people they were. The idea of positive racial representations fulfilled a desperate need of black readers. The resulting actions guaranteed success for a daily edition of the *World*. Black readers in considerable numbers cancelled their white newspapers and then subscribed to the new *Daily World*. The economic pinch was consequential and caused the white press to revisit and revise their reportorial practices. In effect, then, Davis redefined the nature of the discussion and helped the black readership understand that it had alternatives.

By Davis's own account, life in Atlanta had become too routine and the pace too slow. In fact, he felt he had capitulated to "the southern rhythm of life." More likely, Davis was starving for a more active and inspiring creative outlet. Chicago fed this appetite. Chicago was in his blood. The lure of live jazz was seductive and beckoned him to return. The radio broadcasts from Chicago merely whetted his appetite for the actual listening experience. Despite his marriage to Thelma Boyd, an African American woman with whom he worked, Davis felt a deeply spiritual kinship with Frances Norton Manning, a white Chicago socialite who inspired much of his poetry. After much vacillation, Davis decided to return to Chicago. Thelma remained in Atlanta before accepting a job in Washington. They made several efforts to reconcile, but the romance that had culminated in marriage slowly dissolved.

Davis would couch the significance of his return to Chicago in terms of an increased pace of life, a more dedicated commitment to writing and publishing his poetry, and an immersion into the cultural life he so desperately missed when he was in Atlanta. But another, arguably more significant, feature of his return was his evolving news writing and its contribution to enlarging the importance of the black press. To be sure, when Davis returned to Chicago in late 1934 and joined the Associated Negro Press (ANP) in 1935, he was more deliberate, more thoughtful this time as he embarked on a journalistic practice that sought to engage or challenge the status quo or to move a people to better understand why they needed to change the world in which they lived.

The function usually attributed to the black press was "to tell the other side of the story," that which the mainstream press either ignored or distorted. As demonstrated in this collection, Davis's news writing was motivated by other, more significant issues that had a transforming value. For this reason, Davis's work neatly fits into the revised perspective of black journalism history as set forth by recent writers like Todd Vogel and others. That is to say, a reconsideration of the black press shows that it has, among many other functions, "redefined class, restaged race and nationhood, and reset the terms of public conversation" (Vogel 1). This history can no longer be viewed simply or narrowly as merely countering the racism emanating from the white press or covering issues the mainstream press refused to discuss. From this revised perspective, analyses of the black press vividly show how it was dominated with critiques of and proposals for changes in American life and culture. Davis's thought and practice must be viewed through this revisionist lens.

In his memoir *Livin' the Blues*, Davis opened with a retrospective view of his life, and, in so doing, set forth a guiding principle of his political vision, an idea that animated much of his news writing. Reflecting on the meaning of his public school education in Arkansas City, Davis wrote that it prepared none of the students, white or black, for "life in a multiracial, democratic nation" (3). Davis, like most African Americans, placed his faith for social change in the promise expressed in our nation's governing documents: the Declaration of Independence and the Constitution. Principle, as the historical record shows, often ran afoul of practice. Jim Crow was granted imprimatur by the 1896 U.S. Supreme Court decision in *Plessy v. Ferguson*. Conceptually, then, "separate but equal" established the foundation of interracial social and legal relations.

Certainly, Davis railed against Jim Crow and called attention to its injustices. He denounced the supposed guarantees of racial equality as hypocritical, even naming hypocrisy "a national trait of American whites" (Blues 56). But in his mature writing, Davis made his vision do more than "curse the darkness."

He made his vision into a beacon, a light shedding understanding and enlightenment on the problems that denied people, regardless of race, national origin, or economic status, their constitutional rights. In this trajectory of his news writing, he sought to redefine the conversation about segregation, either explicitly or implicitly, by posing a number of remedies to this longstanding problem. For one, he urged the abolition of racial boundaries (and ultimately the concept of race itself) and differences imposed by economic class. To form the more perfect Union promised by the nation's governing documents, Davis used his news writing as a bully pulpit to redefine interracial relations by insisting on the value of cultural differences and the pluralistic character of America's body politic.

While it cannot be fully verified, some evidence of an inchoate development of this practice seems to derive from Davis's tenure with *The Whip* (January to September 1928). The *Whip* had a moderate history of political activism, but to determine the extent to which this history shaped Davis's thinking is nearly impossible. Its editors—Joseph Bibb, A. C. McNeal, and William C. Linton—had conducted a series of forums and a Free Thought Society, into which they infused Marxist-Leninist readings. They made their paper into one of the most militant outlets of post–World War I protest. Using the slogans "Don't Buy Where You Can't Work" and "Spend Your Money Where You Can Work," their campaigns inspired successful pickets and boycotts. The *Whip* forums, as Bill Mullen writes, were one of the first in "a series of political developments on the South Side in which Marxian politics infused black-led protest or interracial radicalism" (6). By the time Davis joined the paper in 1928, its political influence had waned and its financial problems had escalated. In his *Livin' the Blues*, Davis was silent about the *Whip*'s possible political influence on him. Given the paper's history, it is hard to imagine that Davis came away unaffected by its radical reputation.

Davis developed his militancy more fully in his Associated Negro Press years, from 1935 to 1949. In this period, Davis became even more determined to eradicate racism. At the same time, his thinking slowly evolved from a focus on race matters to the economic consequences suffered by all Americans, thus developing a class-based ideology. He came to see that the problem was more economic than racial; and eventually, he linked racism with classicism to demonstrate how both effectively functioned as fascism. Rather than simply "swing at the racists," Davis made his argument more compelling by redefining the terms of discussion so that readers of his word might thoughtfully consider the nature of their oppression.

The ANP he joined in 1935 was largely concerned with collecting, editing, and disseminating the news, effectively functioning as a black equivalent of the Associated Press, United Press International, Reuters, and other news gathering agencies. Against the somewhat conservative politics of Claude Barnett, founder and publisher of the ANP, Davis, as executive editor, first nudged and later pushed the ANP into a more politically assertive posture. In the various columns, editorials, and reporting Davis wrote—representatively reprinted in this collection—he tended to make the news suggest a movement toward racial integration. His early ANP writings were guided by the commonly held idea that if integration were to be achieved, it would take place first because of breakthroughs in athletics and the arts.

For instance, his column "The World of Sports" was more deeply ideological than simply reporting the successes of individual black athletes and teams. He carefully reported on interracial competitions because they clearly demonstrated to him African Americans' potential to compete on par with white athletes. In what was probably his most protracted sports story, Davis followed the life and career of heavyweight boxing champion Joe Louis. Over a period of about five years, Davis reported on all of Louis's goings and comings, not just his ring performances but his personal life too. Louis bore the burden of the race for his generation because he came to represent not just another black boxer, but, on the eve of America's entry into world war, the *nation's* premiere boxer. His fights against the German Max Schmeling ceased to be interracial boxing matches. Symbolically, they represented America versus Germany.

Louis, as has been commonly written, was strongly urged to maintain the image of a respectful, law-abiding citizen and to deport himself in a way that the country would approve. This meant not replicating the interracial daring and "bad niggah" image of an earlier heavyweight champion, Jack Johnson. Johnson's willful defiance of "the racial rules" by cavorting across racial lines for dalliance and sexual relations with and even physical abuse of white women so outraged the white American public that Congress passed the Mann Act expressly to provide a means to arrest and imprison him. If

Louis were to be the nation's boxing hero, he had to be the model of clean living and exemplary deportment. Thus Davis often wrote words of marital advice encouraging Louis to treat his wife Marva with the utmost respect publicly and even privately. Projected in Davis's theory of appropriate nuptial behavior was the sense that marital fidelity and felicity, in theory, would meet with America's approval and expectation for its hero. This image of being upstanding and morally upright would counter many of the negative stereotypes of African Americans and supposedly make African Americans as a group more presentable for inclusion in the American mainstream.

Artistic achievement, similarly, as Davis viewed it, would demonstrate the contributions African Americans had made to American cultural development. In making this claim, Davis echoed an earlier statement expressed by James Weldon Johnson, who, writing in his introduction to the *Book of American Negro Poetry* (1922), proclaimed that: "A people may become great through many means, but there is only one measure by which its greatness is recognized and acknowledged. The final measure of the greatness of all peoples is the amount and standard of the literature and art they have produced" (9). Davis's column "Rating the Records," of course, announced the appearance of new artists and their recordings; but it especially praised the new records that were made by racially integrated groups as an indication of Negro contributions to American art and of the progress music had made toward integrating American society. Black music, in other words, became a weapon for racial integration.

"Things Theatrical" was a wide-ranging, "man on the town" column that afforded Davis the opportunity to offer critical commentary on general news related to the world of black theatrical arts. His eclecticism drove him to review the appearance of new theater acts; critique performances of actors, dancers, and singers; comment on the politics of art, such as the effect of integration and segregation on big bands, the racial implications of such films as *The Green Pastures*, and many others; and even mediate a number of clashes, such as Will Marion Cook's with Louis Armstrong about appropriate Negro humor on the radio or the debate about whether swing music was immoral. At times, his commentaries on sports and arts reflect the racial bias each had to confront. More often than that, though, Davis restaged the terms of debate. He asked how black participation had helped to define the essential Americanness of sports and arts.

By this time, Davis had begun participating in a number of "left of center" organizations. At the height of the Second World War, when Italian dictator Benito Mussolini's resignation revived Allied spirits for victory abroad and the Harlem race riot dampened hope for progress at home, Davis wrote for ANP a column titled "Passing Parade," from September 15, 1943, to July 19, 1944. The title was appropriate, signifying both the military practice of inspection as in "passing muster" and the notion of a public procession of ideas. In the brief ten-month life of this column, Davis carefully probed the intersection of race, labor, and U.S. international relations and their meaning for the war. In so doing, Davis's voice boomed with arguably the most vituperative, hypercritical tone to emerge from the traditional black press. He spoke incisively and dramatically on the major issues of America's involvement in the war, bordering on what some might have considered seditious critique. A profitable way of thinking about his writing is as a courageous extension of a concept initiated by the black press: the Double V Campaign.

When the *Pittsburgh Courier* published "Should I Sacrifice to Live 'Half-American'?", a 1942 op-ed letter from one of its readers, and conceived the mantra "Double V Campaign: Victory Abroad and Victory at Home," Davis took this simple slogan intended to raise the political consciousness of its readers and deeply intensified the meaning of its discourse by offering an acute interrogation. Although John Morton Blum's *"V" Was for Victory* (1976) remains the most incisive book-length history of this concept, Davis's interpretation—revealing a "left-of-center," if not leftist, political vision—stands without peer among journalists who used this phrase to urge black people to develop a consensus on the matter.

Written nearly two years before the end of the war, Davis's "Passing Parade" redefined the traditional discourse of black newspapers by probing with greater intensity the nature of America's postwar international relations. Collectively, the articles in this series asked the question: What are the implications of political choices made *during* the war for determining international, domestic, and racial relations *after* the war? In Davis's analysis of postwar political models, America, most likely, would choose between the ones provided by Winston Churchill and by Henry Wallace. Would Winston Churchill's proposal for a continued Great Britain and American alliance guarantee world peace after the war? Or would this Big Two arrangement, which excluded the Soviet Union and China, merely function as a vehicle for preserving the British empire and therefore extend colonialism? As expected, Davis rejected the Big Two option in favor of Henry Wallace's advocacy of a universal brotherhood of nations. The internationalism revealed here set forth inclusiveness as a goal, one that embraced a partnership with China, Russia, and a postcolonial India.

Despite the urgency reflected in this series, Davis came to see the ANP as too restrictive a medium for his rather frank expressions. In his search for a more militant source through which to present his political vision, Davis connected with Ernest DeMaio and William Sennett to found one of the most outspoken labor weekly newspapers of that day—the *Chicago Star*. Launched the week of July 4, 1946, this sixteen-page paper self-consciously wrapped itself in the holiday's symbolic meaning. "It seems to me," he wrote, "the time has come for a new Declaration of Independence, to be implemented at the polls by the plain people such as you and I, which will remove the chains forged about us by the big money boys and their mouthpieces. I'm for it. How about you?"

Davis's call certainly asked rhetorically for public support. As executive editor who oversaw all of the stages required to publish the paper each week, he also used his column "Frank-ly Speaking" as a forum to comment widely on topical issues. In the brief two-year existence of the paper, Davis located his political vision squarely within Progressive thought. The *Star* defined itself also in terms of Progressive politics and became its voice in Illinois when the chapter was formed there in 1947. With 121, 000 registered voters, the new party set out to influence the judicial campaign that year and, more importantly, to prepare for the presidential election of 1948, backing Henry Wallace. Both Davis and the *Star* strongly endorsed his candidacy.

A careful reading of Davis's editorial opinions in the *Star* reveals an important ideological shift. First, his staunchly prolabor exhortations made him a crucial figure in formulating and disseminating the *Star's* editorial philosophies. In expressing these editorial positions, Davis made a personal decision to work "with all kinds of groups." With this newly articulated commitment, Davis signals his migration from a race-based political grounding to a recognition of the importance of social class. He even issued a discursive call for the elimination of traditional biological definitions of race—a proposal he develops more expansively in an introduction to his *47th Street: Poems* (1948).

Davis's affiliation with numerous labor groups made him an FBI "person of interest." Labor unions had come to be regarded as disruptions to the status quo, supposedly inspired by Communism. The FBI and House Un-American Activities Committee began earnestly keeping alleged subversive individuals and organizations under careful scrutiny. Davis, in their view, warranted close surveillance because of his membership, affiliation, or endorsement of a number of groups, including the Dorie Miller Club (CPA [Communist Political Association]), the Carver Second Ward West Communist Political Association, International Workers Order (IWO), and the Abraham Lincoln School. Another reason is that he had begun preaching the virtues of interracial alliances, arrangements that would force a revision of the old "divide and conquer" theory in which laboring whites were often pitted against African Americans, a problem he dramatizes in his poems "Snapshots of the Cotton South," "War Quiz for America," and "Nothing Can Stop the People." Finally, Davis established a connection between racism and fascism, equating white southerners attitudes toward blacks with the Nazi doctrine of Hitler's Aryan nation. It is little wonder that Davis, who became a closet member of the Communist Party, began to feel the pressure from his radical involvements and decided to take an extended vacation to Hawaii.

Besieged on all fronts, Davis, after thirteen years in Chicago, felt the need for a respite, a break from the urgency that characterized his many political activities. The story goes that his new wife, the white socialite Helen Canfield, suggested a long vacation in Hawaii. Paul Robeson, who had just returned from Hawaii on union business, highly recommended the island territory because of its tolerance for racial difference and, indeed, its celebration of a multicultural world. Davis's largest collection, *47th Street: Poems*, appeared in late summer of 1948, and in December, the couple took off for Hawaii.

Upon their arrival, Davis found not only placid, sun-swept beaches but also workers entangled with management in a "no holds barred" fight over fair wages and working conditions. To contest what he considered a denial of civil and political rights, he became affiliated with the recently founded prolabor weekly newspaper the *Honolulu Record*, edited by Koji Ariyoshi. The *Honolulu Record* (1948–1958) grew out of the history of radical newspaper publishing that had been established by such predecessors as *People's World* on the West Coast and *PM* in New York City. *People's World* (1938–1986), according to historian

Paul Richards, "brought together Communists from California, Oregon, and Washington in a united front of sorts with progressive unionists, especially of the longshore and seafaring trades, and with prominent liberal supporters from Los Angeles to Seattle" (Richards 573). On the East Coast, *PM* (1934–1940) drew from the spirit of the New Deal and the Congress of Industrial Organizations a crusading vision for improving "constructively the way men live together" and for attacking "those who push other people around" (Georgakas 607).

The confluence of both papers is readily discernible in the *Record*. Ariyoshi succeeded in creating his own united front. He published endorsements from such individuals and organizations as United Sugar Workers; Jack H. Kawano, president of Longshore & Allied Workers of Hawaii ILWU Local 136; Ernest Arena, president of ILWU Local 150; and T. Oshiro, secretary-treasurer of the Pineapple and Cannery Workers Union, ILWU Local 152. Through its prolabor position, the *Record* was immediately associated with the Communist Party. This perception was made concrete when Ariyoshi and six others were arrested and charged under the Smith Act in 1951 for allegedly advocating the overthrow of the U.S. government "by force and violence." Their conviction was later overturned, but one point became clear: the verdict seemed vindictive and aimed to punish the radical labor movement and others who rejected management in favor of workers.

To enter this fray, Davis reprised his column "Frank-ly Speaking," once again expressing the voice and vision of the workers, the "common people." In *Livin' the Blues*, he pointedly described his editorial philosophy, which connected the hegemony of management, white supremacy, and imperialism: "In my column, I tried to spell out the similarities between local leaders who thought my fight against white supremacy meant I was antiwhite. I opposed any and all white imperialism and backed the nations seeking independence following World War II" (*Blues* 323). For all his prolabor advocacy, his reward was to be branded by zealous management supporters as a staunchly radical Communist. Later, in 1956, he would counter those accusations before the Subcommittee on Internal Security of the U.S. Senate's Judiciary Committee. It was only after many of the labor issues were settled that Davis was able to write on more diverse topics in the *Record*. While "Frank-ly Speaking" insisted on workers' rights, Davis later commented on subjects as varied as the history of blues and jazz to widen the scope of his political and cultural influence. In effect, this history would serve as a complement to the "Democracy: Hawaiian

Style" series that he wrote for the ANP in 1949. Together, these series worked to forge an alliance between the people of color on the islands and on the mainland and whites who endorsed this collective effort to eliminate racism and classicism.

The decision to take an extended vacation thus evolved into a permanent relocation. Davis concluded that leaving Chicago's political vortex did not signal an abrogation of social responsibility. Among other benefits, the move enabled him to see more clearly the pervasiveness of the struggle waged by the disenfranchised for empowerment. His change of venue did little to mitigate his commitment to fighting the cause of the common people. He became so dedicated to improving the lot of the Hawaiians that it would be twenty-five years before he would return to the mainland. Even then, he expressed no desire to remain in that part of the nation that had nurtured him politically. He had become thoroughly acclimated to his new life in Hawaii. Having lived there since December 1948, he remained committed to Hawaii as his site of political transformation until his death in 1987.

As the nation continues its trek into the twenty-first century, it comes heavily beset with the baggage of debates over race, multiculturalism, (de-) merits of racial and cultural diversity, the politics of art, and more. *Writings of Frank Marshall Davis: A Voice of the Black Press* recovers and reprints a broad range of Davis's news writing that shows how he anticipated many of the major social and cultural issues we discuss today. Conceptually, a "recovery effort," it should be said, is not simply rediscovering or resurrecting a previously well-known author or work. As commonly found in literary studies, to "recover" means rewriting what we recover, giving it meanings that are unquestionably contemporary. It also means to give it a new, discursive life in the present, a life it could not have had before (Nelson 11).

Davis's view on the concept of race is case in point. In one of his early poems, he succinctly expresses what would become the predominant theme defining his vision: "Four puppets / one white / one yellow / one red / one black / amuse the gods." The wry perspective expressed here clearly calls the notion of "race" absurd. It also introduces the inconsistency of Davis's views. Instead of a clear, unambiguous position, up until the mid-forties or so, Davis vacillated on the meaning of race as a vehicle for social change. About 1945, he began to address, historically, the purposes to which race had been made to serve. He found much in the misrepresentation of African Americans that needed correcting. One of the largest distortions was the persistence of black racial stereotypes in the movies, magazines, and social and legal documents. Another lingering misconception that required diligent and assertive refutation was that African Americans came to the "new world" as cultural foundlings, with nothing to contribute to this new amalgam called American culture. In the historiography of W. E. B. Du Bois, J. A. Rodgers, Melville J. Herskovits, Charles Wesley, Carter G. Woodson, and others, Davis discovered a wealth of knowledge that set forth compelling facts about the place of African Americans in the nation's and indeed the world's historical narrative. He emerged from studying their work not only with a more confident knowledge of the racial past but also with cogent reasons for reconsidering the usefulness of race as a delimiting concept.

The history of race Davis uncovered is grounded in biological theory. In a rather unprecedented discussion, he waxed easily through names that have long since lost their currency in science to demonstrate how each contributed to the notion of races categorized by physiogamy. By pointing out the inconsistency of skin color and racial classification, he made his argument that, conceptually, a belief in race as a marker of differences among people is sheer folly. If color as a way of differentiating people is cast out, what is left to fulfill this task? Culture, he boldly asserted, is that way. As he wrote: "Although there is not one iota of evidence to substantiate beliefs in race, there are cultural differences between peoples, even those resembling each other physically" (*Black Moods* 101).

Davis's labor activism, his efforts to wipe out white supremacy and fascism, and his covert flirtation with Communism and popular fronts thus caused him to undergo a conversion. He no longer saw the struggle to overcome oppressive ideologies in racial terms. As he summarized in his poem "For All Common People," "Let the common people smash all foes of the common people; / Let the people fade fascism to a sour memory, / Let the people snort goodbye to empire; . . . . Let us build anew as brothers." The most protracted discussion he conducted of the issue is found in his introduction to his *47th Street: Poems*. For it is there he made his best case for a "raceless society." In this world, people would no longer be assigned to a group based on physical characteristics; at best, he argued, in a raceless society they would be separated by economics into different classes. Davis was less clear in distinguishing culture from class. For this reason, he would never achieve the coherence and logical consistency of writers coming well after him. But because he was a journalist-poet and social activist in an earlier time, it would be unfair to hold him to a standard defined by today's perspectives. Rather, he is to be applauded for helping to set in motion the current conversation now taking place.

Contemporary writers addressing the issues that inhere in Davis's conception of "raceless" culture are more careful in distinguishing "race" from "class" from "culture." In a typical debate, such as the one conducted between Amy Guttman and Anthony Appiah in *Color Conscious* (1996), "culture" is problematic since culture generally assumes a body of commonly shared beliefs, values, and symbols, and not all members of a socially constructed group share these features equally (*Color Conscious* 6). In making their cases, both Guttman and Appiah broaden and extend Davis's position on race into a more theoretically challenging commentary. What if the terms of discussion were shifted to physical features? Both Guttman and Appiah push the question well beyond skin color. Both take their lead from Justice Harlan's dissenting vote in the *Plessy v. Ferguson* (1896) decision when he argues that the Constitution is "color-blind." Appiah ultimately concludes that if the promise of individual freedom and equality is to be realized, "we shall have, in the end, to move beyond current racial identities" (5). Guttman, on the other hand, shows the flaws in the claims for "color-blindness" by arguing for a public policy that acknowledges "color-consciousness" (6).

For Guttman and Appiah, the issue of race is rooted in the philosophical discourse of legal and constitutional interpretation, not biological theory. More specifically, the debate is over a public policy concerning the place of race in American law and what that means for the body politic. In some ways, Appiah's argument confirms the position that African Americans such as Justice Clarence Thomas and educator Shelby Steele hold that racial identity should hold no sway in individuals' achieving progress. More starkly, the argument holds that the legacy of slavery as a determining factor in whether African Americans can succeed should be jettisoned because it has become a crutch or an impediment to self- and group actualization. The mention of slavery supposedly evokes the mentality of the victim, who requires perpetual assistance in order to achieve individual or group social and political advance.

On the other hand, Guttman sees some possibilities in reconsidering the significance of Justice Harlan's "color blind" interpretation of the Constitution. Racial identity, she argues, can never be discounted in public policy matters. Race indeed plays a role but should not be the defining factor in such matters. A more fruitful way of making use of race is to acknowledge its importance in making public policy but not to consider it a handicap to individual or group success. Being aware is not the same as being a victim. Knowing the historic importance of race is not synonymous with being paralyzed by that knowledge. While Davis was less philosophically grounded on race, his ideas clearly presage the current conversation.

Given Guttman's position, we must acknowledge the continuing relevance of Davis and the black press in raising questions about the nation, in "forming and reforming ideologies" and "creating and recreating a public sphere." While the number of black newspapers has declined, the ones surviving still perform the important work of engaging their readership with issues that frame a discourse on national issues affecting their lives. Many of these are routinely found in the various editorial, op-ed, and syndicated columns. Buoyed by a range of positions, from "liberal" to "moderate" to "conservative," readers are provided the opportunity to see all sides of contested issues. There is no denying that parts of most black newspapers are given over to societal and other such matters; nevertheless the larger narrative, the one most like Davis's position, continues to be written.

A paradigmatic shift following the *Brown* decision resulted first in a trickle and then a steady stream of black reporters working at white newspapers. This advance developed into a modified form of inclusion. No doubt some experienced the same dilemma Gordon Parks suffered in his early tenure at *Life Magazine* when he was assigned to report on a black news story: "Am I *Life's* photographer and reporter or *Life's* Black photographer and reporter?" (Parks 93). Parks felt as if he were walking a tightrope. He resolved his dilemma by choosing to be true to himself and to maintain his own integrity. He wanted *Life* to trust him to be "objective"; he needed black people to trust him to tell their truths on their own terms. Thus black reporters simply did not assimilate into the majority or capitulate to the majority's vision. As the white press provided opportunities for black reporting, the issues debated among African Americans were disseminated to a broader audience, thus reshaping or at least affording the nation the chance to reform its thinking about people of color and how those issues affected the nation as a whole. Like all reporters, their work was subject to the license taken by editors. It would seem, though, that even a story written without the edge of critique would still create the possibility for conversation about issues. Despite the potential for editorial interference, black reporters continued to expand the discourse; in so doing, they expanded the consciousness of the country.

Although the *Brown* decision promised racial integration and set in motion the migration of some black reporters to the mainstream publishers, black readers still needed the black press arguably for greater honesty and directness in reporting. History also shows that since the *Brown* decision, black representation in the news industry has become more important than ever. The exponential explosion in black media sources confirms the position that ideas expressed by blacks have entered the public sphere in new and different ways. In television, the Black Entertainment Television (BET) has led a slow but growing procession of visual outlets for public debate. The traditional black radio station has been a staple for stimulating ideas and arguments affecting the lives of blacks and all Americans. Add to these the number of black news and public affairs shows on mainstream television and the proliferation of black news people on traditionally mainstream shows, it would appear that the vision Davis represented—although expressed in new and very different ways—is very much alive.

Instead of stasis, which naturally communicates stagnation, atrophy, or worse, the black press found itself in an ever-evolving world, responding to societal and political changes by reporting with certitude what the mainstream press left untold or distorted in the telling. As we look back and reconsider the meaning and trajectory of the black press, though, clearly the image of the press changes in that the functions it served were multidimensional. It has become apparent today that as the black press raised issues, it inserted itself into the public sphere by offering the stuff of community and national debate. One benefit of this practice is that it gave its readers agency, enabling them to redefine their image and establish their own identity as a people. This racial self-consciousness created an empowered vision of who and what they were. At the middle of the twentieth century, Frank Marshall Davis's writing not only placed him within this historical narrative but it also indicated his shaping influence on the discourse on race and culture of his day. It revealed a writer in touch with the most salient issues defining his era and his desire to insert them into the public sphere. His ideas, perspectives, precept, and example—reshaped and reexpressed in new ways—testify to his enduring significance and firmly establish his place as a major voice in the history of the black press.

John Edgar Tidwell
University of Kansas

Works Consulted

Appiah, Anthony and Amy Guttman. *Color Conscious: The Political Morality of Race.* Princeton: Princeton University Press, 1996.

Ariyoshi, Koji. *From Kona to Yenan: The Political Memoir of Koji Ariyoshi.* Eds. Alice M. Beechert and Edward D. Beechert. Honolulu: University of Hawaii Press, 2000.

———. "A Prospectus." *Pacific Record*, 1 July 1948.

Blum, John Morton. *"V" Was for Victory.* New York: Harcourt, Brace, Jovanovich, 1976.

Davis, Frank Marshall. *Black Moods: Collected Poems.* Ed. John Edgar Tidwell. Urbana: University of Illinois Press, 2002.

———. *Livin' the Blues: Memoirs of a Black Journalist and Poet.* Ed. John Edgar Tidwell. Madison: University of Wisconsin Press, 1992.

Eastman, Max. *The Literary Mind: Its Place in the Age of Science.* New York: Charles Scribner's Sons, 1931.

Evans, Linda. "Claude A. Barnett and the Associated Negro Press." *Chicago History: The Magazine of the Chicago Historical Society.* 12.1 (Spring 1983): 44–56.

Georgakas, Dan. "PM." *Encyclopedia of the American Left.* 2nd edition. Eds Mari Jo Buhle, Paul Buhle, et al. New York: Oxford U. Press, 1998.

Johnson, James Weldon, ed. *The Book of American Negro Poetry.* Rev. ed. New York: Harcourt, Brace, & World, 1931.

Morgan, Stacy I. *Rethinking Social Realism: African American Art and Literature, 1930–53.* Athens: University of Georgia Press, 2004.

Mullen, Bill V. *Popular Fronts: Chicago and African-American Cultural Politics, 1935–46.* Urbana: University of Illinois Press.

Parks, Gordon. *To Smile in Autumn.* New York: W. W. Norton and Company, 1979.

Randall, Dudley. "'Mystery Poet': An Interview with Frank Marshall Davis." *Black World* 23.3 (January 1974): 37–48.

Richards, Paul. "People's World." *Encyclopedia of the American Left.* Eds. Mari Jo Buhle, Paul Buhle, et al. New York: Garland Publishers, 1990.

Vogel, Todd. Introduction. *The Black Press: New Literary and Historical Essays.* New Brunswick: Rutgers University Press, 2001.

A NOTE ON THE TEXT

In news writing, articles are generally disparate and not intended to be read as full, expansive expressions, like poems, short stories, novellas, or novels. Thus the principle of selection I used was to locate a number of articles that, when combined, cohered logically and articulated thematically the vision emanating from Davis's work. To that end, I sought entire series or columns of Davis's news writing, instead of organizing the collection using many excellent but fugitive articles. "Passing Parade," "A History of Blues and Jazz," and "Democracy: Hawaiian Style" were his most complete series. Davis's reviews of African American literature at mid-century, while not intended to form a routinely published column, nevertheless expressed a central theme. Of the nearly fifty book reviews he published, I gathered the twenty-six that most clearly coalesced and complemented the vision he expressed in the other sections published here. Each section is prefaced by a headnote placing the articles in context and guiding the reader intertextually to a central theme.

Today's readers may not be familiar with many names and organizations appearing here, even though they were widely known by readers of Davis's day. As a remedy to possible unfamiliarity and as a further complement to the four sections, I placed a glossary of annotated terms at the end of the text. In choosing these names and organizations, I make no claim for comprehensiveness; I representatively selected the ones that are likely to be most unfamiliar to us today and also the ones most crucial to textual understanding.

WRITINGS OF FRANK MARSHALL DAVIS

A HISTORY OF BLUES AND ALL THAT JAZZ

The disparate articles gathered in this section implicitly form a series, one that coalesces around a controlling theme: that the history of blues and jazz is a political and cultural narrative of the black quest for racial equality in the United States and of the role music plays in constructing this history. In the 1930s and 1940s, when the formal criticism of blues and jazz was emerging, Davis used his ANP columns to shape African American cultural taste by rating the new swing or "hot jazz" records as they appeared. By the mid-1950s, black music criticism had become more systematic, when *Down Beat*, *Metronome*, *Jazz Information*, and other publications regularly offered insightful commentary and debate about new releases. Since black readers were not the intended audience for these periodicals, the work of appealing to black readers was left to the black press and reporters. In 1955, Davis's *Honolulu Record* column, "Frank-ly Speaking," recollected music's history; in effect, it served as a meditation on the meaning of black music and the political vortex out of which it was born.

Davis begins by locating the historical antecedents of jazz in African and European sources, thus countering the prevailing ideas that blacks had no cultural past and had made only a negligible contribution to American cultural development. That African Americans had played a minor role in America's achieving cultural uniqueness was a prevalent view that existed well before Thomas Jefferson and other Enlightenment philosophers questioned the capacity of blacks to reason and to engage in intellectual discourse. In place of intellect, they often conceded that blacks had the potential for creativity, as related to song and instrumentation; however, this potential was never viewed as an indication for altering, let alone shaping, the development of American culture. The principal reason, they urged, was that African Americans landed on the shores of the Atlantic bereft of any experiences that might influence this nation culturally. In 1955, as Davis looked back over his long association with black music and the many shapes and directions it took, he implicitly countered such thinking by setting forth a determining relationship between the music and the social conditions that spawned the music.

The strategy Davis employed is not unlike that of many others who adopted an integrationist political perspective. As it relates to jazz, he argued first that this music was unique and then paradoxically, that it owed its origins to a confluence of African, European, and Euro-American art forms. Rhythm and "a complex set of blending counter-rhythms" were Africa's donation to jazz. To this amalgam, Europe, especially France and Spain, contributed classical and popular music. To these were added English religious songs. All of them were blended like a New Orleans gumbo into a music that was "adapted to suit the needs and musical heritages of the Africans."

In Davis's analysis, this creative act could only have taken place in the cosmopolitanism of nineteenth-century New Orleans where slaves, given a measure of freedom on Sundays, infused their socializing with making music. Much of this process took place in Congo Square, at the crossroads of the different musical forms and cultural practices of slaves kidnapped from many different African nations. In this crucible, jazz had its genesis. It reached its "formalization" a little later in the bordellos of Storyville, New Orleans's "red light district." From there, its influence slowly spread up the Mississippi River to the rest of the nation.

Thematically, several articles reprinted here reveal an important part of Davis's jazz aesthetic. That is, social conditions affected and defined this art form. Initially, Davis conceived social conditions simply as an urgency, as a speedy tempo created by living in the city, which obviously was much faster than the pace of rural living. But Davis expanded the idea of social conditions to imply a protest against existing social practices that fractionalized people and fostered racial discrimination. Out of this idea evolves one of his foundational tenets. That is, for jazz to be authentic, it had to reflect the conditions under which black people lived and how the music became a response to their quality of life. White musicians, according to his argument, were hard pressed to create authentic jazz, because they had not lived the racial discrimination and differential treatment of its black creators. In fact, white groups such as the Original Dixieland Jazz Band and later the Paul Whiteman Band compromised and coopted genuine New Orleans jazz by sucking out its social protest and "sweetening" it, thus making jazz even more popular and commercially appealing. Davis would later express the same complaint when the paradigm shifted from "hot jazz" to bop; he reiterated the argument that social conditions were crucial to the inspiration of genuine jazz. Bop, he maintained, was technically sophisticated but bore little relationship to the lives of the people who inspired jazz's creation.

In yet another way, he argued the political significance of jazz and blues. The technical features of these art forms, he posited, established black cultural uniqueness, which, paradoxically, was also American cultural uniqueness. Could the Chinese have created jazz, he rhetorically asked? Clearly they could not, but almost certainly they would have created their own musical response had they suffered the same social conditions experienced by African Americans. Jazz could only have been created by African Americans, as he said, who were "exploited in an industrialized society." Also, "since jazz is a protest music, nowhere else but in America were there the exact social conditions of an emancipated and transplanted race fighting against discrimination in a society becoming speedily industrialized." Part of protest music is its radical and revolutionary character, which contrasts to the formalism found in most classical music. In "Shocking the Formalists," Davis argues five ways in which jazz differs from classical music: melody by wind instruments, tremolo by horns, improvisation, flatted notes and short intervals, and variation of accent. Davis used these features to show that jazz was distinctive, not derivative, and, essentially born out of social protest.

Davis's divining of the political implications of blues and jazz reveals also his commitment to the commonly held idea that provided hope for many African Americans: that racial integration would take place as a result of progress in arts and athletics. As a journalist, he was quick to point out the possibilities inherent in all events, music, or bands. In Benny Goodman, for example, the renowned clarinetist who so greatly popularized swing or "hot jazz" that he was crowned the "King of Swing," Davis found an outstanding example of how interracial nirvana could be achieved. Goodman's hiring of Teddy Wilson as his band's arranger broke new ground racially. Although racially mixed bands were often found in studios, Goodman's was the first public demonstration of goodwill when he hired Wilson to tour with his group. In the era of de jure and de facto segregation, this simple employment gesture challenged the "rules" prohibiting interracial performances. This defiance signaled for Davis that jazz was inherently democratic and the band promoted equality among all its members. Davis was greatly encouraged by this overture and promoted the practice in other ways. In a radio show, in 1945, he commented on and gave priority to records made by racially integrated bands. Also, he taught one of the first history of jazz classes, in the mid-1940s. Playing excerpts of music from different countries, he traced the development of jazz from its roots in Africa to the current rage in "hot jazz" or swing.

In Davis's historical analysis, the relationship between jazz and religion refutes the binary opposition between the sacred and the secular. Jazz, he argues, became intertwined and therefore reexpressed in gospel music, thus connecting two modes of expression. Jazz was not only functional and a part of the lives of everyday people, but it was also used for religious services. For example, in black funerals in New Orleans, dirges were played enroute to the cemetery but jazz inspired the mourners to "second-line" back home.

Other instances, though, would feature jazz in concerts and clubs, where standards such as "When the Saints Go Marching In" and "Just a Closer Walk with Thee" were crowd favorites. Similarly, the more charismatic churches often depended, either in part or wholly, on the piano, drums, trumpet, guitar, coronet, trombone, and violin to raise their emotions to induce "shouting," dancing, and even "speaking in tongues." For Davis, the jazz-inflected gospel music was a reminder of the old-style preachers of the 1920s. Their sermons not only set forth other-worldly themes but also ones that provided spiritual sustenance for daily living.

Many of the blues and jazz singers crossed over from gospel music or vice versa. Blues singer Thomas Dorsey suffered the tragic loss of his wife and son, which caused him to convert to Christianity, where his considerable fame shifted and he became one of the nation's leading gospel singers and composers. And Sister Rosetta Tharpe excelled not only as a singer of gospel but also of the blues. Politically, this crossover meant that both music forms were empowering. They enabled all who listened or sang to confront the problems of their day and feel hopeful of remaining strong in an often unfriendly world.

As the music paradigm shifted from "hot jazz" to bop, Davis argued that the newer form failed to reflect the lives of the people it was intended for. His opposition reprises the complaint made earlier by critic Max Eastman that modernism in poetry had devolved into the "cult of unintelligibility." In this new expressive mode, writers ceased "talking" to readers and began talking to each other. In its most extreme form, writers were no longer talking to each other; they began talking to themselves (Eastman 57–58). Davis described bop in similar terms. Instead of a democratic, inclusive form of music, bop was self-absorbed, exclusive, and egocentric, thus out of step with jazz audiences. It was a brilliant technical display, but its supposed failure to reexpress the emotions and material conditions of everyday black people made the music accessible to the few, not the many. He articulated these views in heated public debates with Dizzy Gillespie and music critic John Hammond. But the music world changed after the end of World War II, with big bands giving way to smaller groups. Davis eventually came to accept the new music, in part, because the proliferation of bop made it the most widely available music, thus supplanting the mode he had championed for nearly fifteen years.

• • •

JAZZ FOR BEGINNERS

FEBRUARY 24, 1955

As many of you undoubtedly know, one of my major interests is jazz. For this reason, I am especial appreciative of the latest in a long line of excellent books by Langston Hughes entitled *The First Book of Jazz*, just published by Franklin Watts, Inc. and selling for $1.95.

Intended as "an introduction to jazz for young enthusiasts," it is better suited for the older child or for even an adult who would like a sort of primer in this kind of music.

Properly enough, this easily read little volume begins with a story about Louis Armstrong, unquestionably the greatest single figure yet produced by jazz. Telling of the little "spasm band" that Satchmo and three other kids formed with homemade instruments at the age of ten (Louis is now fifty-four), Hughes tells how jazz grew up in New Orleans, its first home "with people playing for fun."

The characteristic rhythms of jazz are traced back to Africa where people did almost everything to rhythm, and a complex set of blending counter rhythms at that, created by big and little drums, gourds, bells, etc. This moving rhythm, unduplicated by any other people, came to America with the slaves.

These varying but blending rhythmic patterns, known as polyrhythms, represent one of the few parts of African culture that were not crushed out by the heel of the slaveowner. Main reason was Congo Square in New Orleans, where the slaves were permitted to sing and dance and make their traditional music. Crowds would gather to watch the dancers, and these gatherings continued for a good many years after the end of the Civil War. Thus this phase of African culture survived.

Mr. Hughes points out: "The African drummers in New Orleans did not have any written music. They played from memory or made up rhythms as they went along, since they were playing just for fun. Today the best jazz is often played without music, from a tune remembered, and played as one feels like playing it for fun at that particular moment."

Although the rhythmic base of jazz is African, there are elements of other music. New Orleans knew many kinds of European music, with French and Spanish being predominant. So this music, both classical and popular, went into jazz. There was also church music. And since the Africans were in a new country, experiencing new musical influences, the various kinds and forms of European music were adapted to suit the needs and musical heritages of the Africans.

The spiritual is a good example. Based primarily on English religious songs, they would often keep European melodic forms but would become African musical expression. With the traditional pattern of moving to music, work songs were created. The blues were born out of a need for expression. All these elements together resulted in the development of jazz some sixty or more years ago. As the author points out, "Nobody else ever made jazz before we did. Jazz is American music."

Mr. Hughes also has chapters on ragtime and boogie woogie before describing something of the nature and use of early jazz bands in New Orleans. A special chapter is devoted to Louis Armstrong. There is also discussion of this new music as it hit Chicago, New York and the rest of the world and how it has affected contemporary composers. Space is also devoted to the swing era, bop and to cool.

In addition to special chapters on "Syncopation," "Jazz Instruments" and "Ten Basic Elements of Jazz," the author attempts to answer that oft asked question, "What *Is* Jazz?" He also lists famous musicians on each instrument as well as a variety of records currently available to illustrate source material and historical stages.

As a first book for jazz beginners, this volume is excellent. However, I do wish Langston had pointed out the social conditions which played a major part in the development of this revolutionary new music. I regret also that he did not go into a description of the differences in technique and approach which made jazz such a radical departure from European musical traditions. I think many beginners would like to know not only effect but cause.

There are brilliant drawings by Cliff Roberts. David Martin selected the music examples. If the book is not available locally, then send $1.95 direct to Franklin Watts at 699 Madison Avenue, New York.

• • •

RHYTHM AND BLUES
MAY 25, 1955

Thus far Hawaii has been spared the battle of rhythm and blues (R&B) now raging throughout the Mainland. Quite likely this is because there is very little genuine R&B music heard locally via the air. The lone exception is KANI, the Kaneohe radio station whose ace disc jockey is Pat Patterson.

R&B might be called the popular music of the Negro people. Since there are few Mainland Negroes in Hawaii, the amount of this music broadcast is correspondingly small. At the same time, since Hawaii is part of America and R&B is the current craze in American popular music generally, the local stations do air it—although generally in its watered down, haole form.

The simple fact is that, with a few notable exceptions, the best R&B music is played and sung by Negroes. And this is the basis of much of the warfare now taking place on the Mainland over R&B.

From around 1920 until a few years ago, the disc makers had what they called "race record lists" which consisted of recordings aimed at the Negro market. At that time few haoles were familiar with such platters. Today many are valuable collectors items. These race records were the R&B discs of former years.

Since World War II, the disc jockey has become increasingly important. Fifteen years ago you could have counted Negro dee jays on the fingers of both hands. Currently there may be that many in one major city. Small record companies have sprouted everywhere, many of them owned and operated by Negroes. The result has been plenty of R&B pouring out of loudspeakers. Some waxings became big hits.

The music business is now really big. When the small labels began producing hits that sold, the major record companies were forced to sit up and take notice. The next step was to cash in on this good thing. So we now find many of the biggest names in the singing profession producing R&B sides. The big music publishers, on the other hand, have been irritated because most of the smash R&B hits bore the imprint of small independents. Naturally, they would like to stop anything in their field that they can't control. Hence the campaign against R&B.

For the first time in history, many Negro singers and musicians are now making a decent living. At the same time, big name white singers are copying original R&B records note for note and getting their synthetic performances on the *Hit Parade*.

The R&B craze really started after a Negro singer name Willie Mabon waxed a side on the small Chess label called "I Don't Know." It was such a hit that one of the major companies put one of its top bands on the number. It was an immediate smash with whites who wanted a strong, rocking beat for dancing.

Right away other R&B hits began sweeping the Mainland, only to be gobbled up almost immediately by white performers. Such recent *Hit Parade* tunes as "Sh—Boom," "Oh, What a Dream," "Good Night Sweetheart, Good Night," "Teach Me Tonight," "Ko Ko Me," and a host of others appeared originally by Negro artists before being taken over by white stars.

And when I say "taken over," that's what I mean. Lavern Baker first recorded "Tweedle Dee." Georgia Gibbs put it on the *Hit Parade*, but Miss Baker is suing Miss Gibbs charging the white star with "stealing" her arrangement note for note. Other suits have been threatened against other top white names in the entertainment field.

In most instances, the original R&B performance is superior to the more popular haole version which you generally hear on the radio. Big Joe Turner's "Shake, Rattle and Roll" was considered one of the top R&B platters of 1954, but the waxing you usually heard was that by Bill Haley and His Comets, a haole group. The Georgia Gibbs version of "The Wallflower" has nowhere near the appeal of the original by Etta James. Ruth Brown's "Mambo Baby" was also in a class by itself.

There is, of course, a reason why most whites fail to touch the best work of Negro R&B artists. As it was phrased by one Negro vocalist: "The whites try to sing 'em but there are only two ways to do the blues—you either cry 'em or shout 'em. Most of them can't do either."

White performers who can do justice to R&B tunes are far between. There are Ella Mae Morse, Vicki Young, Tennessee Ernie and one or two more, but the rest are pale imitations of the real thing. For proof, listen to the platters by white artists over most radio stations and compare them with the original versions aired by Pat Patterson over KANI. And I might point out that there is a desire on the part of some people in Hawaii to hear the genuine, or Patterson would not currently be on the air from 6:30 to 9:00 in the morning and from 9:30 to 12:00 at night. I might also add that probably another big reason why you do not hear more authentic R&B over some other stations is station policy which bans the airing of too many records by Negro performers.

As for me, I much prefer the genuine to the imitation.

• • •

BACKGROUND OF R&B

June 2, 1955

Since last week's column on Rhythm and Blues (R&B) several persons have told me they would like to know more about jazz in general. I have also been asked why white vocalists, generally speaking, are not up to the standard set by Negroes on R&B records.

Although I mentioned no names, I understand that certain of the local disc jockeys (among them J. Akuhead Pupule) have expressed irritation on their programs because I pointed out the general pattern of airing imitative haole versions of R&B hits instead of the usually superior Negro originals.

There are at least five basics needed by singers to be good in R&B. They include (1) timing: the ability to place a word or phrase either before, on or after the best for the greatest possible effect; (2) rhythmic imagination: shortening, extending and curving a word or phrase up or down to add excitement, emphasis and variation to the basic beat or pulse; (3) voice quality: the sound of a singer's voice, the warm kind of tone which blends with jazz band instruments and the way in which they are used; (4) emotional experience: whether the words in a vocal are sufficiently close to the singer's own personal experience that he can make them sound valid; and (5) improvisation: the ability to vary the melodic time and still retain the feeling of the original.

Most white singers, no matter how talented, lack one or more of these basics. On the other hand, all five are common to even second rate Negro R&B vocalists. This is undoubtedly due to the difference in cultural background between whites and Negroes in America's dual society.

Jazz was born of the musical experience of the Negro people in America. Into it went the highly complex rhythmic patterns and musical conceptions native to those sections of Africa from which the black man came: the spirituals, blues and secular music developed in America following contact with European music patterns in the New World, and the social and psychological experiences of a minority group struggling for equality. The background is not common to whites, although many have learned its characteristics.

White popular music has been influenced increasingly by ragtime pre-jazz pianos and jazz itself for the past century, but the sounds and rhythms of jazz found in white popular music are watered down in comparison with similar elements found in Negro popular music which is still strongly influenced by the blues. Currently, R&B is a novelty element in white popular music; on the other hand, R&B is Negro popular music. White singers have to learn it whereas it is the stock in trade of Negro vocalists.

However, let no one get the idea that I am an all-out R&B fan. Some performances stink, no matter who does them. I am often annoyed by the Johnny one-notes on tenor sax, the fourth rate boogie piano and the vocalists who can't carry a tune in a five gallon can. As is typical of all popular music, much stuff is put out which really should have been put down.

But why do I say that the best R&B performances today will compare favorably in years to come, with corresponding records made twenty-five or thirty years ago and which are now valuable collectors' items? There is no doubt in my mind that Joe Turner's "Shake, Rattle and Roll" or Big Mama Thornton's "Hound Dog," to name only two, will join the list of jazz classics.

Unfortunately, white America is still not ready to give colored America its due. Negroes had been playing jazz in and around New Orleans since the 1890s but this revolutionary new music was not accepted by America until the Original Dixieland Jazz Band, a white outfit, came out of the South. Yet there were at least a dozen colored bands immeasurably superior to this white group.

Big Negro bands such as those of Duke Ellington, Fletcher Henderson, Bennie Moten, Louis Armstrong, Jimmy Lunceford, Don Redman and a number of others had been swinging merrily for years, but it was not until Benny Goodman based a big white band on Negro style that swing became popular with white America. Although the piano style called boogie woogie had been known since the early 1900s and perhaps its greatest exponent, Pinetop Smith, had died, the general public accepted it only after Bob Crosby included "Yancey Special" and "Honky Tonk Train Blues" in his book.

During the 1940s, there was a new development in jazz known as Bop created by Dizzy Gillespie, Thelonius Monk, Charlie Parker and a number of other Negro musicians. Today bop is dead but white musicians are making money with "cool" and "new sounds" which is, actually, bop with an extra shot of European musical tradition.

It has been the same with R&B. For an R&B number to make the *Hit Parade*, it must be performed by whites even though the white version may be copied note for note and the actual performance inferior to that of the Negro original.

The point I am trying to make is that white America, by and large, will give only partial acceptance to Negro music rendered by its creators. The element of race too often outweighs merit which ought to be the determining factor. White disc jockeys and station owners, when they limit records by Negro artists or play inferior haole versions of R&B hits, are therefore following the pattern, even though it is a shock to many to learn that this policy is one of prejudice.

• • •

MY FINICKY FINNY FRIEND
JUNE 9, 1955

I have been quite amazed at the unusually wide interest shown in my comments on rhythm and blues. And I have also been astounded by the resultant attacks from my finicky finny friend, the morning disc jockey known as Aku.

Battles with mere men I can take. But nowhere along the line have I learned the technique of combat with precious fish who have their own radio programs.

What are the Marquis of Queensbury rules to an encounter of this nature? Are fist and fin rated equal as weapons? If I am finned in the throat, do I have the return privilege of thumbing a gill? Are we both expected to scale the same weight? I await the answer to these and similar puzzling questions with baited breath. Meanwhile, let's listen to the newest recording by Tommy Dorsal—er—Dorsey.

I had no idea that this highly unusual attraction would develop when I made my original comments about local disc jockeys who play watered down haole versions of rhythm and blues numbers instead of the originals by Negro performers. So far as I know this was taken hook, line and sinker only by Aku. I shall not comment that this is a natural ichthyological trait.

I must confess that I have not personally heard any of Aku's comments, so I have had to get my information second hand—and from a lot of second hands at that. I have not heard Aku because at the time of his morning show, I am listening to Pat Patterson's program over KANI.

Let me assure you that this is no reflection against either Aku or his air show. I have never met Aku. For that matter, I have never met Patterson. Aku has a good program for those who prefer commercial music. As for me I like my music hotter.

In all sincerity, I think Aku is quite gifted. He has performed a number of noteworthy services for the people of Hawaii. As an emcee and comedian he ranks with the best. Few can match the apparent spontaneity of his humor.

He is also a master of the difficult art of satire. One of my brightest memories is of an election day broadcast (1952, I think) where he brilliantly satirized a candidate appearing for votes. In fact, last fall before the primaries he had an unusually clever routine involving a mayoralty aspirant.

Aku also gets a dry, down to earth quality in his running comments. The way he uses everyday language shows that he is a gifted actor—for I refuse to believe that the grammatical monstrosities which come over the loudspeaker are his normal speech habits.

As you can see, I have nothing against Aku. Of course I disagree with many of his expressed positions on various matters, but then I don't expect everybody to think alike. Since my heart is filled with Aloha for the residents of Hawaii, both on the land and under the sea, I am at something of a loss to understand why he has reacted as he has.

My original comments were not aimed at any particular disc jockey. Since apparently nobody but Aku has taken up the matter, I am placed in the position of fighting against the conclusion that he considers himself the only real dee jay here.

Speaking of disc jockeys in general, the best I have heard here was Kini Pope when he had his early morning radio show. Kini Pope had a most mature sense of humor plus good taste in jazz and ability to mix jazz with the most alive commercial releases.

When I was listening to Aku, I got the impression that my finicky finny friend does not like jazz. That is, of course, his privilege just as it is mine not to like most commercial music. But we are currently in the midst of a period when one phase of the kind of music I like keeps popping in the middle of the music Aku offers over the air. The position I took two columns ago and which I maintain is that, if a dee jay is going to play R&B, he ought to play the best available.

The big labels have many excellent R&B releases by Negro artists which are available to all dee jays. As for the smaller record producers, if KANI can get some of their platters, why can't KOU?

• • •

WHAT JAZZ IS
AUGUST 11, 1955

After my recent columns on rhythm and blues, it was my intention to steer clear of jazz. But apparently my comments were at least provocative. And I find it easier to go into a more extensive discussion of jazz itself in this space than to orally answer individual questions.

This can also serve as a warning to you who are not interested in the subject to read, no further. But if you would like to know more about jazz, which came into being as the urban folk music of the Negro and has since spread throughout the world, meanwhile undergoing many changes and having lasting impact on the "serious" creations of contemporary composers, then keep going.

Let me point out, first of all, that nobody has yet come up with a definition of jazz that will be accepted by all. Several years ago in Chicago I recall serving with a panel of "experts" at a series of discussions, with records, on jazz. Among those present were such well known authorities as S. I. Hayakawa, George Hoefer, Paul Edward Miller and several others. We were getting along splendidly together until someone in the audience requested a definition of jazz. It was a signal for war. We couldn't agree, and peace returned only when we agree to pass on to something else.

One of the main difficulties lies in the various schools of jazz and their die-hard followers. At one extreme are the purists, known as "moldy figs," who discredit anything not in the basic New Orleans tradition of collective improvisation. At the other end are the modernists of the cool school who consider anything recorded before one o'clock this morning as "old-fashioned" and "dated."

Nevertheless, I have lately evolved a kind of definition which can serve as a basis for judging the two extremes, as well as everything in between. Here it is: Jazz is music based on the blues tonal scale, with a recognizable beat or foundation either real or implied, and with variable rhythmic impulses. It must also have virility and it must swing.

Let me expand upon this. In the blues tonal scale, the third and seventh tones tend to be flattened. The degree varies. These blue notes came into existence outside of Europe. They cannot be reproduced accurately on any European instrument with regular tones, such as the piano. On this instrument the closest approximation is the striking of two keys near the desired tone. The introduction of the blues tonal scale provided a logical basis for the dissonances found in jazz. Without the framework of the blues tonal scale, the new dissonances would have been completely out of place in American music which is basically a mixture of the music of Western Europe.

Now take the matter of beat. Jazz is basically functional music to be used primarily for dancing. This demands a regular number of accents per measure, usually counted off by drums, guitar, bass and piano. This also enables the melody instruments to function with a foundation beneath. When the rhythm instruments for some reasons or other do not play, or do not mark the beat, the listener nevertheless should get a feeling of tempo from the horns, which is implied beat.

A large measure of the excitement in jazz comes from the lavish use of counter rhythms, provided mainly by the horns or melody instruments. Basic New Orleans jazz, like the bulk of African music, is rhythmically highly complex. When the trumpet, clarinet and trombone are improvising collectively over the basic beat, there is a wealth of variably rhythmic impulses. Big band jazz does not permit this variety, but the use of riffs (repeated rhythmic phrases) and counter-rhythmic section scoring, plus the improvisations of the soloists, does produce variable rhythmic impulses. So, for that matter, does the work of the coolest of the cool and experimental schools when it really is jazz.

What I mean by virility is a feeling of aliveness and flowing strength. A sense of virility is essential to jazz. And when I say it must swing, I do not refer to a kind of jazz called swing. I mean that the music must move with the impact of rhythm upon tempo in such fashion as to produce a positive emotional response in the listener. The best jazz also has a feeling of freshness, of being created as it is performed.

That is what I mean by jazz music.

• • •

UNDERSTANDING THE BLUES

AUGUST 18, 1955

Actually the blues are the mother of jazz. To understand jazz, you need to understand the blues.

Nobody knows when the blues began, but they are a folk music developing in the rural South and becoming identifiable as a specific type of American Negro secular music some time after the Civil War and before the 1890s.

Basically, they are personal songs of protest and rebellion, growing out of individual needs. They may have any subject matter ranging through love, politics, current events, race relations and what not. They may poke fun or they may be deadly serious. A true blues is always realistic: it is never maudlin or escapist.

If you think of blues at all, you are likely to think of them as being concerned almost exclusively with sex. That is the result of the Tin Pan Alley influences. After the businessmen who control the music business found in the early 1920s that there was good money in blues and that the public would pay especially for risque material, the blues were diverted from their original channel into primarily sex songs. But it is still possible to find blues about other subjects.

At first the blues were sung without accompaniment, as a spontaneous expression of the way the singer felt about any topic which moved him deeply. Most of the early blues singers couldn't afford instruments anyway. Then gradually they began using whatever was available as accompaniment: banjo, guitar or whatnot. Out of this grew jazz.

Jazz developed because of the structure of the blues. Last week I mentioned the distinctive blues tonal scale in which the third and seventh tones tend to be flattened. This was revolutionary in European music. But in addition to introducing new tones, the blues also provided new structures and techniques.

Most genuine blues consist of twelve bars of music in common time, divided into three equal groups of four bars. The first group of four is on the common chord on the keynote, the second four-bar grouping is on the chord of the sub-dominant and the third on the chord of the dominant seventh.

Each group of four bars has a line of verse. This line of verse rarely fills the entire four bars, often ending on the first beat of the third bar. Usually this same verse is repeated for the second group of four bars. This is done because, at the outset, the blues were completely improvised at the very moment of singing. By using the same words twice, the singer had time to compose on the spur of the moment a third and rhyming verse to fit the concluding group of four bars of music. For example:

I'd rather drink muddy water, sleep in a hollow log
Said I'd drink muddy water, sleep in a hollow log
Before I'll stay in Honolulu, treated like a dirty dog

Since each line of words did not take up the full group of four bars, the accompanying instruments had to fill in the remainder of the four bars as they saw fit. In other words, they were forced to improvise.

Meanwhile Negroes were flocking to New Orleans by the end of the last century. Life was faster and there were more jobs and better times than in the rural areas. By now there were many blues which had taken form and were common property. Not everybody wanted to sing the words; some preferred instead to use the musical instruments for the entire blues instead of merely to fill out a four bar phrase. They tried to make their instruments sound like the human voice, thus creating the kind of intonation associated with hot jazz. And since life in New Orleans moved at a far faster tempo than it did on the plantations and small towns, the music also increased in tempo from slower blues; the improvisation now extended over the entire bars. Thus it was that new music to be known as jazz came into being in the 1890s.

The blues, however, have continued to flourish both vocally and instrumentally. Weed out the phony and the cute, and today you can find numerous authentic examples of blues on every conceivable subject, many rich with highly imaginative folk poetry. Since the blues are basically protest music, they will meet an emotional need so long as there remain conditions which call for protest.

• • •

JAZZ IN NEW ORLEANS
SEPTEMBER 8, 1955

After the columns on other topics, I'll get back to jazz this week. In previous discussions I tried to tell something about what jazz is and to provide a basis for understanding the blues. This time I want to talk about New Orleans jazz, the parent style.

Jazz first took an identity of its own in New Orleans where it was, in every sense of the word, a music of the plain ordinary Negro. This was sometime in the 1890s.

There were many good reasons why jazz was born in New Orleans and no other place. The Louisiana metropolis was a sort of Mecca for Deep South

Negroes who came there from the rural areas in search of better jobs and a little less prejudice. It was also cosmopolitan, being a major port with strong Spanish and French influences.

But most of all, it was the one place in America where African music and dancing was permitted to survive. In all other sections, efforts were made to crush it. In New Orleans there was a place called Congo Square where the slaves were allowed to go and to sing and dance as they had done in Africa. Even after Emancipation, Congo Square maintained its unique distinction and freed men would still come there. Thus they kept alive African musical patterns.

All of these factors together created the conditions out of which jazz came into being. This, plus the fact that New Orleans was a musical city.

The Negroes who flocked to New Orleans from the country brought with them a tradition rich in blues. In the Louisiana city the blues were put to practical use. Men who drove the coal carts, selling this fuel by the bushel basket; peddlers of fish and other items brought little dimestore tin horns, removed the mouthpieces, and learned how to blow blues tunes to attract the customers. It was often possible to identify a peddler by sitting in a room and listening to what blues was being played.

Buddy Bolden is credited with having the first jazz band, somewhere in the 1890s. His was the most prominent of that period, although many existed and others began trying to play like him. Bolden himself was a cornetist, with a tone reputedly so powerful that it could be heard for several miles.

Buddy's band, as well as the others, was not used exclusively for dancing. Music was functional. These jazz bands were used for parades, funerals and advertising in addition to dances. Most Negroes belonged to lodges or burial societies. Funerals were big events, and the procession would be led by a jazz band. Marching to the cemetery, the music would be a slow dirge. But after the grave-side rites, the band would wait until it got a respectful distance from the burial ground and then it would break into a fast stomp, usually playing a number called "Didn't He Ramble," of which a number of good records are currently available.

Sales, grand openings, etc. called for the use of jazz bands. A wagon would be used to haul the musicians, whose playing of beat tunes would attract crowds. So as not to interfere with other musicians when he moved his slide back and forth, the trombonist was seated by himself at the tailgate of the wagon. Since then, the style of alto-horn playing associated with New Orleans jazz has been known as tailgate trombone.

Instrumentation of the typical New Orleans jazz band was clarinet, trombone, one or two cornets, drums and occasionally tuba. The piano was not used, since nobody could march playing a piano. The saxophone, now an integral part of the jazz orchestra, was taboo. As a rule the pianist played alone, usually in saloons or sporting houses.

The dances where these jazz bands worked were patronized primarily by the working class. Jazz itself appealed to and was played by the ordinary Negro. The upper class Negro shunned it like the plague.

Meanwhile, as jazz developed in New Orleans and became part of the pattern for living of the common Negro, whites gradually came under its influence. It is significant that the whites who took to jazz and became most proficient at this revolutionary music in New Orleans were also members of the most exploited and underprivileged white groups there.

Jazz could have been created only by Negroes exploited in an industrialized society. No other group had the background of African rhythmic complexities and music patterns which we find in jazz; nowhere else in the world was there the proportion of interplay between African and the various kinds of European music taking place in an area foreign to both. And since jazz is also protest music, nowhere else but in America were there the exact social conditions of an emancipated and transplanted race fighting against discrimination in a society becoming speedily industrialized.

In my next article, I want to go into what these jazz musicians did that caused jazz to be so revolutionary as well as so bitterly fought by those trained in Western European musical traditions.

• • •

SHOCKING THE FORMALISTS

SEPTEMBER 15, 1955

Formally trained musicians were shocked when they awoke one morning and found jazz in their midst. Here was a music that violated virtually every tradition and precept in Western European music. Jazz was radical, revolutionary and thoroughly democratic. It was as great an upheaval in the music world as was our own Revolutionary War and the founding of American democracy, the French Revolution and the decimation of the nobility or the Russian Revolution and the ending of the reign of the czars.

Had you been trained in a conservatory and then had gone to a dance hall in New Orleans in 1910 and heard Buddy Bolden's band for the first time, these are some of the things that would have shocked you:

1. MELODY BY WIND INSTRUMENTS. Cornet carried the melody with lacy embellishments up high by clarinet and lower voiced fill-in by trombone. In traditional western music, the melody was carried by strings with reeds and brass used only to give texture, depth and color. Most of the early jazz bands used no strings at all.

2. TREMOLO BY HORNS. Traditionally, the tremolo was used only by stringed instruments such as the violin; never by horns. But in jazz, the vibrato is used by all horns. In order to get what is called "hot intonation," jazzmen developed strong vibratos. They were trying to imitate the human voice on their instruments with all its expressiveness.

3. IMPROVISATION. Buddy Bolden used no score so there was no music read by the instrumentalists. They composed collectively on a given and memorized theme as they played. This was contrary to formal musicians who read and rendered each number note for note. For more than a hundred years, improvisation had been a lost art in Western European music.

4. FLATTED NOTES AND SHORT INTERVALS. Formally trained musicians tried to tailor each note to a sound predetermined by the authorities in that field. Sometimes a note would be slightly sharpened to increase its brilliancy. There were no such rigid requirements in jazz: instead the musicians might flatten notes in varying degrees to increase the effect of hotness. Further, there was a limit to the intervals recognized by formal music: the jazzmen violated this completely by introducing intervals of a 32nd, a 64th, etc. and by gliding from one to the other with perceptible break.

5. VARIATION OF ACCENT. Formally trained musicians had to play each note precisely where the composer had placed it. Jazz musicians, on the other hand, put a note where they felt like placing it. If they played a note slightly before it was expected to return to the basic tempo or beat, it was called anticipated accent: if they played it after, it was called retarded accent. Both devices give added excitement and vitality to jazz.

The foregoing is merely a few of the radical departures from Western music found in jazz and help explain why the maestros trained in the conservatories of Paris, Rome and Berlin, as well as their progeny, were shocked at jazz.

One of the main reasons why the first jazz players launched the revolution—unintentional as it might have been—was because they had not been trained to follow European traditions. Coming from the ranks of ordinary working class Negroes, they were self taught. Since nobody had had told them for instance, that it was wrong to produce a tremolo on a wind instrument, they went ahead and did it. They played the way they felt like playing—which meant there were African musical patterns given free rein. These innovations have even come to be accepted by the "serious" contemporary composers.

Traditional music still has no provision for writing down some of the new devices inherent in jazz. Nobody can reduce to paper the anticipated and retarded secrets, the variations in pitch and interval and the differences in intonation and vibrato which are basic parts of jazz.

No written arrangements were used in early jazz which was the reason for its complete democracy. The player was at least as important as the composer. A band of cornet, clarinet, trombone, bass and drums depended for success upon the ability of all the players to create equally well and to be able to understand each other thoroughly.

When you remember that jazz reached the world at large at a time many of the leading composers were trying to break away from the restrictions of traditional music, which they considered decadent, and were experimenting with new scales and tone colors, and these composers found in jazz what they had been hunting, you can see how the entire course of world music has been changed in the past few decades.

• • •

COULD CHINESE HAVE CREATED JAZZ?
OCTOBER 6, 1955

Mind if I return to jazz this week? My last column on this subject September 15 listed some of the more important ways in which jazz musicians broke with tradition and shocked the formalists by such innovations as variation of accent, flatted notes and short intervals, improvisation, tremolo by horns, melody by wind instruments, etc.

Let me remind you again that this radical new approach to music, this revolutionary method of using instruments was created by musicians with little or no formal training. For the most part they could not afford to study at the music schools because they were of the working class of the most exploited and downtrodden group in America, the Negro people.

I cannot help wondering what our music would have become had history been changed with the slave traders bringing in Chinese or East Indians instead of Africans. What would we have had in place of jazz? Would we have had an entirely new music rising from the impact of the music of India or China upon that of Western Europe?

I think so. But I cannot begin to imagine how it might sound.

I think we would have had a music new to both China or India and America but evolving from both cultures because of the necessity for finding a means of social protest.

Let us imagine that several million Chinese had been shipped to America as slaves beginning in 1619. On the plantations, all of their traditional culture other than music was systematically squelched. They were allowed to sing because this was essential in the new religions forced upon them but these songs had to be sung in English and then mainly as part of the ritual in connection with the new religion.

Meanwhile in New Orleans there was one place called Hong Kong Square where the Chinese slaves were allowed to congregate weekly and continue the kind of musical activity in their native tongue which was part of their culture in China.

And then came emancipation, with the Chinese bondsmen given their freedom. All that they had left of their cultural tradition after 250 years of bondage was in the field of music, and this had been somewhat altered by contact with the music of France, England, Germany, Spain, Portugal and the other nations whose people had settled in America.

After Reconstruction during which the Chinese freedmen were instrumental in bringing the South its first democracy, the North made a deal with the South and let Dixie, with all its slave psychology, resume its complete mastery of the Chinese—who by now had varying amounts of white and Indian blood in their group makeup.

The Chinese freedmen, facing extreme prejudice at every turn and denied decent jobs and education in a South becoming more and more industrialized, began turning toward New Orleans where there was a little less prejudice and a little more economic opportunity, and where life moved at a speedier pace than in the rural areas.

In New Orleans there were Chinese who were extremely interested in music. By economic necessity, they were self-taught. But they played the instruments they had come to accept through several generation of slavery: piano, cornet, trombone, clarinet, etc. Culturally, however, because of the existence of Hong Kong Square, their musical conception was Chinese.

And so they began playing, out of a necessity to express themselves. Their music had militancy and protest, because of the constant battle against white supremacy; it was a new folk music with Chinese survivals that was brought into being as a result of bitter experiences as the most exploited group in America. In short, it was a revolutionary fast-paced music the likes of which had never before been heard in the world because never before had there been conditions like these.

Of course there are other elements which would have to do with the music itself created by free Chinese in America as compared with that originating among freed Africans. I refer to rhythm and function of music and dance in Chinese culture compared with that of Africa. But after all this involves the physical structure, not the emotional need to create a new method of musical protest by a people fighting against race discrimination in a land which blandly boasts of equality for all.

To those who are stymied at contemplations of Chinese music in such a context, let me assure you that its tonal scale and structures are no harder or easier than African music for the Western European encountering both for the first time.

The important thing is that if jazz had not been created, some equivalent music would have come into existence under the same socio-economic conditions. Because people of African ancestry were the ones in the situation, we do have jazz. The point is, it could have been another equally revolutionary music had there been Chinese ex-slaves in industrialized American instead of African.

• • •

JAZZ AND RELIGION
NOVEMBER 3, 1955

I, for one, am glad to see that an Episcopal minister, the Reverend Alvin Kershaw of Oxford, Ohio, not only chose jazz for his category on that TV quiz show, *The $64,000 Question*, but realized the place of this music in our society.

Only a few decades ago, "respectable" white people just didn't listen to real jazz. They might bend an ear to the musical meanderings of Paul Whiteman who never could play jazz, or perhaps listen to Gershwin's "Rhapsody in Blue," which was 95 percent foreign to both jazz and the blues, but that was as close as they ever got.

Hidebound critics and musicians, steeped in the traditions and adhering to the standards of Western European music, had little or no patience with African-rooted sounds and techniques which rebelled against everything they had been taught.

But despite all its enemies could do, jazz grew and became not only the music of America but of all sections of the world influenced by American culture. And now we have a minister who not only is a student of jazz but who has brought it into his church.

If you saw the feature article on the minister in last Sunday's [*Honolulu*] *Advertiser* and were shocked by the revelation that he actually invited George Lewis and his New Orleans band into his church to play certain tunes, you shouldn't have been. Back in the early days in New Orleans, jazz was often used as church music.

In previous columns I mentioned that in New Orleans, jazz was functional. It was part of the everyday life of working class Negroes. And it was also used for religious services.

"When the Saints Go Marching In" and "Just a Closer Walk with Thee" are two of the religious tunes still played by New Orleans and Dixieland bands. In the old days, jazz was accepted and both ministers and congregation expected certain songs to be jazzed. It was only when jazz scattered all over America that certain ministers, who had not been brought up in the New Orleans tradition, became shocked and protested loud and long when they heard hymns and gospel songs recorded by hot bands.

When I was a kid back in my home town of Arkansas City, Kansas, I would go at night to the revival meetings of the Holy Rollers because I liked the music. The meetings were in a tent, and I remember the band consisted of piano, kazoo and harmonica. The summer I finished high school I went to Wichita, and spent a lot of time at night around another Holy Roller revival with a bigger band composed of piano, drums, trumpet, guitar, cornet, trombone and fiddle.

In both instances they played spirituals and hymns and gospel songs, but so far as I was concerned this was just plain jazz. In fact, it was better jazz than you could hear from most of the jazz bands available there at the time. Let me assure you this was not merely my opinion, not only youngsters but many older persons came out just to listen to hot music. When the bands got going, church members danced, shouted, clapped their hands and had "seizures"—but it was supposed to be religion and nothing else. All the rest of us could do was pat our feet. And I have no doubt that some listeners joined church only so that they could dance uninhibitedly to the music.

I have recordings made by some of the old-style preachers back in the 1920s. One of the best was a Reverend Gates, an Atlanta minister whom I later came to know personally. When these preachers get going, they produce as good hot vocalizing as you will hear anywhere. I also have a satire recorded in the late 1930s called "Preachin' Trumpet Blues" which recaptures in a frankly jazz performance the spirit, timing and general feeling of the work of Rev. Gates, et al.

Currently there are a good many vocals who have won equal prominence singing spirituals and blues: Sister Rosetta Tharpe is one of the top gospel singers of the day, yet for several seasons she was star vocalist with Lucky Millinder's swing band. Marie Knight is still another. And many choirs and small religious vocal groups get a better rock and have a stronger and more incisive beat than most of the out and out rhythm and blues singing units.

Yes, jazz and religion have been buddying around together for over fifty years. I am glad the Reverend Kershaw is helping bring the facts of the alliance into the open.

• • •

MIRROR OF JAZZ

NOVEMBER 17, 1955

Listen to a people's music, and you get a picture of their social structure and living conditions. Music mirrors the social forces at work within a culture.

That is why what is called the rhythm and blues craze will not die down among the Negro people, despite the wishful thinking of many persons. There may be alterations and adjustments to fit the changing patterns and there will be a lessening of the purely commercial stuff, but the mainstream of R&B will continue so long as the Negro must fight for full equality and is not completely assimilated by white America.

There are some differences between the "race records" of thirty years ago and the R&B discs of today, because there have been important changes in America and in the status of Negroes. Negroes are no longer recent migrants from the rural South to the urban North; segregation has significantly declined in many aspects of national life. Greater group sophistication and more complex living demand a musical outlet with more urbanity and instrumental complexity than most of the blues and rhythm tunes popular in the 1920s.

At the same time, there is still a demand and appreciation for blues in the strictly classical manner. One of the top R&B hits of the year is "Walkin' the Blues," by Champion Jack DuPree and Mr. Bear. DuPree for the last quarter of a century has been one of the leading folk blues pianists and his style remains unchanged.

The important thing is that there still exist the socio-economic conditions which led to the birth among Negroes of a revolutionary new music called jazz. As a group, Negroes are still segregated and must keep on fighting to win full and equal status as Americans.

Jazz and blues popular in New Orleans almost sixty years ago had the same basic psychological ingredients as the best R&B today. There was and still is the feeling of social frustration, of loneliness, of getting a rotten deal, coupled with protest often distilling into anger and outrage over existing conditions; there was and still is a feeling of defiance, of saying in music: "Look, you can't keep me down. I know I'm as good as you are any day. Just watch the way I strut and learn something!"

It is this feeling of being kicked around and of revolt against rejection which characterized early blues and jazz, the race records of thirty years ago and the best R&B today. It mirrors in music the long-time status of the Negro people and our group attitude towards life in America. It contains both realism and hope and determination for the future.

I think, frankly, that the reason why the kind of jazz known first as be-bop and then more simply as bop did not catch on with the masses of Negroes was its lack of optimism. Bop came into prominence during the mid-1940s around the end of World War II. It mirrored not only the frustration of Negroes in their quest for first-class citizenship but was a vivid portrait of America and a chaotic world. But bop was a music without hope and confidence for all its graphic commentary, and thus was not acceptable to the Negro masses.

What I mean to say is that the Negro people have not and will not give up the fight for full equality in America. As a group we are determined to keep on fighting for the time when there can be no more cases anywhere in our land like that of Emmett Till, the fourteen-year-old boy lynched by two white half-brothers in Mississippi. A music that does not reflect this determination does not mirror Negro life and therefore is rejected by the majority of Negroes.

Ten years from now in Negro homes, night spots and taverns you will still be hearing music that is spiritually akin to the rhythm and blues of today. You'll still be hearing songs of derision: you'll get bitterness and irony and realism mixed with defiance and the sheer joy of being alive. You'll find this kind of music popular among Negroes no matter what Tin Pan Alley and the multimillion dollar music business have been able to palm off on the rest of America.

In future articles, I hope to discuss some of the content of the blues which points up the differences between white and Negro living conditions as well as ways in which jazz has helped break down racial barriers.

• • •

THE BLUES ARE REAL

NOVEMBER 24, 1955

There is a vast difference between the words found in genuine blues and the words in popular songs. Broadly speaking, it is the difference between realism and pretense.

Love in a popular song is, as a rule, romantic love. Sir Galahad boy meets wide-eyed, innocent girl beneath a moon in June. Everything is such enchantment, way up high in the sky. Knight and fairy princess stuff.

The blues assumes that male and female are flesh and blood people, behaving in an everyday, earthy way. In other words, the blues lyrics accept sex as a perfectly normal activity in male-female relationship while the popular song evidently is written on the assumption that sex doesn't exist—or, if it does, is indecent and must be ignored.

The frankness of Negro blues songs in comparison with the pretense of the popular song reflects the basic difference between life in white and black America. A people forced to live life in the raw with no trimmings, as was the case during slavery and even today in the rural areas down South and the slums up North, has no need for nor inclination to fool itself. White America insists on hypocrisy. A society which talks democracy and actually practices discrimination could logically be expected to have the same pretense extended to its popular songs.

In addition to frankness about sex, blues lyrics often have a dry and bitter humor possible only among a group used to getting the dirty end of the stick. Often they are pungent folk poetry. But most of all, they must express commonly held ideas or they won't get to first base.

About as pithy a farewell as you'll find anywhere is in these words of a blues song:

> *"When you see me leavin' pin crepe on your door*
> *Said when you see me leavin' pin crepe on your door;*
> *I won't be dead but I ain't coming back no more."*

Here is another, equally brittle:

> *"I asked the brakeman to let me ride the blind*
> *Asked the brakeman to please let me ride the blind*
> *He said 'I'm sorry, little girl, but this train ain't none of mine.'"*

It is true that a large portion of blues lyrics are concerned with sex. But so, for that matter, is a large part of adult life. In addition, since in pre–Civil War times it meant more slaves and even today means an abundant supply of cheap labor, for generations sex was the main source of pleasure permitted Negroes by white America.

Even so, the sex blues have been built up out of proportion for commercial reasons. Back in the 1920s when the music business learned there was a lot of loot to be taken from blues with off-color or suggestive words, it encouraged this type and has recorded or pushed only a comparative smattering of other kinds of blues on the ground that they "aren't commercial enough." The singers and musicians, who like to eat regularly, have found it profitable to go along.

But there have been and still are many great blues songs that have nothing to do with sex. Blues lyrics can often present a biting social commentary as, for instance, Josh White's famous *Southern Exposure—an Album of Jim Crow Blues* which was marketed by a small company some fifteen years ago after the major recording firms turned thumbs down.

The range of possible subject matter for blues lyrics is as wide as the day-to-day experience of the Negro people themselves. Bad housing often means unsanitary living conditions and such pests as bedbugs. One of the best known was a number called "Mean Old Bedbug Blues" which had a number of verses in the following vein:

> *"Bedbugs big as a jackass will bite you, stand and grin*
> *Yes, bedbugs big as a jackass will bite you, stand and grin*
> *They'll drink up all the chinch poison come back and bite you again."*

One of the great Bessie Smith's most famous hits was called "Backwater Blues" and was written about the Mississippi River floods of 1927 which destroyed the homes of some 700,000 persons. One of my favorite blues— and it was so popular that it has been reissued twice—is called "Going Down Slow" and is a sort of last letter from the tuberculosis victim in the final stages of the disease.

These and many other blues which have found a ready response in the hearts of Negro America have nothing to do with sex. The point I'm trying to make is that blues subject matter is limited only by Negro experiences and that even sex blues are based on realism. Study the lyrics of genuine blues and you can get a picture of Negro life in America.

• • •

FIFTY AND '56

DECEMBER 29, 1955

Like most people, I approach a new year with optimism. No matter how rotten the previous twelve months, no matter how dismal the immediate future, most of us have a kind of blind faith that somehow, some way the coming year will be better.

Undoubtedly I should know better by now. Exactly one hour before midnight ushers in 1956, I reach the half century mark. If you're ever going to get any sense, you should have it then. And yet, only a few breaths short of fifty, I find myself anticipating the new adventure of 1956 with the same relish that thirty years ago I awaited 1926.

When I was in high school back in Kansas, I was convinced that I would never reach the advanced age of forty-five. I often wondered what went on in the feeble mind of such an ancient. Today, I would like to reach back some thirty-three years in time, tap the adolescent me on the shoulder and say:

"Son, when you reach fifty your biggest regret will be that you're not likely to stick around for another half century to watch and take part in man's struggle with himself and the world around him. You will thank your lucky stars for having lived in one of the most exciting and fruitful periods in mankind's history. You will have seen such inventions as the phonograph, motion pictures, radio, talkies, television and the airplane grow up and become commonplace; you will have heard the labor pains at the birth of a new atomic age.

"You will have seen this new music called jazz roar out of New Orleans and spread all over the world. It will have been your privilege to have seen and heard in person such greats as Ma Rainey, King Oliver, Freddie Keppard, and the rest; you will have seen and heard such fabulous things as Louis Armstrong and Fats Waller at the old Vendome Theatre, Jimmy Noone and Earl Hines at the old Apex in Chicago in 1927, and Bennie Moten battling George Lee at the Paseo Dance Academy in Kansas City—events not chronicled in jazz histories and known to younger enthusiasts only through the printed word.

"You will have learned that you are nowhere near the ball of fire you thought you were at twenty-five; the world will not come a-blaze at your genius. You will find that no matter how good you are, there are many others who are far better at anything you can name.

"You will have taken an active part in the struggle of Negroes for full equality in America, you will have seen the barriers of race crack and give way at many places. And you will have realized the kinship between all darker people seeking to overthrow white supremacy, you will have understood that the triumph of Asians and Africans in their battle against colonialism aids the Negro people of America and vice versa.

"Your ego will have been salved by the praise given three published books of your poetry and the translation of your work into foreign languages. And yet there will still be so much you will want to say in books that at times you will want to despair of living long enough to get more than a fraction of it on paper.

"Somewhere in your thirties you will learn that despite what your friends call your cast iron stomach, you cannot get rid of it as fast as the distilleries can make it. Women, you will have found also in your thirties, can be almost as exasperating to you as you are to them.

"And when you reach fifty you will find that physically you feel little different from how you did at thirty-five."

That's how it is as I approach the double header of a fiftieth birthday and a new year. I just don't feel fifty. And I'm still giddy enough to think things will be better next year. Maybe the rank and file of the new AFL-CIO can bring about the election of enough new lawmakers to Washington to produce a government favoring the ordinary citizen instead of the monster corporations. Maybe also the anti-colonialism force banding together at Bandung will gather sufficient momentum to deal another major blow to white supremacy. And maybe the big nations will agree to halt the mad race to create bigger and better instruments of mass extermination.

And maybe also we will have more songs of the type of "Sixteen Tons" on the *Hit Parade*. In this connection, I want to publicly thank the young woman who phoned me about the recent Billboard article on this number.

It seems, according to this trade publication of the theatrical and amusement world, that residents of the mining towns in Pennsylvania and West Virginia have been buying this record in large quantities. The stores in these towns are mainly company stores—who, because of the demand and the profit are placed in the uncomfortable position of a record aimed directly at them!

• • •

MODERN JAZZ IS A FOLK MUSIC THAT STARTED WITH THE BLUES

DECEMBER 25, 1955

It was good to see that an Episcopal minister, the Reverend Alvin Kershaw of Oxford, Ohio, not only chose jazz for his category on that TV quiz show, *The $64,000 Question*, but realized the place of this music in our society.

Only a few decades ago, "respectable" white people just didn't listen to real jazz. They might bend an ear to the musical meanderings of Paul Whiteman, who never could play jazz or to George Gershwin's *Rhapsody in Blue*, which was 95 percent foreign to both jazz and the blues, but that was as close as they ever got.

Jazz was born of the musical experience of the Negro people in America. Into it went the highly complex rhythmic patterns and musical conceptions native to those sections of Africa from which the black man came, the spirituals, blues and secular music developed in America following contact with European music patterns in the New World, and the social and psychological experiences of a minority group struggling for equality.

The background was not common to whites, and hidebound critics and musicians steeped in the traditions and adhering to the standards of Western European music had little or no patience with African-rooted sounds and techniques which rebelled against everything they had been taught.

As a matter of fact, white America is still not ready to give colored America its due. Negroes had been playing jazz in and around New Orleans since the 1890s, but this revolutionary new music was not accepted until the Original Dixieland Jazz Band, a white outfit, came out of the South. At the time, there were at least a dozen colored bands immeasurably superior to this white group.

Negro bands such as those of Duke Ellington, Fletcher Henderson, Bennie Moten, Louis Armstrong, Jimmy Lunceford, Don Redman and a number of others had been swinging mightily for years, but it was not until

Benny Goodman based a big white band on Negro style that swing became popular with white America.

Although the piano style called boggie-woogie had been known since the early 1900s, and, perhaps its greatest exponent, Pinetop Smith, had died, the general public accepted it only after the Bob Crosby band included "Yancey Special" and "Honky Tonk Train Blues" in its repertoire.

But despite all its enemies could do, jazz grew, and became not only the music of the U.S. but of all sections of the world influenced by U.S. culture. And now we have a white minister who not only is a student of jazz but who has brought it into his church.

The blues are the mother of jazz. To understand jazz, you need to understand the blues.

Nobody knows when the blues began, but they are a folk music which developed in the rural South and became identifiable as a specific type of U.S. Negro secular music after the Civil War and before the 1890s.

Basically, they are personal songs of protest and rebellion, growing out of individual needs. They may have any subject matter, ranging through love, politics, current events, race relations and what not. They may poke fun or they may be deadly serious. A true blues is always realistic; it is never maudlin or escapist.

At first the blues were sung without accompaniment, as a spontaneous expression of the way the singer felt about any topic which moved him deeply. Most of the early blues singers couldn't afford instruments, anyway. Then gradually, they began using whatever was available as accompaniment—banjo, guitar or whatnot.

The blues have a distinctive tonal scale, in which the third and seventh tones tend to be flattened. The degree varies. These "blue" notes cannot be reproduced accurately on any instrument with regular tones, such as the piano. On this instrument, the closest approximation is the striking of two keys near the desired tone.

In addition to introducing new tones, the blues also provided new structures and techniques. Most genuine blues consist of twelve bars of music in common time, divided into three equal groups of four bars. The first group of fours is on the common chord on the keynote, the second four-bar grouping is on the chord of the subdominant and the third on the chord of the dominant seventh.

Each group of four bars has a line of verse. This line of verse rarely fills the entire four bars, often ending on the first beat of the third bar. Usually this same verse is repeated for the second group of four bars, for example:

I'd rather drink muddy water, sleep in a hollow log:
Said I'd rather drunk muddy water, sleep in a hollow log.
Before I'd stay in Mississippi, treated like a dirty dog.

Since each line of words did not take up the full group of four bars, the accompanying instruments had to fill in the remainder of the four bars as they saw fit. In other words, they were forced to improvise.

Meanwhile, Negroes were flocking to New Orleans by the end of the last century. Life was faster and there were more jobs and better times than in the rural areas. By now there were many blues which had taken form and were common property.

And since life in New Orleans moved at a far faster tempo that it did on the plantations and in small towns, the music also increased in tempo from slow blues; the improvisational now extended over the entire bar. Thus it was that a new music, to be known as jazz, came into being in the 1890s.

• • •

BACK TO THE EARLY DAYS OF JAZZ
JULY 15, 1936

Dusky musicians are awaiting with just as much interest as palefaces the return to the "Rhythm" scene of the Original Dixieland Jazz Band which first made this form of dance music palatable to the public on a wide scale. Although most students give the Negro credit for inventing the term and style, it took whites to make it popular—just as it has taken Casa Loma and Benny Goodman to make America and Europe "swing" conscious despite the term's invention by Louis Armstrong.

In spite of contributions of colored artists both before and since, jazz may properly be said to have its popular beginning with the Dixielanders. Formed in 1917, these five white boys for four years were the jazz sensations of the day. It had so happened that W. C. Handy's authorship of the brand new form of music called the blues gave these Dixielanders much-needed themes.

In addition to such Handy classics as "St. Louis Blues," "Memphis Blues," "Joe Turner Blues," "Hesitation Blues," "Beale Street Blues," the Original Dixieland Band popularized such wild compositions as "Livery Stable Blues," "Barnyard Blues," "Dixieland Jazz Band Blues" and others. Today these records are rare collector's pieces and are revered by all students of jazz.

Members of the original orchestra were Nick LaRocca, trumpet player, who afterward became a New Orleans contractor; Larry Shields, clarinet; Eddie Edwards, trombone; Tony Sbarbaro, drums; and Henry Ragas, pianist, who died in 1919. J. Russell Robinson, who succeeded Ragas, is still alive. These five are the honored old gentlemen of jazz and the ones who will attempt to come back to a modern world. This will consist of a dance tour, a CBS radio buildup, and possibly a sequence in Paramount's *Big Broadcast of 1937.*

These five white boys were masters at the art of improvisation. They scored nothing. No piece was played exactly the same way twice. As a rule, a number consisted of one chorus rendered together, then each member would take a hot chorus, and there would be a final one together. Robinson, who has authored the currently popular "Swing, Mr. Charlie," says that swing today is basically no different from that of 1917–1921. Today it is arranged, although technically improvised, because of a larger combination of instruments. But with five pieces, arrangements aren't necessary—if you're dealing with real swing musicians.

Contemporaries of that day included Wilbur Sweatman, clarinetist, who also had a five piece combination; W. C. Handy, who led his band as well as composed, and Lieutenant Jim Europe, back from the World War. Obviously, this was pre-Henderson and pre-Ellington. The Dixieland owes its foldup to the craftsmanship of Paul Whiteman who changed jazz from a wild, hot style to a symphonic and sweet manner. As everybody knows, Jim Europe was headed for the same goal.

The revival of the Dixielanders is laid at the door of swing music— which, if nothing else, proves that even jazz has its cycles. Negro swing enthusiasts steeped in the tradition of Armstrong, Teddy Wilson, Chick Webb, Barney Bigard, and Benny Morton will surely enjoy hearing how a quintet of hot white men played—men who did the pioneer work for the sepia swing artists of today. While the Dixielanders may have lost some of their technique through age and general rustiness, they will at least be interesting.

• • •

LAMENT FOR THE BLUES
SEPTEMBER 29, 1937

It was quite a relief to the ear when they went out of fashion, but today I can't help but yearn wistfully for an occasional auditory meal of those mean, low down, gutbucket, barrelhouse, slow draggin' blues which blared from nearly every phonograph just about fifteen years ago.

In 1937 we have torch songs, double meaning ditties, and our lonely ballads with only a mild dash of indigo coloring. No more do any of the Smiths—Mamie, Bessie, Trixie, Sippie or others of the husky voiced clan—shout to the world about their two-timin' daddies what done 'em wrong. None of the gals today is "Gulf Coast bound," Michigan water has stopped tasting "like cherry wine," and it seems that the "mean black snake" has gone entirely out of the bitin' business to live on its old age pension.

For this, I shed a tear. I've got the blues because there ain't no blues.

And much as I tired of them when every month saw dozens of platters issued starring these same Smiths, Ma Rainey, Sippie Wallace, Alberta Hunter, Ada Brown et al., that now is forgotten. Maybe that is why I welcome hearing Lionel Hampton's "Vibraphone Blues" out by the Benny Goodman quartet.

Some of the greatest and sincerest jazz ever recorded is on these old platters, many of which are currently collector's items bringing high prices. On them you hear Louis Armstrong playing music instead of exhibiting his trick horn; Fletcher Henderson when he was the world's greatest pianist; Earl Hines at his peak; and other demi-gods of the swing world. Ethel Waters leaped into fame by her "Down Home Blues," released in 1921 by the ill-fated Black Swan company. And that same disc is also valuable, in case you have one lying around.

Blues looked on when jazz was born. Indigo chants were popular in the Deep South before W. C. Handy made history with his "Memphis Blues," the first ever written down. It ushered in a new form of music, a natural for the infant called jazz. That Handy's own band, King Oliver, Papa Celestin, and the Original Dixielanders should have taken to the blues was not surprising. Composers saw the public falling for it, and hurriedly produced more and still more. After a few years the public tired and the market dulled.

Then began our stomps, one of the most popular being "Sugar Foot Stomp." In rapid succession appeared the Charleston and Black Bottom with music of their own, and finally Duke Ellington with his jungle rhythms. Cab Calloway suddenly showed up with his scat singing. Meanwhile sweet music was pushing hot jazz aside and it was not until a couple of years ago, with the rise of Benny Goodman, that it returned to the general public under the guise of "swing." And now it has gone modernistic, what with "Twilight in Turkey" by the Raymond Scott Quintette setting the pace.

Unless you stray far from the beaten path, your blues fare today is likely to consist almost exclusively of the St. Louis, Basin Street, and Limehouse Blues. They're all right. But I, for one, must go 'way down to the basement when the mood strikes and get a bunch of mournful "Tishamingo Blues" or something of that sort. Otherwise there is little relief.

• • •

MORE MIXED BANDS NEEDED
FEBRUARY 24, 1937

Now that Benny Goodman has smashed tradition and demonstrated that interracial orchestras can be accepted in person by the best circles, who will be the next American dance band leader to follow in his foot steps? Will he be white, or will he be colored?

You will notice that I speak of accepting an interracial orchestra "in person." That has been the trouble. It is a matter of history that mixed orchestras have been waxing discs for Victor, Columbia, the old Okeh and other companies for a dozen years or more, but of course the buyers couldn't see who was doing the playing. In Europe, Asia and other parts of the world, sepias and ofays have been playing together out in the open for many, many months.

Goodman is at the top of the swing music heap because he has hired musicians instead of skin coloration. He wanted the best men available, not just the best white men. It took nerve and a fight to make Teddy Wilson and Lionel Hampton regular members of his organization and acceptable everywhere. At first the Camel company objected, California didn't want them, and it took a firm hand to get them into the Hotel Pennsylvania in New York.

But success has crowned Benny's efforts. Reynolds Company executives have just sent through an order authorizing the use of Wilson's and Hampton's names, and insisting that either the trio or quartet be featured every week in the Camel air show.

That is as it should be. An orchestra leader should want to get the best man available for his kind of music, whether that individual be an Aframerican, a Jap, an Indian or a Caucasian. For the same reason, a football coach should use the best players for his team, irregardless of color. Brad Holland, for instance, should be used at end on the Cornell varsity because he is the best man for that spot—and for that reason actually is used in place of an inferior white boy. Similarly, if Don Redman wants a white musician and Jimmy Dorsey wants a sepia, they should be free to get them if possible instead of bowing to race prejudice and absurd tradition.

In addition to Goodman, two other outstanding hot white musicians have broken the ice by using a mixed band. One is Joe Marsala, one of the world's greatest clarinet artists, who is unlike most other stars of Italian extraction in that he seems to lack prejudices. The other is Eddie Condon, sensational banjo and guitar virtuoso. Together they give New York what is considered its first interracial band, playing at the Hickory House. The great Henry "Red" Allen opened with them on trumpet, and when the press of other obligations took him away, his place was filled by Otis Johnson, another iron horn star. Unfortunately, the bunch has been broken up.

Marsala, incidentally, was recently seriously considering going even farther than Goodman has by joining as a regular member of Lucky Millinder's band. His purpose was to be near Red Allen, for he admits no player in the world inspires and brings out the best jazz in him as does the trumpet ace.

White boys who record with mixed bands often do so under the names of colored orchestra leaders. For instance, a recent Teddy Wilson disc uses Allen Reuss on guitar and Vido Musso on tenor, two ofay lads. Billie Holliday has used Artie Shaw and others on her wax works. At the same time, sepias often record with bands bearing white names. Allen, Louis Armstrong, Buster Bailey and many more are included.

I long for the day when there will be no color distinction in America. But this goal can be reached only a step at a time. Just as colored boys help overcome prejudice and give Caucasians another view of the race by their successes on the football and track teams of white colleges, so can musicians help by means of mixed bands. When it becomes commonplace instead of an oddity to see sepia and ofay musicians seated side by side on the same bandstand, it will mark another significant milestone in our fight for recognition as full-fledged American citizens.

AFRICAN AMERICAN LITERATURE AT MID-CENTURY

Davis's book reviews reveal a determining relationship between racism and fascism and demonstrate how creative and nonfiction literatures participate in dismantling these political constructs. As a critical act, book reviewing became more widespread and important beginning in the New Negro Renaissance, when journals such as *Opportunity*, *Crisis*, *The Messenger*, and a whole host of "little magazines" began reconsidering the significance of book production as a marker of racial progress, cultural transformation, and political consciousness-raising. Initially, this practice came from academically trained scholars, critics, reviewers, and historians. In fact, except for a small, specialized group as diverse as post-Victorian Benjamin Brawley and the New Negro poet-fictionist-reviewer Countee Cullen, the majority of book reviewers were scholars whose training in a specific academic discipline nevertheless required them to read and review works beyond their areas of academic preparation. However, there were also the occasional reviewers, a group to which Frank Marshall Davis belonged. Davis wrote nearly fifty reviews off and on from the early 1930s to the mid-1950s. Thematically, these pieces are connected by political necessity, a thread that complemented and extended his other news writing.

Davis reveals his "theory" of art most pointedly in discussions about poetry, but this aesthetic vision describes his concept of fiction and other prose expressions too. As an occasional reviewer of poetry, from 1937 or so to 1947, Davis labored in the long shadow cast by such formally trained academic critics as Alain Locke, Nick Aaron Ford, and J. Saunders Redding and by such poets as Langston Hughes, Sterling A. Brown, and Arna Bontemps. For these writers, whose analyses and reviews found expression in journals such as *Phylon*, *Opportunity*, and *Crisis*, poetry was often considered an art form that used language more beautifully than prose and that thematically sought the universal in human experience. The point that fractured this very simple unity was the conflict over the extent to which social issues should be revealed in poetry. Without their training and forums, Davis nevertheless managed to participate in these formal conversations in his reviews, released largely through the ANP, and to provide excellent descriptions and interpretations of poetry collections.

For Davis, the role of the fiction writer was not only to move readers to a deeper understanding of the human condition, but also to combine character, plot, setting, style, and other elements into a text that raises the consciousness of people and make them more politically aware of the material conditions of their lives. The danger here is that Davis's vision might be misconstrued as reductive, since it seems to create an uneasiness between art and social issues. Davis's reviews clearly demonstrate how he managed to escape the trap of propaganda or bombast as evaluative standards. Instead, he was able to demonstrate how the boundaries between art and social issues are fairly elastic.

This point, arguably, can be made fairly easily by assessing his reviews of Richard Wright's books. Davis made his own contribution to the reputation of Wright as being the most important writer of the era and therefore to the so-called Richard Wright School of Fiction. Beginning with *Uncle Tom's Children* (1938), Davis could hardly contain his enthusiasm for Wright's prose. Despite the contradictory metaphor, he praises Wright's writing as "the muscular economy of words characteristic of Ernest Hemingway at his best." Indeed, Davis celebrates Wright for being the peer of "any Caucasian master of rugged realism." Apart from questions of style, this review tells us that Davis considered "Fire and Cloud," the last story in the collection, to be the best one because it demonstrated a Communist-inspired protest march, featuring African Americans and poor whites. It is a union consistent with the political focus Davis advocated.

Davis's appreciation of Wright's *Native Son* (1940) is ecstatic. Viewing it as a "realistic-psychological story," Davis effusively praises Wright for creating a novel that "tells in detail the entire psychology and background that makes such things" as the depravity that gives rise to the potential for the creation of actual Bigger Thomases so realistic. Like many other reviewers of the novel, Davis found "the episode by Defense Attorney Max at Bigger's trial . . . one of the greatest documents ever written on interracial relationships in our society and by itself is a tremendous contribution to literature." Davis's enthusiastic appreciation of the sociopolitical theme in the novel leads to an easy deduction of Davis's own flirtation with Communism. As reflected in his review, for him, Communism was potentially a transformative political and social force in American life and culture. Even in his review of Wright's *12 Million Black Voices*, Davis praised "the naked realism that characterizes Mr. Wright's work" and the picture of American democracy that "cannot be beautiful and be accurate."

But it is in his review of Wright's autobiography *Black Boy* (1945) that Davis not only mitigates his enthusiasm for Wright the writer, but he also states unambiguously his own standard of art. This book, in Davis's view, was rooted in a realism that led to an unbridled exposure of blacks' social ills, raised people's consciousness, and, in turn, inspired political and cultural transformation. Yet it was a book out of step with a war-torn world. His principal claim was that "Wright's book has little to do directly with the fight for democracy, when it could easily have been an important contribution." Oddly enough, he felt *Black Boy* merely accentuated "the unholy pattern of southern race relations without suggesting a solution, even by indirection."

Davis's displeasure developed from Wright's apparent move away from group progress to the position of a complete individualist. His apparent desertion of a collectivist vision for solving political problems left Davis and other South Side Writers' Group members in an uncomfortable position, of being forced to agree with Wright's new political vision. They felt that if Wright couldn't have his own way, then he would desert them and their causes. Moreover, Davis was greatly disturbed by what he perceived as the book's gratuitous sex, its rampant commercialism, and especially its failure to confront fascism. He felt Wright should have shown "the strong connection between southern racism and Hitler race theories." This failure represented for Davis a stumbling block in the work to create a racially integrated armed forces. Even though the Department of War opposed this military arrangement, on the grounds it was a mere sociological experiment, Davis felt a more agreeable relationship might be reached, one that would encourage the formation of such troops. Wright's representation of black-white southern life, in Davis's view, clearly exacerbated interracial tensions and therefore hindered the creation of a racially mixed armed forces.

In reviews of Arna Bontemps's fiction, Davis shifted temporarily to a more lyrical expression to compliment Bontemps's less acerbic treatment of war in *Black Thunder* and *Drums at Dusk*. *Black Thunder*, he writes, is "a gallery of vivid and clear pictorial etchings," while the substitution of "gentle understatement" in *Drums* increases the effect of vivid scenes. Although Davis appreciates the achievement of Bontemps's lyricism, he finds himself drawn to "the hardboiled school of fiction," that is, "fiction written with a vigorous realism." In these representations, race doesn't necessarily matter, as he writes of William Attaway's *Let Me Breathe Thunder* or Waters Turpin's *O Canaan*, two works in which the principal characters are white. Sinclair Lewis's *Kingsblood Royal* even underscores for Davis the folly of race. Overall, his aesthetic is best summarized in his description of Willard Motley's *Knock on Any Door*: it is a polemic against poverty, insecurity, and inequality, "as much as a social treatise as a gripping, powerful novel." A similar view of art characterizes his reviews of poetry.

To Davis, the best poetic expression derives from social and literary realism, mirroring, in some ways, the lives of readers and written in terms the reader would find accessible. In reviews of three works by Langston Hughes, he clearly struggles for words of praise because *Shakespeare in Harlem* and *Fields of Wonder* fall short of Davis's expectations. Their impact is mitigated either by an unhelpful universalism or by rhyme. *Montage of a Dream Deferred*, though, evinces more of Davis's vision of poetic excellence, since it was written to be read by the people, not a small "corps of intellectual snobs." While he doesn't apply this critique with the same language, Davis finds Tolson's *Rendezvous with America* historically grounded but undermined by a tendency to be bookish, intellectual, and mystic.

The sine qua non of poetry for Davis is achieved by a number of new writers, led by Margaret Walker's *For My People*. The influence of the realistic Midwestern school of expression, best exemplified by Carl Sandburg, enabled Walker to write a socially conscious verse that spoke to the people. In much the same way, he finds force and fire in Owen Dodson's *Powerful Long Ladder*, since it mirrors the inequities of Negro life with strong drama. This obvious privileging of realism in poetic expression not only informs his own poetic practice but differs from the aesthetic of a handful of black critics, such as Nick Aaron Ford, who were unwilling to grant that a realistic mode was different from pure propaganda. Although Davis never engaged their argument directly in his reviews, he nevertheless held fast to the position that realism was not synonymous with the dull drudgery of rhetorical bombast and propaganda.

For Davis, the most highly esteemed nonfiction writing is that which complements ideas and arguments found in his news writing. His reviews of books on jazz, for example, reveal the extent to which this mode of expression extends the news writing collected here as "A History of Blues and Jazz." His article "Back to African Music" begins with the premise that the black public knows little of its racial heritage, which means it also needs to develop a greater respect for its African ancestry. *The Aesthetics of African Music* and *The Philosophy of African Music* fill this lacuna in black cultural history and become, in their own way, sources that engender racial pride. Read intertextually, *Jazzmen, Jazz Record Book*, and *Jazz: A People's Music* discursively present ideas that augment his narrative on jazz as a weapon of racial integration.

Davis's foray into African American literary history is brief but helpful in bringing visibility to the legacy of this literature and how, in different eras, it was made to serve the needs of a people. Thematically, it restates in yet another way, the importance of making known the cultural contributions of African Americans. Unwittingly, Davis presents a critical clash over the meaning of African Americans in American culture. His review of Herskovits's *Myth of the Negro Past*, one that resonated with previously discussed books, carefully lays out its origins in the Carnegie Study that culminated in Gunnar Myrdal's *An American Dilemma*. Davis's appreciation of Herskovits and his establishment of a cultural past for Negroes has been widely documented. But Communist historian Herbert Aptheker did not share Davis's enthusiasm; in an eighty-page pamphlet, he challenged the very grounds on which *An American Dilemma* rested. Aptheker resists the idea that the racial problem can be defined, as Myrdal does, in moral terms; in his view, it has to be considered in economic terms. That Davis makes no evaluative statements about Aptheker's conclusions suggests that Davis was himself presented a dilemma, between Herskovit's history of a black racial past and Aptheker's communist interpretation of that history. His appreciative review of Kennedy's *Southern Exposure* enables a clearer view of the importance of economics to Davis's formulation. For *Southern Exposure* tells us about Big Business and its efforts to gain more profits by extending World War II.

Collectively, then, these reviews tell us much about Davis's view of art and especially art in the era of world war. His vision that all efforts must be directed toward the goal of complete democracy is manifested in this section. What this means is that the war at home and the war abroad must be contested vigorously and with an equally concerted effort. Davis's position offered hard choices. His desire to expose racism risked exacerbating racial tension. At the same time that he called for national and racial unity, he also sought reasons for and solutions to the alienation of African Americans from the American mainstream. For Davis the book reviewer, these contraries posed an enormous dilemma. Initially, of course, the purpose he fashioned for a review was that it should be descriptive. That is, it should introduce and generally describe a book. But even though his reviews sometimes offered the more rigorous critical act of interpretation or textual analysis, the reviews were usually rooted in the need to see the books within the context of cultural contributions African Americans were making to an amorphous American cultural mainstream. In the end, the determination of a book's worth was often evaluated in terms of its relative success in demonstrating its contribution. These are lofty goals for a book review published in a weekly black newspaper, especially when subscribing newspapers were free to print all or only a part of the whole review. Notwithstanding, Davis's nearly fifty extant reviews, judged on their overall merit, are remarkably consistent.

• • •

RICHARD WRIGHT'S PRIZE VOLUME, *UNCLE TOM'S CHILDREN*, IS STRONG AND BRILLIANT

MARCH 30, 1938

Divided into four complete short novels, *Uncle Tom's Children* is the most absorbing fiction penned by a Negro since George Schuyler's *Black No More*. Richard Wright, the twenty-nine-year- old author, writes with the muscular economy of words characteristic of Ernest Hemingway at his best; indeed, Mr. Wright is the peer of any Caucasian master of rugged realism. His prose is so alive and gripping that the reader is likely to forget it is fiction and consider himself actually looking at the southern scenes unfolded.

Each story reveals the deep South and its constant race struggles. The first three are definitely tragedies. Only the fourth shows some ray of hope, and that through united action of white and black masses for a common purpose.

First of the short novels, or novellas, is "Big Boy Leaves Home." It first appeared in *New Caravan*, published in 1936, and immediately placed Mr. Wright in the literary limelight. It tells of four boys, carefree under the southern gun, who go swimming on forbidden property. A white woman appears and during their efforts to get their clothes and run away, she screams. A male companion appears and kills two of the foursome. In a scuffle, Big Boy grabs his rifle, shoots the white man, and flees. Realizing a mob will hunt him, Big Boy hides that night knowing he can get a ride North next morning. Bobo, the fourth boy, is to meet him. But the mob catches Bobo and lynches him within sight of Big Boy's hideout. Big Boy himself is saved only because he chokes with his bare hands a bloodhound hunting him, and after a night of terror gets safely out of the community.

"Down by the Riverside," second novella, is the story of a Mississippi flood. Mann, the main character, after a night of battle against the raging waters and increased racial passions during which he heroically rescues many marooned whites, is killed by soldiers after a white family he had saved from death point him out as the slayer of their husband and father earlier that night. Mann had killed to save himself and wife after being attacked with a gun, but in this community it was no defense.

The third story, "Long Black Song," tells of Sarah and her baby, awaiting the return of Silas, her husband and small independent farmer, from town where he went to sell cotton. A white salesman stops, seduces Sarah, leaves a phonograph to be bought on installments and promises to return next morning to see if the deal will go through. When Silas returns that night, he ingeniously discovers the seduction despite his wife's denials, smashes the machine, and drives out Sarah with a whip. His hate for whites causes him to kill the salesman next morning but the latter's companion goes back to town, returns with a mob. Silas grimly refuses to flee and shoots as many of the posse as he can until his house is set afire. Silas refuses still to leave his burning dwelling, and dies in the flames without even a cry of pain as Sarah looks on from afar, then carries the baby to her aunt in town.

"Fire and Cloud," the concluding novella, finds the Negroes of a small town aroused because they are starving and relief is denied them. Desperate, and influenced by a white and a Negro Communist, they plan to march in protest. Rev. Taylor, colored leader, is visited by the mayor and other officials who demand that he use his influence to change their minds. Although really afraid, he refuses. That night he and other Negro leaders are kidnapped one by one by white men and brutally beaten, and the Communists jailed. But they are determined more than ever to march, and next day for all their bandages they lead a demonstration joined by starving po' whites of the town. The mayor, frightened, gives in. The story ends on Rev. Taylor's exulting words, "Freedom belongs to the strong!"

Uncle Tom's Children is not for those with Pollyanna minds, or those who picture Dixie as a place of picturesque cottonfields and banjo-strumming plantation hands. These stories are strong fare, beautiful with the beauty of naked truth, harsh as a tornado, authentic as life itself, as elemental and burning as a forest fire. Every white person and every Negro should be forced to read them, both for the artistry and as an insight into southern race relations as they really are.

The volume won Mr. Wright a $600 first prize from *Story Magazine* in competition with five hundred other authors, most of them white. It couldn't have been awarded for a more deserving book.

• • •

NATIVE SON GREATEST NOVEL YET BY AN AMERICAN NEGRO

MARCH 6, 1940

Put down *Native Son* by the brilliant young Richard Wright, published March 1 by Harper Brothers and current Book of the Month club selection, as the greatest novel to come from the pen of an American Negro. In fact, it ranks with the best work of any modern American and is likely to prove as controversial as Steinbeck's *Grapes of Wrath* with which it is going to be quite generally compared.

Chief character in this realistic-psychological story is Bigger Thomas, twenty, who for five years has lived in Chicago with brother, sister and mother in a one-room kitchenette. Born in Mississippi, reared in the midst of this nation's color prejudices, ringed by white restrictions, he is anti-social in a society hostile to him. White people he hates and fears. His outlet is petty crimes. Forced to work or be cut off relief, he becomes a chauffeur for the Daltons, rich philanthropists who have given millions to Negro education—and who own the kitchenette building where Bigger Thomas pays exorbitant rent.

The Dalton daughter, Mary, is pro-Communist. First night there he drives her to meet Jan, her sweetheart, a Red organizer, who tries to get Bigger interested in the Communist Party. Mary becomes dead drunk, Bigger takes her home, and is forced to carry her to her bedroom. Mrs. Dalton, blind wife of the philanthropist, enters the room. Thinking only of what it would mean to be found in a white girl's bedroom, Bigger places a pillow over her head to keep her from talking to the mother and accidentally suffocates her. Knowing that no one would believe his story of accidental death, he takes the body down stairs, burns it in the furnace, and tries to blame Jan for the disappearance, knowing the public attitude toward Reds as gleaned from the daily press. Bigger also tries to collect ransom, but after the murder is discovered he flees, killing his gal, Bessie, to keep her from telling. Restricted to hiding on the Southside, he is soon caught, tried and sentenced to die.

Certain sections of this book have an all too-familiar ring to Chicagoans. Not long ago a white woman was killed and after a strenuous manhunt two Negroes were arrested and executed. In his novel Mr. Wright has copies of newspaper stories about Bigger's crime and tells how a lynch attitude was incited in Chicago. Actually this did happen in the recent Nixon case and the fictionalized newspaper stories about Bigger are almost identical with those printed about Nixon. This should make Chicago daily editors blush with shame.

Lest anyone think "Native Son" is merely a sensational yarn about a depraved Negro criminal, let it be said that America is full of potential Bigger Thomases, hounded by white persecution, victims of circumstances they cannot control. Mr. Wright makes this plain; he tells in detail the entire psychology and background that makes such things exist; the episode by Defense Attorney Max at Bigger's trial is one of the greatest documents ever written on interracial relationships in our society and by itself is a tremendous contribution to literature.

• • •

[*12 MILLION BLACK VOICES*]

DECEMBER 3, 1941

Turning from fiction in which he has won international acclaim (*Uncle Tom's Children* and *Native Son*), Richard Wright makes a moving, brilliant appeal for the millions of inarticulate Duskymericans in his new book, *12 Million Black Voices*.

The author has done an excellent job of gathering data and observing the Negro both North and South and of interpreting this material sociologically, albeit with definite Marxian leanings. He has dramatized his argument, what with his "Lords of the Land," "The Bosses of the Buildings," etc., and has made the book as readable as a novel.

There is no getting away from the driving force, the naked realism which characterizes Mr. Wright's work. His words live and breathe; witness his description of the South.

> *In summer the magnolia trees fill the countyside with sweet scent for long miles. Days are slumberous, and the skies are high and thronged with clouds that ride fast. At midday the sun blazes and bleaches the soil. Butterflies flit through the heat; wasps sing their sharp, straight lines; birds fluff and flounce, piping in querulous joy. Nights are covered with canopies, sometimes blue and sometimes black, canopies that sag low with ripe and nervous stars. The throaty boast of frogs momentarily drowns out the call and counter-call of crickets.*

The picture Mr. Wright paints of the Negro in our American democracy is not beautiful. It cannot be beautiful and be accurate. But Mr. Wright, although he says in his foreword that he is speaking for only the masses and not the talented tenth, cannot tell the entire story unless he tells also of those Duskymericans who, like himself, have overcome the handicap of color to win the acclaim and admiration of the white world. And then, too, other Negroes are in some measure responsible for the race's plight; let the dusky brother get the change and he will exploit his less fortunate kind as much as does the money grabbing white.

Some very fine photographs set off the book. They are so fine and realistic that it is just possible they might defeat their own purpose as in the picture of the domestic who leaves the broken down, germ ridden kitchenette to cook in Miss Anne's beautifully appointed and sanitary kitchen. Instead of being horrified that a human has to live in such circumstances, the white reader of means may be horrified that one who comes from such surroundings cooks his food, and solve the problem simply by firing his colored domestic.

• • •

DYNAMIC NEW CHICAGO NOVEL BY WHITE WRITER HAS INTRODUCTION BY WRIGHT: *NEVER COME MORNING*

APRIL 15, 1942

It has long been a common practice for outstanding white writers to prepare forewords to books by Negroes, but it is a distinct novelty for a colored author to write the introduction to a volume by a Caucasian. Yet this has happened with *Never Come Morning*, a dynamic novel by Nelson Algren with an introduction by Richard Wright, author of *Native Son*.

That Wright and Algren should join forces this way is fitting. Both young men are warm personal friends, both worked together on the WPA writers' project in Chicago, and both have written powerful, moving stories of Chicago. Wright's Bigger Thomas, a killer of the Southside, is matched by Bruno Lefty Black, a killer of the Polish district, main character in Algren's novel. A major difference is that *Native Son* has a definite and obvious message and everything is built toward that end. *Never Come Morning* is a subtle and impersonal indictment of social conditions in general.

Bruno Black, popularly known as Lefty Bleeps, is the muscular seventeen-year-old hoodlum son of a widowed mother. A leader of a small gang, his main interests are dodging a WPA job, pitching baseball and boxing. He has dreams of being the White Hope who will knockout Joe Louis and give the Poles a fighter to remember along with Stanley Ketchell and Joe Choynski. He betrays his girl, Steffi R., into a house of prostitution and kills a Greek while so doing. After his arrest in a robbery and a six month prison term, while awaiting fights he acts as tout for the "refined" house where Steffi works, finally gets a chance with Tucker, ranking brown light heavyweight contender, and as he rests on his dressing room table after his kayo of Tucker, is arrested for the Greek's murder. Says Lefty: "Know I'd never get t'be twenty-one anyhow."

Mr. Algren has done a brilliant job in breathing life into his many characters. Beside Lefty and Steffi there are Mama T. and the girls in her house; the Barber; Casey; Bibloback; the Finger; Police Captain Tenezarn and a number of others. They become real flesh and blood people; the section of Chicago where they live is made as vivid as if you were actually there. And his description of the showup at detective headquarters and of Lefty's bout with Tucker are masterpieces of description. He combines humor with pathos. It took a powerful lot of minute observation for this sharp word photography. As for his style, it is a mixture of hardboiled realism and poetry.

This is not alone a story of immigrant Poles and their offspring; it is a story that could and does happen to underprivileged peoples of all nationalities who are forced through some economic necessity to face big city life in the raw, be they Italians, Negroes or native-born whites. This is a dark but important part of American life; Duskymericans will find *Never Come Morning* as virtually interesting as will any other segment of the population.

• • •

RICHARD WRIGHT'S NEW BOOK, *BLACK BOY*, OUT OF STEP WITH WAR TORN WORLD

FEBRUARY 28, 1945

Your reaction to Richard Wright's autobiography up to his seventeenth year, *Black Boy*, will be largely conditioned by your conception of the role of a writer. Should he feel free to write at any time about whatever comes to mind? Or does he, in the midst of an all-out war against fascism, when every intelligent person knows that words are weapons, have the moral duty to use his art to further the fight for democracy?

I pose this question because Wright's book has little to do directly with the fight for democracy, when it could easily have been an important contribution. His three previous volumes, *Uncle Tom's Children*, *Native Son* and

12 Million Black Voices served a useful purpose. His latest creation merely accentuates the unholy pattern of southern race relations without suggesting a solution, even by indirection.

No escapist, Richard Wright is still the realist, writing dramatically, pictorially and brilliantly of his early life. From the age of four, he recalls clearly incident after incident as he moved from town to town, never adjusting himself to hunger and poverty, the religious fanaticism of his Seventh Day Adventist family, the desertion of his mother by his father, or the status of black folk in Dixie. With only a few years of formal schooling, he developed a passion for reading, determined to be a writer, and had his first story published in three installments in the Negro paper at Jackson, Mississippi, incurring the wrath of his family. After graduation from the ninth grade as valedictorian, he struck out alone, going to Memphis where an anxious mother sought fruitlessly to persuade him to marry her sex-mad daughter. At the end of the book he is preparing to come north for the first time.

As you read the book, you understand the forces which made Richard Wright what he is today. You see the making of a complete individualist, even one who is determined to have his way if at all possible even though it means desertion of man and causes when they do not conform to his opinion of what they should be.

But I am disturbed by Wright's preoccupation with pornography. Certain incidents are related at considerable detail, it seems, only for the salacious offset. They cause the reader to lose sympathy for Wright, the boy. But perhaps the author and publisher had their eye on possible banning in Boston and a resultant sales increase, particularly among the dirty minded. As a matter of fact, the title, *Black Boy*, reeks with commercialism. The original title, *American Hunger*, had both dignity and appropriateness, for the book tells of Dick Wright's quest to satisfy his hunger, both physical and spiritual.

It seems to me that the author, in his frequent commentaries throughout the book, could easily have showed the strong connection between southern racism and Hitler race theories, instead of taking the long chance of having it drawn by only the small, observant minority among the thousands who will read *Black Boy*. A craftsman of the stature and ability of Richard Wright could have done this effectively and memorably, thereby making his work a guide to action in remedying such conditions.

Instead he spends his time excreting such inaccurate generalizations as this gem found on page 33:

After I had outlived the shocks of childhood, after the habit of reflection had been born in me, I used to mull over the absence of real kindness in Negroes, how unstable was our tenderness, how lacking in genuine passion we were, how void of great hope, how timid our joy, how bare our traditions, how hollow our memories, how lacking we were in those intangible sentiments that bind man to man, and how shallow was even our despair. After I learned the other ways of life I used to brood upon the unconscious irony of those who felt that Negroes led so passional an existence! I saw that what had been taken for our emotional strength was our negative confusions, our flights, our fears, our frenzy under pressure.

I could speak of the egotism which causes Wright to believe that the story of his life up to the age of seventeen is more important at this moment in history than the world-wide struggle for human freedom and the stake of the Negro in this war.

When *Native Son* appeared in 1940, I termed it the greatest novel yet produced by an American Negro. Even despite my dissatisfaction with *Black Boy*, I still consider Richard Wright our greatest master of prose. I hope, therefore, that in the future he will again use his amazing talent for the benefit of the people at large. And if he has another book like *Black Boy*, let it wait until after the war or tie it in with the war.

• • •

BONTEMPS' *BLACK THUNDER*—AN IMPORTANT BOOK
FEBRUARY 5, 1936

Recapturing the atmosphere of Virginia in 1800, Arna Bontemps, the young Negro author, has given us a most important book in his *Black Thunder*, just published last week by the Macmillan Company. The plot, simple enough, deals with a massive young slave, Gabriel, who dreams of being America's Toussaint L'Ouverture, freeing the bondsmen and setting up a black empire in Virginia. Ready to march on Richmond at the dead of night with 1,100 followers, the plan is frustrated by a thunderstorm. Before his "army" can strike again, plans are revealed to the whites by two followers—similar to what goes on today—and the rebellion is nipped with the leaders hanged.

Black Thunder represents a distinct advance over the author's other book length story, *God Sends Sunday*. Obviously Bontemps went to considerable research to build an authentic atmosphere. His description is often poetically beautiful, his style subdued. Instead of rising to a grand climax through a succession of intense and passionate scenes, Bontemps presents his story through a gallery of vivid and clear pictorial etchings, each distinct in itself although related to its fellows. This is undoubtedly best: a rip-snortin' novel calculated to make its readers see red would arouse useless passions in 1936 about a situation existing in 1800.

Besides Gabriel, whose counterpart is said to have actually existed, other well drawn characters include Juba, his slim-waisted and high spirited mistress; Pharoah, who revealed the plot because Gabriel wouldn't let him lead a column into Richmond. Ben, a personal servant of Mr. Mosely Shepard; Melody, a free mulatto enchantress who consorted with a white planter's son and radicals, and the Jacobins, French-born whites blamed for fostering the rebellion. But Gabriel, afraid of nothing, not even death, dominates all.

Bontemps' uses of dialect is unique. It is a mixture of every day English with colloquialism. Because of the fine writing, the insight into black and white thought in those years, and the graphic portrayal of slave-time Virginia by a talented Negro author, *Black Thunder* takes its place as an important book that ought to be read by both races.

• • •

BONTEMPS' NEW NOVEL TELLS OF HAITIAN SLAVE REVOLT
May 17, 1939

On the publication slightly more than three years ago of *Black Thunder* by the same author, Arna Bontemps, became generally recognized as the first American Negro to write an historical novel. It dealt with an ill-fated slave insurrection in our own United States. *Drums At Dusk* tells of the successful slave revolt in Haiti, during the era of the French revolution, which brought Toussaint L'Ouverture to power and renown.

Although the story covers only a few days from immediately prior to the uprising through the first battle between government soldiers and insurrectionists, a solid background of the causes of this epic struggle is given. In developing his plot, Mr. Bontemps has used a camera technique, moving from clear picture to clear picture with Hollywood dexterity.

Haiti at that same time was a troubled island of 500,000 Negro slaves, 10,000 white aristocrats, 30,000 low class whites and 40,000 mulattos sired by these aristocrats. Most of these slaves, unlike those at the Breda plantation who had a kind overseer, suffered from cruelty; even at Breda those wailing from a strange fever were subjected to a stomach turning emetic. But rebellion was in the air. Secret meetings were held at night. Even some of the whites risked the deadly danger of being pointed out as Friends of the Blacks to actively aid the cause of freedom.

Suddenly one night while a big party was in progress at Breda, the storm broke. Slaves wreaked a vengeance on their masters that was equaled only by what these same slaves had previously undergone. Fortunate members of the aristocracy fled to the garrisoned nearby city, leaving their mansions looted and burning. The slaves have sated their first lust for blood and pillage and await the ascendancy of a leader as the book ends.

Several characters stand out; there is young Diron Desautels, Friend of the Blacks, about whom most of the volume is woven; Celester, his sweetheart; Toussaint, already fifty and a coachman at Breda, who later was to win undying fame; Count Armand de Sacy, middle-aged libertine visiting from Paris; Captain Frounier, slave trader; Mme. Visard, sinister and beautiful, and M. and Mme. de Libertas who run the Breda plantation.

The reader's chief regret is that Mr. Bontemps chose to end his story where he did. Unless he plans a sequel at some later date, he might have included in this work the story of the entire revolution and the career of Toussaint. There was tense drama throughout this historic struggle, and Mr. Bontemps, who has long been a student of Haitian history and recently did research work there on a Julius Rosenwald fellowship, is capable of congealing the entire story in unforgettable prose.

This author's style and technique are surer with each new book. Around a dozen years ago he won first prize in a national poetry competition held by *Opportunity Magazine*, and his prose displays frequent passages of rich imagery akin to poetry. A disciple of restraint, in *Drums at Dusk* he forswore the obvious chance to engage in blood and thunder narration substituting gentle understatement, thereby increasing the effect of such vivid scenes as the cock fights at Breda and the death of Count de Sacy. His language is smooth flowing and easily read.

Born in Louisiana thirty-six years ago, Mr. Bontemps now makes his home in Chicago. *Drums at Dusk* is his third novel. He has had several books for children published, his most recent being *Sad Faced Boy*, and has written other children's stories and one or two plays with Langston Hughes.

• • •

NOVEL BY NEW NEGRO WRITER IS OF REALISTIC, HARDBOILED SCHOOL
JUNE 28, 1939

Most novelists of ordinary means dream of making enough money by sales of their published work to spend all their time at writing. Negro novelists seldom reach this goal because their work, for the most part, appeals to a rather select group of readers. William Attaway, young author of *Let Me Breathe Thunder*, published last Friday by Doubleday Doran, has the best chance of obtaining financial success of any recent novelist of color.

Mr. Attaway's book is not a Negro book, for its main characters are not Negroes nor does it deal with interracial problems. It is the kind of book that could have been written by a white person with sympathy for the minor colored characters who are in the story, and represents one of the few times in American literary history in which a Negro has forgotten race and written of his Caucasian brother.

Let Me Breathe Thunder tears a period of several weeks from the lives of Step and Ed, two depression youths drifting from town to town in the West. With them is Hi-Boy, a Mexican lad of ten whose past they cannot fathom. The story is of the two older youths and their young pal who touches in them fine emotions they hadn't dreamed they possessed and his tragic death while the three hobo from Oregon to Denver. Ed relates the narrative in the first person.

The result is gripping realism of the "hardboiled" school. In this it is akin to Cain's *The Postman Always Rings Twice* and McIntyre's *Steps Going Down*. It's a story snatched from life itself, and so powerful as to defy being laid aside until all 267 pages have been read.

Mr. Attaway has written a book which most of our famous white writers might be proud to author. He has a natural easy style, economy of words, a flair for strong imagery and the ability to make his characters come to life on the printed page. At twenty-five, this brilliant young writer, a graduate of the University of Illinois who has done a stretch of hoboing, looms as one of the brightest new stars on the whole literary horizon.

• • •

O CANAAN! NEW NOVEL BY TURPIN, PICTURES MIGRATION TO CHICAGO

SEPTEMBER 23, 1939

Those who contend that in order to have fiction published a Negro must write of the lowest classes or else play to traditional white attitudes toward the race will find this theory blasted in *O Canaan!,* a second novel from the pen of Waters E. Turpin whose first book was *These Low Grounds.*

In this volume of 311 pages, just published by Doubleday Doran of New York, Mr. Turpin is not concerned about pandering to Caucasian slants on Aframericans. Instead he is occupied with the story of a family which migrated from Mississippi to Chicago during World War days, rose to wealth and prominence, lost nearly all in the stock market crash of 1929, and out of the debris went on to again find itself.

Big Joe Benson, forty, over the protests of his wife, Christine, takes her and their five children north to Chicago in 1916 along with many others lured by the promise of big money in industry. He sets up a store, goes to night school, buys real estate, watches his fortune rise, and moves into a white neighborhood. Later comes the 1919 race riots in which he loses his oldest son, Sol. Afterward comes Prohibition. In partnership with a Jew he becomes a big bootlegger, riding high until his arrest which costs him a pretty penny. But the family is now wealthy and "in society." He helps start a bank just before the depression and loses all his money in an effort to save the enterprise. Although wiped out and suffering from a bad heart, he never loses his nerve and becomes a Pullman porter which he still is as the story ends.

Christine, his wife, can't stand reverses and returns home. Lem, another son who becomes a social worker, finally dies of tuberculosis and Junior, family black sheep, succumbs to syphilis. Connie marries a young doctor and Essie, his youngest daughter, turns their mansion into a rooming house and after meeting Paul Johnson, graduate of a southern college caught in depression's whirlpool, starts a beauty parlor in partnership on his policy winnings and finally marries him.

It is refreshing to find an author willing to write of Negroes outside Harlem or the deep South. Chicago is exceedingly rich in source material, just heretofore little of it has been used. Mr. Turpin deserves credit for transcribing an authentic picture of Negro life in America's great inland metropolis.

O Canaan! is interesting and easy to read, although the author now and then becomes a bit flowery in his phrases. His use of dialect is skillful and never boresome. Mr. Turpin's book should appeal to those who want a good, readable story of a Negro family with no more interracial conflicts than those which customarily beset the lives of most Duskymericans.

• • •

KINGSBLOOD ROYAL SHOULD SCARE ANTI-NEGRO WHITES

June 11, 1946

If I were white and possessed the usual quota of prejudice against colored people, and then by chance happened to read *Kingsblood Royal*, I think I would be scared almost witless by the fear of Negro forebears. For there are few people who can trace all their ancestors back even three generations and definitely identify all eight great-grandparents.

When you go back five generations—a mere 125 years or so—you find you have some thirty-two foreparents. Among those thirty-two people might have been almost anybody from China to Timbuktu, from Siberia to South Africa. Maybe, if you try real hard, you can dig up the lowdown on half a dozen or so. But that's a minority out of thirty-two. What about the others?

It so happened that Neil Kingsblood, a young banker of Grand Republic, Minnesota, made the mistake of looking up his forebears. To please his father, who thought the Kingsbloods were descended from English royalty, Neil investigated. But instead of British nobility on his father's side, he found an ancestor of his mother was a full blooded French Negro.

The story, then, is that of a young white bank executive with the right connections, a socially prominent wife, a darling daughter, and the usual attitudes toward Negroes, and what happened after the 1/32 part of African blood made Neil into a Negro in accordance with our queer American laws.

There are those who will think Neil's reactions unreal. With that, I cannot agree. He is painted as a young man not particularly brilliant but fundamentally honest. I have an idea that an honest person would try to find out all he could about the "inferior" people to which he suddenly finds himself belonging, and the realization of the raw injustices against Negroes could easily produce the John Brown kind of militancy that caused Neil to openly commit himself.

It is in his descriptions of racial patterns, of white ideas on Negroes, and in his American creed, that the author's satire becomes devastating. This took a lot of observing; Mr. Lewis etches these observations in acid.

Of course Neil loses his job, is kicked out of his club, and runs into the difficulties common to most Negroes. Finally a mob comes to oust him from his home in an area covered by restrictive covenants; the story ends with Neil, his wife who stuck with him and assorted friends being carted off to jail for having the audacity to defend themselves.

This is the kind of story that everybody should be forced by law to read and discuss, particularly white Americans. After this, nobody but a professional idiot could still believe the mumbo jumbo of race.

• • •

KNOCK ON ANY DOOR MIRRORS WEAKNESS OF OUR SOCIETY

JULY 23, 1947

The new realistic novel that is making such a tremendous impact on literate America, *Knock on Any Door*, is not merely the case history of a young Italian named Nick Romano who was put to death at twenty-one in the electric chair. It is primarily a mirror held up to our society and shows how poverty and the slums create young killers and hoodlums. In a land as rich as ours, there is no excuse for either poverty or slums.

Nick, born in Denver, reared in the Catholic church as an altar boy, started along the hoodlum path when his father lost his business and was forced to move to a blighted area. Nick, learning how to steal, went at fourteen to a reform school that didn't reform. Coming to Chicago, he learned the trade of strong-arming, of armed robbery, capitalized on his good looks with both women and men, and adopted as his philosophy, "live hard, die young, and make a good looking corpse."

He married but his wife committed suicide after Nick was unable to adjust himself to seeming respectability. Following a holdup, he killed Officer Riley in the notorious "Skid Row" area of West Madison street, was arrested, defended by a brilliant lawyer, convicted and sentenced to die. The story ends with Nick strapped in the electric chair.

Nick Romano might be any one of thousands of youths. *Knock on Any Door* in the underprivileged sections of any big city and you will find the counterpart of Nick. The jails and the underworld are full of Nicks, both black and white. Of course not all those reared in this kind of environment become "anti-social," but the number is sufficiently large to merit the most serious attention. And only when poverty, insecurity, inequality, etc., are eliminated can we halt the creation of new Nick Romanos.

As a graphic writer, Willard Motley ranks with the best. His description is photographic in its detail and on many occasions becomes sheer poetry. With this volume, which is as much a social treatise as a gripping, powerful novel, Mr. Motley takes his position in the forefront of contemporary writers.

• • •

NEW HUGHES BOOK SHOWS PITHY PORTRAITS IN POETRY

MARCH 25, 1942

After authoring volumes of short stories, a novel, an autobiography and several plays, Langston Hughes returns to his first love, poetry, in his new volume,

Shakespeare in Harlem. And if all of this implies that Mr. Hughes is extremely versatile, that is just what is meant. Mr. Hughes is at home in any medium of expression and is one of those literary rarities: a creative writer able to live purely by his pen.

This new book is intended to be a volume of light verse. It is. What's more, this reviewer suspects it was slanted particularly for the Caucasian reader—highly desirable, if Mr. Hughes and Mr. Knopf want to sell it. But no matter: Mr. Hughes paints pithy portraits for heavy handed propaganda for Solution No. 999 to the Race Question; you can skip this book.

The Associated Negro Press considers it an honor to have released some of the poetry prior to its publication. Other compositions appeared originally in *Esquire, Poetry, The New Yorker* and other periodicals. All of it is worth reading time after time. Give ear to what Mr. Hughes suggests in the frontispiece: "Blues, ballads and reels to be read aloud, crooned, shouted, recited and sung. Some with gestures, some not—as you like. None with a far-away voice."

Section headings give a key to the content: Seven Moments of Love, Declarations, Blues for Men, Death in Harlem, Mammy Songs, Ballads, Blues for Ladies, and Lenox Avenue. As for individual poems—which range from pungent two line epigrams to narratives of several pages—the title poem for the section, "Death in Harlem," strikes this bystander as being most impressive. It's a ballad in a Frankie and Johnnie mood, but there the resemblance ends. The Hughes creation is genuine poetry, memorable and alive. So for that matter, is just about all of the book. It will be your loss if you fail to read *Shakespeare in Harlem.*

• • •

DISARMING CHARM TEMPERS NEWEST HUGHES POETRY

JUNE 4, 1947

Langston Hughes writes with such ease and disarming charm that many people who ordinarily would have little patience with poetry are completely captivated by his work. That, I think, is the secret of his popularity which has made him the most widely read of Negro poets for some two decades.

His fifth and latest volume [*Fields of Wonder*], recently published, is devoted to lyric poems. Brightly polished they are, and carefully cut like small diamonds. They range from pure imagery to glimpses of reality. Best of all, they communicate directly with the emotions.

Of course, Mr. Hughes is modern, having a command of both rhyme and free verse, but giving rhyme the living feeling of today instead of the stiffness of the departed past. For instance, here is his "Little Song":

Lonely people
In the lonely night
Grab a lonely dream
And hold it tight.

Lonely people
In the lonely day
Work to salt
Their dream away.

In this volume Mr. Hughes is not preoccupied with what is known as "the race problem." He uses a universal approach, on behalf of all humanity, so that the reader may see the world through the eyes of a poet who happens to be a Negro instead of as an open propagandist. There are just enough verses that could have been written only by a Negro to assure the successes of this indirect approach.

• • •

MONTAGE OF A DREAM DEFERRED IS LANGSTON HUGHES' FINEST VOLUME OF POETRY

February 28, 1951

For a quarter of a century, Langston Hughes has been in the forefront of contemporary poets. And now, with a world reputation that is almost legendary, he has authored a new book that is easily his finest among a series of fine volumes of poetry.

Montage of a Dream Deferred, published February 19 by Henry Holt, is the title. It borrows liberally from the terms and feeling of contemporary hot jazz and bop to create a movingly realistic picture of Harlem as it is, with its joys and its dreams deferred.

As was the case with *Simple Speaks His Mind*, this is primarily a book for Negroes. That, to me, is a good thing, for the tendency too often is to write about Harlem primarily for the white reader.

Like other of Hughes' work, the style is disarmingly simple—so simple that often the brilliant artistry may be overlooked. Yet this conversational simplicity makes for the charm and readability that produces a wide audience. It is only rarely that one encounters the obscurantism that too often hangs like a heavy cloud over the work of certain other highly regarded poets.

It seems to me that any poetry woven out of the daily lives of people should be written to be read by the people instead of by a small closed corps of intellectual snobs. Apparently this is also Langston Hughes' belief, for I have yet to see anything from his pen that could not be read and understood to those whose formal education ended in the lower grades.

Consider, for instance, this in "Children's Rhymes":

> *By what sends*
> *the white kids*
> *I ain't sent:*
> *I know I can't*
> *be President.*

Hughes has his ear attuned to jive talk and uses it for sharp portraits, as in the conclusion of "Dead in There," describing the burial of a sharp cat:

> *Squares*
> *Who couldn't dig him,*
> *Plant him now—*
> *Out where it makes*
> *No diff' no how.*

The volume also contains "Freedom Train" as well as a number of other widely known poems not previously available in book form. The book is so uniformly excellent that it should bring one of the year's top literary awards to Langston Hughes—if such awards are to be made on pure merit without any other considerations.

• • •

FOR MY PEOPLE BEST POETRY VOLUME IN FIVE YEARS
NOVEMBER 25, 1942

It is a distinct pleasure to read this new volume of poetry by Miss Margaret Walker, for her *For My People* is far and away the best book of poetry written by a Negro to be published in the last five years. It deeply deserves its selection as the 1942 winner in the annual Yale Series of Younger Poets contest.

Miss Walker has plenty to say, and a personal and dynamic way of saying it. She is modern in style and approach with the first section entirely in free verse, and has developed her own kind of sonnet, on display in Section III. She also has a good ear for folklore as her humorous ballads demonstrate. Unfortunately, however, she occasionally repeats a word or phrase in such a way that it dulls the emotions of the reader. But this is a minor fault that can easily be corrected.

Having lived in Chicago for some time, Miss Walker has come under the influence of the early, realistic Midwestern school of expression and in more than one instance shows traces of Carl Sandburg, Through it all she shows keen social consciousness coupled with nostalgia for the southland of her nativity. In "Sorrow Home" she says:

> *I am no hot-house bulb to be reared in steam-heated flats with the music of "L" and subway in my ears, walled in steel and wood and brick far from the sky.*
> *I want the cotton fields, tobacco and the cane. I want to walk along with sacks of seed to drop in fallow ground. Restless music is in my heart and I am eager to be gone.*
> *O Southland, sorrow home, melody beating in my bone and blood! How long will the Klan of hate, the hounds and the chain gangs keep me from my own!*

Without question, this young writer's poetry is smooth, easy flowing, dynamic and rhythmic, always majestic and occasionally rhapsodic. Her title poem, incidentally, was first printed in the esteemed *Poetry, A Magazine of Verse* where it excited considerable controversy a few years ago, and was also chosen for *The Negro Caravan*.

Her section of ballads, written in a semi-dialect, semi-colloquial style, has a spiritual kinship with work in similar vein of Langston Hughes. Miss Walker not only sings of such traditional favorites as John Henry and Stack-O-Lee, but also paints portraits of such characters as "Poppa Chicken," "Kissie Lee," "Molly Means" and others. Here is part of her saga of "Teacher:"

> *Women scarred his upper lip:*
> *Nearly tore his head*
> *Off his shoulders with a gun*
> *Kept his eyes blood-red.*
>
> *Women sent him to his doom.*
> *Women set the trap.*
> *Teacher was a bad, bold man*
> *Lawd, but such a sap!*

A word about the author, Miss Walker, who is professor of English at Livingstone College, Salisbury, North Carolina, is just twenty-seven years old. Born in Birmingham, she went to school there and in Mississippi and New Orleans before finishing Northwestern University in 1935 and taking her master's degree at Iowa two years ago. With such a start as that made in *For My People*, she seems destined for a brilliant literary career.

• • •

NEW BOOK OF POETRY SHOWS STRENGTH, MASTERY OF TECHNIQUE

SEPTEMBER 20, 1944

Melvin B. Tolson, who directs drama and debate at Marshall College, down Texas way, has authored a book of poetry which should establish him in the forefront of contemporary writers of verse. His first volume, *Rendezvous with*

America, just published by Dodd, Mond and Company, reveals strength, maturity, and mastery of technique.

Mr. Tolson lives in no ivory. His title poem treats of America today; his best known work, "Dark Symphony," which won the national poetry contest sponsored by the American Negro Exposition in 1940, tells particularly of the Negro, and his final composition, "Tapestries of Time," is a cosmopolitan preachment against world fascism. A preoccupation with contemporary problems is found through the volume.

His style is lean and hard. He has eliminated unnecessary words, often using short punchy lines to build additional power as in "Song for Myself." Most of his poetry is in rhyme, but it is a rhyme as modern as tomorrow. He has also a remarkable gift for epigram. Consider these lines from "The Ballad of the Rattlesnake:"

> *The blond man lies*
> *Like a bar of lead*
> *No hiss or laugh*
> *Can vex the dead.*
>
> *The desert holds*
> *In its frying pan*
> *The bones of a snake*
> *And the bones of a man.*
>
> *And many a thing*
> *With a rock in its tail*
> *Kills the nearest thing*
> *And dies by the trail.*

Mr. Tolson has read and studied. This shows in his use of history. Unfortunately, it also crops up occasionally in his use of words, for now and then this poet has a tendency to get bookish. And his entire style of writing, so often intellectual and mystic, will undoubtedly prevent a wide appreciation of his brilliancy. Unfortunately, he is as yet too complex for the masses. If ever he can develop a style as simple and direct as that of Langston Hughes, for example, to go along with his strength and beauty and insight into life, he can well become the poet of all the people instead of the discriminating few.

• • •

POWER AND FORCE CHARACTERIZE YOUNG POET'S FIRST VOLUME

SEPTEMBER 28, 1946

For their first venture into the field of poetry publishing, the new firm of Farrar, Strauss and Company chose the works of Owen Dodson, young Negro writer, who for several years has been making an enviable reputation for himself. The finished product shows that the choice was wise.

Powerful Long Ladder is a powerful good book. Mr. Dodson has force and fire and is a realist rather than an escapist. He mirrors the inequities of Negro life with strong drama. His most ambitious effort is in the section called "Three Choruses from a Verse Drama: Divine Comedy." Remembering the current wave of anti-Negro terrorism, consider this passage:

> *PRIEST:*
> *The Lord's children are never alone or angry.*
> *Prayer changes things. Go home and pray.*
> *CHORUS:*
> *We have prayed in the solid night,*
> *But still our children rub their skin in terror*
> *And stare at their hands.*
> *There are faces at our windows,*
> *Nooses in our hallways.*
> *PRIEST:*
> *Go home and pray.*
> *CHORUS:*
> *We have no home!*

Mr. Dodson has a feel for the plight of all plain people as his "Jonathan's Song" shows. This poem was written after seeing the Jewish pageant, "We Will Never Die." He also has a sensitivity and a way with words that stands him in good stead, although now and then he grows a bit mystical and occasionally does not use utmost care in finding the precise word.

This thirty-one-year-old author is a happy addition to that small but increasing group of Negro writers who have something important to say and who can stand on their merits with the creative artists of other groups.

• • •

BACK TO AFRICAN MUSIC
OCTOBER 21, 1936

Two volumes by N. G. T. Ballanta of Freetown, Sierra Leone, entitled *The Aesthetics of African Music* and *The Philosophy of African Music* will, on their appearance, be of tremendous importance to every musician as well as to the Duskymerican public which has an all too little known racial heritage.

Mr. Ballanta, who has spent over twenty years of research on the subject, first became interested in 1914 when, in Gambia, he noticed that a flutist of the Bambara tribe produced a tone in his instrument midway between B natural and B flat. He tried to reproduce the tone on his own small harmonium but could not.

This caused Mr. Ballanta to do some thinking. Suddenly he realized that up to that time no attention was ever paid by any of the musicians in West Africa to the music of the native tribes and they were all engaged in copying European music for the expression of their ideas.

His interest thoroughly aroused, a year later he traveled into the Bo district and found the songs of the Mondi people ended on the second of the scale—"do" instead of "re." After giving this strange discovery deep thought, Mr. Ballanta concluded that "European music is not African music and one is quite different from the other. Both cannot be governed by the same laws." He then decided to seriously study to find out what caused the difference.

He came to the U.S.—and found white Americans also baffled by the technique of the spirituals. At the suggestion of Clarence Cameron White, he wrote an article on African music which appeared in the *Musical Courier* and eventually brought him a scholarship. Since 1924 he had been collecting data as he traveled through Africa.

His books should settle many questions about American Negro and African music, both dance and religious. And they ought to create greater respect for our African ancestry.

• • •

JAZZMEN IS AUTHORITATIVE NEW BOOK ON HISTORY OF JAZZ AND ITS MAKERS
NOVEMBER 8, 1939

Jazz, a new art still in a formative stage, has its traditions and heroes. Its historians are constantly turning up new evidence on origins and artists, and different authorities may reach opposite conclusions from the same or similar sets of facts. *Jazzmen*, the new book just published on the history of this form of music and its exponents and written by several men, surprisingly enough has only a few instances of this kind.

The editors have worked with exceeding care, interviewing every living musician who could contribute factual material, checking back, consulting other authorities, and making the sum total of material available to each chapter author. The result is the most informative tome on jazz and its players that this reviewer has yet read.

Jazz, the book sets forth, began among New Orleans Negroes who, after the Civil War, began playing by ear on the white man's instruments, fusing the music of their former masters with traditional African material. By the 1890s they had developed this style of playing to the point where Buddy Bolden, the granddaddy of all hot cornetists, was able to produce history's first jazz band. Improvisers, as all jazz artists must be, they played in unison what they felt. Before the Spanish American War, Buddy was the man of the hour, playing his new music at picnics, dances, funerals and parades. After him came such other cornet greats as Bunk Johnson, who taught Louis Armstrong, Freddie Keppard and Joe Oliver. The latter three helped carry jazz north.

How jazz and the slow blues were played in Storyville, the red light district of New Orleans created in 1897, how Jack Laine (with two "passing" Negroes in his band) pioneered jazz among the whites, its introduction north along the Mississippi River, its debut in Chicago in 1911 and in New York later on, and its development among white and colored players up until the present day is told in exciting and intensely readable fashion. There is also a chapter on record collecting and another on jazz critics.

E. Simms Campbell has a chapter on the blues, much of the material coming from Clarence Williams. Blues were played before jazz; it becomes evident that W. C. Handy's recognition is not for creating this kind of music but for being the first to write it down as well as the first to formally compose in this field. As for boogie-woogie pianistics, just "discovered" generally a scant three years ago, one author in *Jazzmen* says it was originated in Texas years ago and bore the name of "western blues" or "fast blues;" another writer credits Jim Yancey, now groundkeeper at the Chicago White Sox ball park, with furthering this style.

An interesting sidelight on jazz is that while some of its great artists, notably Bix Beiderbecke, Frank Teschmaker, Bessie Smith and King Oliver are dead, others of its legendary pioneers are alive and struggling for existence in New Orleans. Bunk Johnson, who played with Bolden in 1895, is still there; "Big Eye" Louis Nelson, who in 1905 was the inspiration for Jimmy Noone, Johnny Dodds and Sidney Bechet, was playing great jazz on a broken-down clarinet at the last Mardi Gras.

However, some of the foremost players are not mentioned. The names of Mildred Bailey, Billie Holiday, Roy Eldridge, Lester Young, Red Norvo and several others are omitted. As a matter of fact, this book could have been five times its total of 360 pages and then would not have come near exhausting the vast amount of material available on jazz and its interpreters. That so much important matter has been crammed between the covers is a tribute to the expert editing of Ramsey and Smith.

What I would like to see produced is a work having sections devoted to the various instruments in a jazz band, chief soloists on these instruments with short biographies and critical appraisal, and lists of records showing these musicians at their best. Perhaps Ramsey and Smith may eventually get around to authoring this some day.

• • •

NEW BOOK GIVES SHORT HISTORY OF JAZZ AND LISTS RECORDS TO HEAR

April 1, 1942

Most books on hot jazz—or "swing" if you prefer—have treated this form of music historically or critically or else have concentrated on records. It is therefore a pleasure to have available a book which not only gives some of the highlights of jazz history, distinguishes between styles of playing, but also lists outstanding hot records that illustrate these schools as well as difference between individual musicians.

Such a volume is the newly published *Jazz Record Book*, written by a group of men who know their way around in the field of swing music. Not only that, they have an expert knowledge of what is called "serious" music and the "classics," and therefore are able to evaluate the playing of jazzicians in terms used by technicians who idolize Bach, Beethoven and Brahams. That they have this foundation in the conservatory and yet look upon hot jazz as a true art form should give pause to those die-hard Duskymericans who sniff contemptuously at jazz because it is basically a Negro music and was not born in sixteenth-century Germany.

Dedicated to the late Jelly Roll Morton, a pioneer and truly remarkable composer-pianist, the volume is divided into two parts; "Jazz History" and "Recorded Jazz." Under the first those titles are listed: New Orleans and the River, the Parent Style, Chicago Breakdown, New York and Harlem, Blues and Boogie Woogie, Seven Brass and Four Reed, and They Still Play Jazz. Those titles are repeated in the second section which describes individual records illustrating these styles.

Around a thousand records are listed. The beauty of it is that most of these discs are currently available or soon will be through reissue. Some were waxed in the latter half of 1941, just to show you how current his book is. And while the critical reader may not agree with the authors' evaluation of each platter, there is no denying that the choice of hot wax is uniformly excellent.

• • •

BEST BOOK YET ON JAZZ WATERS DOWN NEGRO BACKGROUND
JANUARY 26, 1949

It is especially lamentable that the new book *Jazz: A People's Music*, glosses over the African background of the American Negro, for this volume is without question the best study yet published about hot music and its reason for being.

Mr. Finkelstein knows and understands jazz. He understands the socio-economic forces that made this music a revolutionary development, a method of protest against the continuing oppression of the Negro people and a sharp weapon in the struggle for democracy; he understands also the attempt by Tin Pan Alley and the large commercial music interests to rob it of its guts and sting. Herein lies the volume's chief value.

But either he does not know or does not understand the individual qualities of African culture that made jazz the different kind of music it is. If African civilization and music had the same customs and standards of European music and civilization, there could be no argument with his approach. But there are major differences.

Jazz is actually a blending of the European with the African, two greatly different kinds of musical experience. Jazz originated among the Negro people who maintained strong strains of ancestral culture. Therefore to ignore the African background is even more serious than ignoring the European.

But outside of this and a few other controversial issues, including the significance of "bop" music, the book is completely sound. It should be revealing to those Negroes who look down their dusky noses at jazz as something to be ashamed of, for here they can see in black and white why hot music is tied up not only with the Negro's struggle for equality, but with the democratic aspirations of all other peoples.

Spirituals and the blues, forerunners of jazz, are brilliantly analyzed by Mr. Finkelstein. He also treats of individual musicians and styles, discusses the future of this still fluid music, and lashes hard at the restrictions and discrimination which handicap the Negro.

Fittingly, he concludes with: "Jazz is the living embodiment of the creative power of the people. It is especially the product, and gift to America, of the most poverty-stricken, hounded and exploited of the country, the Negro people. In it we can find the growing consciousness of the Negro people of their own solidarity as a people, a sense of national traditions, history and culture, born not out of Africa but out of their struggles against slavery, and out of the part they took in every struggle for the progress of American democracy from the War of Independence onward."

• • •

ASSOCIATES PUBLISH THREE IMPORTANT BRONZE BOOKLETS

SEPTEMBER 14, 1938

There is no excuse now for any Negro to say that lack of finance keeps him from knowing more about his race. To a list of three important titles, the Associates in Negro Folk Education at Washington, D.C., have just added *Negro Poetry and Drama* by Sterling Brown; *The Negro and Economic Reconstruction*, by T. Arnold Hill; and *The Negro in American Fiction*, by Sterling Brown.

Negro Poetry and Drama, a book of 142 pages, sells for twenty-five cents each copy, less if more than ten copies are purchased. Mr. Brown, professor of English at Howard University, Guggenheim Fellow, and one of America's foremost poets and critics, has condensed in this volume a critical appraisal of virtually every capable Aframerican poet from Jupiter Hammon and Phillis Wheatley to bards of the present day, gives illustration of their work, offers discussion questions, and lists additional reading matter.

Two chapters are given to the writing of white poets on Negro life with similar critical treatment. The section on Negro drama discusses the development of plays on Negro life by white and black authors, minstrels, folk drama and the realistic and problem drama, including *Green Pastures*, the works of Eugene O'Neill and WPA theatre productions. The entire volume is a comprehensive, though condensed, history of the race's poetic and dramatic efforts since arriving on these shores.

The Negro in American Fiction, a longer volume of 210 pages, sells for thirty-five cents, less in lots of more than ten. In this book Professor Brown's keen analytical powers and his exhaustive study of the Negro character in stories by whites and of works by colored authors are evidenced. He shows the development of the Negro character from the status of clown, inferior or menial, on through the Harlem Renaissance to the present day when such noted writers as T. S. Stribling and William Faulkner are striving for accuracy and closes with the statement that current trends indicate "the Negro character in fiction may meet with the justice that has so long been deferred."

The Negro and Economic Reconstruction has eighty pages of exceedingly readable facts and statistics on the Negro worker since coming to America as a slave. The author, T. Arnold Hill, is director of the Department of Industrial

Relations of the National Urban League and is qualified to speak with authority. It is his conclusion that the race must use mass protest to correct economic injustices, and must support and be active in progressive movements. The book sells for twenty-five cents per copy, less for orders of more than ten.

These volumes are known as the "Bronze Booklet Series" and are aimed to bring within reach of the average reader basic facts and progressive views about Negro life. Previously published were the titles, *The Negro and His Music*, by Dr. Alain Locke; *Negro Art: Past and Present*, by Dr. Locke, and *A World View of Race*, by Professor Ralph J. Bunche. Each of these contains in simple, direct language information on the Negro that previously could be obtained only by long hours of wading through many other volumes. All of them should be read by every person who is the least bit interested in the accomplishments of Duskymericans. They may be ordered from the Associates in Negro Folk Education, P.O. Box #636, Ben Franklin Station, Washington, D.C.

• • •

FOR SHORT COURSE IN LITERATURE READ
THE NEGRO CARAVAN
MARCH 4, 1942

Dwarfing all previous efforts to present an omnibus of Aframerican literary creations is *The Negro Caravan*, a huge book of more than a thousand pages obviously published with an eye toward classroom and reference use as well as for the private library. Three college professors labored to bring this ponderous volume into being and they should be proud of their achievement for here they have a nearly complete history of American Negro literature.

I say "nearly complete" because there is one serious omission. Nowhere is there mention of *The Pedro Gorino* written by the late Captain Harry Dean in collaboration with the eminent white critic, Sterling North. Captain Dean, who died in Chicago during 1935 at the age of seventy-one, was one of the most interesting Negroes in our history and, so far as I know, the only Duskymerican to own and sail his merchant ship on the seven seas. Pedro Gorino recited his exciting adventurers in all parts of the world, adventures which included arrest by the British for running guns to the African natives.

But this omission is not enough to condemn *The Negro Caravan*. Not only does it give examples of the work of better known writers from Phillis Wheatley and Jupiter Hammon to such recent arrivals as Richard Wright and William Attaway but includes excerpts from such historically important but comparatively unknown early figures as David Ruggles, Mrs. Keckley and others of the pre-Emancipation period.

The compilers have arranged the volume in sections, with a keenly analytical preface to each section and a biographical sketch preceding the excerpt from each other. These divisions include short stories; selections from novels; poetry; folk literature; drama; biography and autobiography, and historical, social, cultural and personal essays. To make the anthology even more complete, the appendix contains a chronology of certain historical and literary events in America together with important events in the history of literature of the American Negro.

Quite naturally, the many writers show wide variations in style and treatment of subject matter, and yet all hang together because of the common attention to the color question with which white America has forced us to temper our lives. This has resulted in the creation of a literature that follows the patterns of American writers as a whole but at the same time is Negroid, just as the work of the Midwestern school is in the American idiom but at the same time carries the flavor and strength of the prairie states.

Since it is unlikely that any individual or library is likely to have all of the books, articles and verses contained in the *Caravan*—and if they did, they would still lack the critical appraisal contained therein—ownership of *The Negro Caravan* becomes essential to any person who is the least bit interested in the colored American or his contribution to the literary wealth of this nation.

• • •

THE MYTH OF THE NEGRO PAST

November 7, 1942

It is generally believed that the American Negro has no African background worth mentioning. Some students of the racial problem have advantageously used this premise to show that the Duskymerican is the same as all other Americans except for color. Such distinguished men as Dr. Alain LeRoy Locke of Howard University and others have accepted this belief and amplified it. To such persons—and that obviously includes most of us—Dr. Herskovits' new volume will come as a shock.

The distinguished professor belongs to that small group of scientists who are both friends of the Negro and seekers after truth. For more than twenty years Herskovits had painstakingly studied the Negro in both the New World and Africa. Results of his significant research have appeared previously in books and articles. This new volume, the first of a series on the Negro in America and sponsored by the Carnegie Foundation under the editorship of Dr. Gunnar Myrdal, is his greatest achievement to date where the black man is concerned.

What Herskovits disproves are such widespread beliefs as these: (1) that Negroes are naturally childlike and adjust easily and happily to the most unsatisfactory social conditions; (2) that only the poorer stock of Africa was enslaved; (3) that Negroes were brought from all parts of Africa and so mixed up in their American distribution as to lose tribal identity; (4) that even if Negroes of a given tribe had been able to live together and had the desire to continue tribal customs, their culture was so low and savage that it would have been lost in contact with superior European civilization.

Briefly, the anthropologist has the data to show, in answer: (1) the complex economic and social character of African civilizations permitted the Negro to fit into slavery, but even this was under protest. Slave uprisings, revolts and escapes plagued the New World. Slaves killed themselves and consistently practiced a work "slow down" which gave rise to the popular fallacy of the race's "inherent" laziness; (2) slavery engulfed every strata of native African life; (3) most slaves came from areas near the west coast of Africa. These west coast people consisted mainly of four large tribes which perpetuated their cultural outlines through being numerically superior to slaves from other African tribes and assimilating them, and (4) west coast African civilization ranks high among the world's nonmachine cultures, is in some ways more practical and realistic than European civilization which in certain aspects it resembles, and its patterns are today found in varying degrees of strength in North and South America and the Caribbeans.

Why is the Baptist church the most popular of faiths among Negroes? What causes the strong interest in big funerals, burial societies and ritualistic fraternal orders? Why do many Negroes turn their heads when they laugh and refuse to look a person of higher position or authority in the eye? Why is the mother instead of the father so often the head of the family? These and many other questions have their answers rooted in African customs and habits.

Dr. Herskovits makes the important observation that a people with a past of which they may be proud cannot be called inferior. The Negro has such a past with strong traditions and behavior patterns. And understanding of this background should mean as much to the Duskymerican as does an appreciation of his homeland to the Irish-American or the Italian-American. America has knowingly accepted many of their traditions in becoming the melting pot of all peoples; all unknowingly certain patterns of African custom have been woven into the national life. An American is a blend of many backgrounds.

The Myth of the Negro Past should be required reading in schools everywhere. Let such books as this become the intellectual fare of the nation's young and a major victory will have been won against race prejudice and intolerance.

• • •

GUNNAR MYRDAL CONCLUSIONS WRONG, SAYS HISTORIAN IN [NEW] BOOK
NOVEMBER 6, 1946

Gunnar Myrdal's long two volume work, *An American Dilemma*, accepted as the last word on Negro-white relations, is dangerous and full of erroneous conclusions. This is the belief of Dr. Herbert Aptheker who takes the Swedish scientist to task in a well documented and illuminating eighty-page critique from the press of International Publishers, New York.

For those who may not know Dr. Aptheker, he ranks high as a scholar. He is the author of four important pamphlets on "The Negro in American History" and of the book, *Essays in the History of the American Negro*.

Furthermore, he wrote the document on Negro oppression which has been submitted to the United Nations by the National Negro Congress and which may prove decidedly embarrassing to the U.S. delegation.

Myrdal began his study with the wrong title, Aptheker contends. A "dilemma," he says quoting *Webster*, "is a situation involving choice, especially in actions, between equally unsatisfactory alternatives." This means that Myrdal thinks the Negro-white problem can never be satisfactorily solved.

What is more, the Swedish social-scientist considers that "the American-Negro problem is a problem in the heart of the American." That is completely untrue, Aptheker declared, and serves only to fortify those propertied forces fighting to retain control of the socio-economic system. For, if it is a moral problem, then eliminating the economic conditions that lead to human exploitation, racism, the Ku Klux Klan, and white supremacy will not bring about equality.

Being a Marxist, Aptheker blasts the Myrdal approach and contends that the status of the Negro in America is determined purely by the nature of our economy in which the financial rulers find it profitable to keep alive strife between Americans. Using divide and rule tactics, they foster divisive ideas of race so that Negro and white will fight each other instead of uniting for their common good. This, says Aptheker, makes the Negro problem an economic one instead of "moral."

Aptheker is also highly critical of many of Myrdal's conclusions and accuses him of plain distortion of facts. Furthermore, he accuses Myrdal of completely ignoring exhaustive studies made by authorities on specific problems, and making statements that are the exact opposite of what those authorities found. The list is astounding.

Says Aptheker in his conclusion: "In summary, we find Myrdal's philosophy to be superficial and erroneous, his historiography demonstrably false, his ethics vicious and, therefore, his analysis weak, mystical and dangerous.

"We do have a situation involving choice, but the alternatives are not equally unsatisfactory. The choice lies between the attempted preservation of our existing exploiting system, which nurtures the oppression of minority peoples, or the introduction of fundamental and vital changes now, and the consequent hastening of the transformation of our society into a pattern of socialism."

By all means, read it.

• • •

AUTHOR EXPOSES BIG BUSINESS TIE WITH DIXIE RACISM

DECEMBER 11, 1946

If ever we have a fascist America, it will rise in the South, hotbed of hate groups. But race discrimination and organized prejudice are not purely sectional products; they are financed by big business groups who use the hate technique as a weapon to maintain economic control.

Only twice before the present period have there been serious and widespread efforts to unite black and white in Dixie. Once was during reconstruction which ended when the North sold out to the South in the Rutherford B. Hayes election. The other was during the time of the Populist movement, founded on interracial cooperation. In this era, Negroes and whites worked closely together. It ended after Tom Watson of Georgia, its chief evangelist, reversed himself completely and became a champion of white supremacy.

Today there is a third attempt at unity and it is union-based. And if the threat of fascism is defeated and democracy prevails, a major share of the credit will go to the CIO which is slowly conquering the difficult problem of placing workers together in the same unions without discrimination. Such organizations as the Southern Conference for Human Welfare and Southern Regional Council are also carrying the ball. This is part of what *Southern Exposure* tells you.

Stetson Kennedy's fascinating, easily read volume is divided into provocatively titled sections and chapters such as "The Squalid South," "Freedom Road Closed," "The Southern Revolt," "James Crow, Ph.D." and others. In them he treats of political demagogues and financiers, of the plot against naming names and places. He spares none who has helped uphold the fascist tendencies of Dixie. He is for full equality, knows what it takes to get it and how it can be won. And he concludes:

> As it did after the Civil war, the south stands at the crossroads. It can continue down the path of prejudice, with poverty and privation for all but its exploiters. Or it can take the high road to democracy—political, economic,

racial; for democracy is indivisible—and proceed full speed ahead to the promised land of liberty and justice for all.

America and Negroes in particular need many more Stetson Kennedys. The best way to get more is by supporting those we have and backing them to the extent of at least three dollars.

PASSING PARADE AS POLITICAL CRITIQUE

In "Passing Parade," his most unsubtle series, Davis challenged the very assumptions of patriotism and reset the public conversation about the meaning of democracy, at a time when economic and social contradictions disenfranchised people of color and laborers. At the height of World War II, the flagging hopes for an Allied victory abroad were revived, while, at home, race riots disillusioned people of color in their quest for full racial equality. In the midst of this flux, Davis wrote "Passing Parade," from September 15, 1943, to July 19, 1944. While his column was not intended to have the cachet, say, of Gunnar Myrdal's *An American Dilemma*, as news writing it cogently questioned not only the American creed as related to its black citizens but also the place of America in international relations. In raising these issues, Davis, in comparatively shorter space, distilled the analyses posited in longer, scholarly studies and arguably reached more everyday nonacademic readers than the most sophisticated social science studies of that era. His work demonstrates the power of the black press to expand the knowledge of its readers about domestic and international affairs and to set forth the relevance of these issues for their lives. Through Davis's vigorous engagement with the presumed status quo, his column enabled readers to participate in the larger conversations influencing their place in the world.

The "Double 'V' Campaign" represented the black press's most concerted entry into resolving the conflict between patriotic spirit and the quest for equal rights. A profitable way of thinking about Davis's column is as an extension of this concept. When the *Pittsburgh Courier* published "Should I Sacrifice to Live 'Half-American'?", a 1942 op-ed letter from one of its readers, and conceived the mantra "Double V Campaign: Victory Abroad and Victory at Home," Davis took a simple slogan intended to raise the political consciousness of its readers and deeply intensified the meaning of its discourse by offering a more probing interrogation of the major issues that blacks and workers should be aware of—both at home and abroad.

From his examination of issues in the domestic sphere, we can infer how important a left-of-center political perspective was to Davis's analyses. The character of Davis's interrogation was often cast in reactive or confrontational terms. Congressional leaders who invoked the power of their offices and the FBI found themselves the subjects of Davis's careful scrutiny. Predating the 1950s, the era made infamous by Senator Joseph McCarthy, was Martin Dies, who chaired the House Committee on Un-American Activities. Among his many "investigations," Dies disingenuously characterized the interned Japanese Americans' resistance to their imprisonment as a conspiracy against the nation. He also intentionally blamed the 1943 Detroit riot on Communist instigators, when the real issue in this civil unrest was overcrowded, segregated housing. Davis also used his column to mount a vigorous opposition to others, such as ultraconservatives Gerald L. K. Smith and Westbrook Pegler, who cast aspersions against the likes of Henry Wallace for holding philosophies that might lead to social equality. They branded such liberal positions as "Communist," thereby fusing, in Davis's view, the discourse of racial segregation with anti-Communist rhetoric. In effect, this "red baiting" was a contrived distraction, designed also to undermine the labor union movement.

Davis saw America's postwar international alliances decided ultimately by a number of cartels, combines, and mega-corporations. The success of this infrastructure abroad depended in large part on exercising economic control at home. Davis posited a determining connection between the nation's financial centers and white supremacy. The economic interests of companies and corporations signified by Wall Street in New York and LaSalle Street in Chicago were, in Davis's mind, enhanced by racial and labor divisiveness in the South. Northern-owned industry moved south, where race prejudice fueled an anti-labor union fervor. With both black and white workers suffering from low wages and increased competition for the few available jobs, the investors reaped more profits. The problem, as Davis simply states, was that "Black worker and white worker have refused, except in a pitifully few instances, to plan and act together for the common good."

Davis's solution, a call for interracial cooperation among laborers, acknowledges the difficulties of bridging differences. The American Federation of Labor (AFL), for instance, contributed to interracial strife because its own union rituals excluded blacks. Even when the AFL tried dancing around its own restrictions by setting up auxiliaries for blacks, many black workers refused to join because the often equal membership dues were offset by an inability to vote and to exercise other privileges. A greater degree of interracial harmony was achieved by the Congress of Industrial Organizations (CIO). But the cooperation often suffered the designation of being a Communist-front organization. By forcing labor to contest those false charges, owners effectively kept labor on the defensive and thus unable to pursue more significant issues such as fair wages and other benefits.

As Davis makes clear in another article, the battle royal designed to forestall the achievement of racial equality was furthered exacerbated by the traditional American two-party system. Except on infrequent occasions, American politics generally featured a system consisting of Democrats and Republicans. But Davis probes beneath the respective partisan political positions and discovers what, for him, is a more precise oppositional stance—reactionaries versus progressives. These terms defined for him a coalition between reactionary Republicans and anti-Roosevelt Democrats who united to oppose the racially friendlier New Deal program of President Franklin Delano Roosevelt. For Davis, the line demarcating progressive from reactionary was determined by who wants "a better deal for the common man." In this scenario, no hope could be held out for support by the reactionaries. Their position consisted of Democrats, say from the "solid South," voting with like-minded Republicans around issues of mutual interest.

For instance, northern and southern industrialists, according to this argument, maintain their hegemony as a result of "conservative" social policies. This generally meant using the oldest divisive trick, of "divide and conquer," to keep white and black laborers from seeing the benefits of cooperative action. Much northern capital had been invested in southern business and manufacturing. In order to maximize profits, it was to the owners' advantage to keep labor unions from organizing the work force. And advantageous it was! In citing one example that generalizes into a pattern of profit-making for all of Big Business, Davis notes that Bethlehem Steel "made $19,260,000 after taxes as an annual average from 1936 to 1939. For 1942, the profit after taxes was $38,188,000." This led Davis to conclude that such increments in profit convinced most manufacturers that extending the war was an obvious financial advantage for them. Never mind the moral issue of making weapons to take the lives of other human beings; morality was jettisoned for financial gain. Part of this issue was tied to the notion of tax increases for individuals. The question Davis put to his readers was whether support for the war should come from proposed tax increases on individuals or from the profits made by giant corporations.

Moreover, this unholy alliance between anti-Roosevelt advocates had other economic consequences for African Americans and workers. The issue was what would be gained or lost in a protracted war versus a negotiated peace. Davis cites one compelling argument for an early negotiated end to the war: "The longer World War II lasts, the bigger [the rising tide of American fascism] becomes." Because the tide of fascism was steadily growing worse, an early settlement by negotiation would rob fascism of its momentum. Even this argument, Davis had to admit, was not without flaw: a negotiated peace still left some semblance of the Axis's infrastructure intact, which might possibly be resurrected later. Davis believed, though, that any hope for eradicating homegrown fascism depended on curtailing that growth abroad. The sooner it was arrested abroad, the easier the task at home.

Davis's writings did more than expose issues; he also proposed solutions. "Why not form a council against racism?" Davis asks in one installment of "Passing Parade." The need for such an organization reiterates his perception of America's most critical problem: "A belief in racism and racial differences is a springboard to fascism." For Davis, Americans had succumbed so long to pseudo-science and popular ideas that race and racial difference had become topics with little value for distinguishing human beings. His solution, which may have seemed more radical in his day and time, was to jettison race altogether as a social category. Too many misconceptions had flown in the face of legitimate science, thus opening the door of myth and stereotype as means for separating people. Anyone born or naturalized in America, he argued, was an American. Case closed! It is a position that he would argue more expansively five years later in his poems and in his introduction to *47th Street: Poems* (1948).

Davis also found merit in allowing soldiers engaged in war the opportunity to vote. The 1943 debate in the Senate over the Soldier Voter Bill is a case in point. At stake in this legislation was whether special voting provisions should be made for soldiers actively involved in the war. The reactionary position coalesced around two quite different interests: Southerners saw an extension of the franchise as a threat to their poll taxes because new African American voters would assuredly vote to replace the tax system. Northern Republicans perceived that a sizeable majority of their soldier voters were supporters of President Roosevelt's Democratic administration, so withholding the vote would withhold support from the Democratic Party.

The progressive position would therefore seek inclusiveness, not exclusion. Not to pass the bill would then leave the crucial decision about federal voting to each state. The absence of a federal law would open the door for the exercise of states' rights, which, for African Americans in the South, spelled doom. For Davis, withholding the right of franchise from black soldiers was a deeply moral issue. Can compelling a soldier to die in war while denying him the right to vote be sustained? In this argument, no amount of justifying and qualifying could support withholding this right. As he states: "If a gun is to be shoved in one hand, then let the other reach for a ballot."

Accountability was also important to Davis. He recognized that African Americans had the potential to effect change. The challenge was to act responsibly, committedly when placed in positions of authority. In this spirit, Davis publicly chided Congressman William Dawson, the longtime black elected representative from Chicago for, as Davis says, ". . . muffing one opportunity after another to make both his voice and the sentiments of Negroes heard in a place where it would do a lot of good." Davis wanted from Dawson a more concerted effort to refute "the white supremacy doctrines and divisionist tactics of the congressional reactionaries."

At the same time that he chides Representative Dawson for taking virtually no action, Davis commends whites of conscience for acting out the courage of their convictions. Lillian Smith, for instance, was the subject of one installment of "Passing Parade." Smith edited *The South Today*, a publication that challenged the very grounds on which southern racism rested; however, it had fallen on bad economic times. Because Smith was southern, white, and a woman, Davis admiringly acknowledges the risks she took and held her up as a courageous friend of African Americans. "Imagine," he writes with unmistakable respect, "a white woman taking democracy and the Constitution seriously!" Davis indicated his unconditional support of Smith by making known her request for subscribers to *South Today*. At one dollar per year, this cost was a miniscule sacrifice compared to the enormity of the racial problem.

Finally, Davis was encouraged by some governmental activities, especially the Fair Employment Practices Commission (FEPC). Born as a result of A. Philip Randolph's threatened protest march on Washington in 1941, the FEPC was both hope and conscience. For blacks and other racial minorities, the FEPC signified the first genuine effort by the federal government to make possible ethnic and racial minority participation in nonmilitary ways in the war. More than this, the FEPC was the nation's conscience, the regulator of what was right and wrong. It not only provided hope but was charged with protecting it too.

In yet another way, "Passing Parade" functioned to redefine the terms of discussion for its readers. In addition to an interrogation of domestic issues, Davis pushed black public discourse on the war even higher by examining the globalization of the nation's postwar political relations. Collectively, the articles on this subject asked: What are the implications of political choices made during the war for determining international, domestic, and racial relations after the war? In his analysis of possible postwar political models, Davis foregrounds as most likely a choice between the ones provided by Winston Churchill and by Henry Wallace. Would Winston Churchill's proposal for a continued Great Britain and American alliance guarantee world peace after the war? Or, would this Big Two arrangement, which excluded the Soviet Union and China, merely function as a vehicle for preserving the British empire and therefore extend colonialism? As expected, Davis rejected the Big Two option in favor of Henry Wallace's advocacy of a universal brotherhood of nations.

Wallace, a liberal politician, served as vice president under Franklin Delano Roosevelt. Philosophically, though, this Iowan defined himself against the rather conservative economic policies that might lead to America's emergence from isolationism into full-fledged imperialism. When *Life Magazine* publisher Henry Luce called on the United States to "assume leadership in the world," a number of editorials made it clear that Luce was referring to a manifest destiny like the doctrines of Rudyard Kipling and Winston Churchill. Wallace opposed this notion of empire-building and proposed a new-age alternative: ". . . that the century on which we are entering—the century which will come out of this war—can and must be the century of the common man."

This stark challenge, anchored in the philosophy of progressive thought, inspired Davis to seek through Wallace's commentary a goal for African Americans. For Davis, Wallace's "century of the common man" spoke to social arrangements that postwar America should seek because it represented a true international commonwealth, not Anglo-American domination. Choosing a commonwealth also meant thinking of a coalition of at least the Big Four nations: the United States, Great Britain, the Soviet Union, and China. Davis perceived that a movement to establish an "Anglo-American combine" had already begun. Because the "combine" favored a capitalist economic arrangement, Davis saw in the formation of different cartels and monopolies, such as Continental Oil Company of Europe, an obvious result of Big Business's power. The purpose of these mega-corporations quite simply was to "dominate both synthetic and natural fuel after the war."

The position Davis advocates effectively foregrounds a postwar world he describes as "without exploitation or inequality." Accordingly, China, once wrested from Japanese control, would be returned to the Chinese, and India would ultimately be given its independence from British rule. Quite obviously the freedom Davis advocates for these "nations of color" differed considerably from goals of imperialist philosophies. What Davis reveals in this forum is the connection that the international environment has to domestic policies. In sum, Davis's leftist political leanings reassert his personal commitment to ensuring human rights and his public commitment to refashion the nation's creed to match the rhetoric of its professed democratic principles. In communicating his own vision in "Passing Parade," Davis inspires a redefined black public discourse on domestic and international political issues and points the way to a solution that benefits all Americans, not just a few.

• • •

CHURCHILL OR WALLACE WORLD?: PART I
SEPTEMBER 15, 1943

Two influential leaders of the United States and Great Britain, Vice President Henry Wallace and Prime Minister Winston Churchill, are moving in opposite directions toward a postwar world. Wallace wants peace and security for all the people in a universal brotherhood of nations; the only people Churchill gives a rap about are the white people of the British Empire and America he thinks, ought to use strongarm tactics to bludgeon all other countries into submission.

What kind of a peace we get concerns you and me. The Negro will soon have one million men in the army and navy, some of whom will not come back. There's little they can do but follow orders and fight. It is up to us on the home front to make ourselves articulate, to help guide Congress and Washington into those channels which will bring peace and security in future years.

Isolationism, despite the loud outcries of the *Chicago Tribune*, Gerald L. K. Smith, certain congressmen and the America Firsters, is all but dead. I think it's pretty well understood that this nation can't climb back into its former shell. So the issue, really, is what kind of alliance the United States must make to give peace a reasonable chance of taking a long term lease on this planet.

Here is Churchill's idea, as stated in a recent speech at Harvard:

"It would be a most foolish and improvident act on the part of our two governments, or either of them, to break up this smooth running and immensely powerful machinery the moment the war is over. For our own safety, as well as for the security of the rest of the world, we are bound to keep it working and in running order after the war, probably for a good many years, not only till we have set up some world arrangement to keep the peace but until we know that it is an arrangement which will really give that protection we must have from danger and aggression."

By "our two governments," Churchill means the United States and Great Britain. He does not mean the Soviet Union, which now is acknowledged to have the greatest land army in the world, nor does he mean China, most populous nation in existence, and which because of modernization induced by the war is destined to become one of the strongest countries in the globe.

Now go back over Churchill's statement and re-read it, substituting "the United States and Great Britain" for "we." Get it? It comes out as a pattern for Anglo-American world domination, for super-imperialism. And don't forget that Churchill has publicly stated that he has no plans for breaking up the British empire, that every parcel of land taken by the Axis nations must be returned to Great Britain.

Churchill means that the British and American armies and ships and planes should continue to be used together after the war ends. This mighty military force will be available to enforce whatever those two nations want enforced. If Britain and America decide to divide up Asia and the Pacific islands as they see fit or ring Russia with an order of rightist buffer states or establish semi-fascist governments all over Europe as they have done in North Africa and Sicily, through AMGOT, then they will have the armed might to make the rest of the world like it.

And only when they have annexed or so weakened the rest of the earth that there is virtually no danger of any threat to continued Anglo-American imperialist domination will this super-army be disbanded, by Churchill's own admission.

I don't know how far we have been committed to such a policy. But I do know that certain important former isolationists have come out for continued collaboration with Great Britain, that Governor Dewey of New York and some other presidential possibilities favor an alliance with the British, and that Secretary Hull's recent speech was so general that it could be interpreted as backing an Anglo-American combine or favoring an international commonwealth including everybody from the Eskimos to the Hottentots.

Big business, of course, would like to see it. You know, big business such as Standard Oil of New Jersey which, according to Wallace, thought more of its obligations to German firms than to America in the matter of synthetic rubber.

Already cartels and monopolies are being formed. In Switzerland recently a new corporation called the Continental Oil Company of Europe was organized. Listed as owners are subsidiaries of the Royal Dutch Shell, Rockefeller and Texas Company. Concerns—all British and American capital. The purpose? To dominate both synthetic and natural fuel after the war.

And don't forget that Ethiopia, which surrendered its freedom to Italy, has all but surrendered its freedom to Great Britain as the price of "liberation" from Mussolini. And who gets control of the former Italian possessions in Africa?

Thus far there is no record of President Roosevelt having agreed to the Churchill ideology. He still talks of the Atlantic Charter and the Four Freedoms. But the British have a way with them, and plenty of powerful interests back the dream of Anglo-American imperialism.

It becomes increasingly obvious that what stand is taken by our president will depend upon you and me and the rest of us, as exemplified through instructions to our congressmen. In World War I, Woodrow Wilson gave mankind on his own a pattern for peace, then came home to Washington to find it rejected by a recalcitrant Congress. Roosevelt is too smart to make that kind of mistake.

• • •

BEN AND THE REDS
SEPTEMBER 17, 1943

Benjamin J. Davis, Jr., attorney and associate editor of the *Daily Worker*, also county chairman of the Communist Party in New York, is running for the city council in the hope of replacing the Reverend A. Clayton Powell, Jr., who has his eye on Congress. Ben may not win, but I don't believe Harlemites can elect a more honest and fearless fighter.

I first knew young Ben some twelve years ago in Atlanta. Complications which developed then dogged us both for several years. People had a habit of confusing us, although how they do so will always be a mystery. I'm much smaller physically, for in all my life I never weighed more than 247 pounds. But anyway the same last name and the failure of astigmatic individuals to see that little Frank Marshall Davis was never more than a *Readers Digest* version of large Ben Davis, Jr., plagued us there, as well as at the first convention of the National Negro Congress in Chicago in 1936 when Ben was congratulated several times for authoring my *Black Men's Verse* and I was praised for his legal work in the Angelo Herndon case.

It was this Herndon case which showed young Ben's idealism. With his father's still existing prestige and importance in Republican politics, Ben could have taken the easy way. He admitted there was plenty of money to be made by a capable lawyer in Atlanta who was willing to follow traditional southern behavior patterns. But the young attorney was too intellectually honest. Believing firmly in the Communist doctrine, he renounced easy gold for manhood. He became an avowed Red in open defiance of the witch hunters and went all the way with young Herndon, fighting to eventually win him freedom in the United States Supreme Court.

Even in deep Dixie, young Ben made no compromise with reaction. He even sought to use the facilities of the state law library, on the ground that it was maintained by all the taxpayer's money, and was as caustic in his communications with Governor Rivers as Rivers was with him. And if a man has the courage to stand virtually alone for his and the people's rights in Georgia, to take the thorny path of personal economic insecurity when he would have traveled the smooth highway to comparative wealth, neither his courage nor his honesty can be successfully challenged in liberal New York.

Maybe we ought to get more savvy about the Communists anyway. A social system that can mold Russia from a huge weakling in twenty-five years to what is today the strongest and most united nation in Europe, a people who has borne the full brunt of the terrible Nazi war machine and has flung it back, must have something, fundamentally sound.

You have probably noticed here at home that practically every social advance made under the Roosevelt regime has been labeled "Red." You may have noticed also that practically everybody who yells, "Communist" is himself anti-Negro or anti-labor, that whenever a white person makes a bold and determined fight for full racial equality and justice, he is painted as a "dangerous radical taking orders from Moscow."

Only last week in Chicago at a meeting of the America First Party, Gerald L. K. Smith, the hate-inciting Detroit rabble rouser who is held responsible in large measure for the recent race riots in the Michigan metropolis, denounced Vice President Wallace as "a Communist" because that great humanitarian, who has often openly blasted tenaciously held theories of racial differences, has told the world that "this is the century of the common man" and is trying to bring this nation to see the necessity of creating a postwar world without exploitation or inequality.

When you look at the kind of people who have hoodwinked the public into believing that Communism is something despicable and its followers are unshaven anarchists who want to seize the government and murder everybody who has a dollar left over the following payday—men like Martin Dies, Gerald L. K. Smith and Westbrook Pegler, the press prostitute—and then consider the persons so designated, such as Wallace and Dean William Pickens and Mrs. Bethune and the NAACP, it makes you think that one of the major needs of this nation is a hell of a lot more Communists, if that's what these people really are.

Out of curiosity I have read the constitution of the Communist Party of the United States of America, adopted in 1938 and amended in 1940, and certain sections ought to set at rest the minds of those who believe the Reds are anarchists, whether you believe or disagree with their general theories.

Says Section 10 of Article VI on "The Party's Rights and Duties of Members."

"It shall be the duty of party members to struggle against the national oppression of the Negro people; to fight for complete equality for Negroes in all phases of American life and to promote the unity of Negro and white toilers for the advancement of their common interests."

That means that race prejudice is outlawed among Communists. Have either the Republicans or Democrats, also political parties like the hated Reds, ever taken such a stand?

Article IX—"Disciplinary Procedure"—says in Section 5C "Party members found to be strikebreakers, degenerates, habitual drunkards, betrayers of party confidence, provocateurs, persons who practice or advocate terrorism, sabotage, espionage, and force and violence (read that again), or members whose actions are otherwise detrimental to the party and the working class, shall be summarily dismissed from positions of responsibility, expelled from the party and exposed before the general public."

As I was saying, I think Ben Davis, Jr., would make a good councilman. He's got to have the interests of the ordinary people at heart, people like you and me, to be a Communist. And you won't find many politicians who give a hoot about the rest of us except around voting time.

• • •

CHURCHILL OR WALLACE WORLD?: PART II
SEPTEMBER 22, 1943

Last week I stated that the postwar world envisioned by Prime Minister Churchill is obviously Anglo-American imperialism and global control, whereas that desired by Vice President Henry J. Wallace is one of peace and security obtained by a universal brotherhood of all nations.

I am against the Churchill conception because I honestly believe that it can but lead to a bigger and greater war. If America and Great Britain alone intend to dominate the world, they are going to have their supremacy challenged by other nations led by the Soviet Union and China. To keep in power, England and the United States would have to maintain the biggest military force ever dreamed—and despite their resources, would find themselves eventually going broke doing so. When that time came, whether ten years or fifty years hence, they would be easy prey for the sullen rival nations.

There can be no plan for permanent peace that does not call for a coalition between the Big Four nations—Britain, America, Russia and China—with guarantees of equality for smaller states and dominion status for populous India and the other areas when they are found to be ready for self government. Although Wallace has not said so, it seems to me that this is what he has in mind.

Too little stress has been placed upon the importance of China in postwar planning. Here is a huge nation of 500,000 colored persons kicked around and exploited by the great powers since the domination of western materialistic civilization. Caring little for modernity, the Chinese were all but helpless. But her twelve years of warfare with Japan have changed all that.

Today we see signs of a powerful China rising, phoenix-like, from the ashes of war. Her men have become fighters in the modern manner. Strong foundations for a democratic peoples' government have been laid. Industrialization is taking place. And with the spirit of nationalism imbedded in Chinese minds, the postwar China will be no weakling like the China of old.

Churchill has said he expects the return of Hong Kong to the British empire. All who believe the Chinese will cheerfully surrender this valuable and strategic bite of the Orient to London after the Japanese are forced out will hold a convention in a telephone booth.

There is also a vast psychological advantage to be obtained in accepting China on a basis of full equality. The Japanese are currently having great success in pointing out to Asiatic peoples that she is a champion of all colored persons, that she is crusading against white domination. This had its effect in the easy conquest of Malaya, Burma, the Dutch East Indies, etc. There are a few Chinese who favor Japan for the same reason. But if China is today and in the future accorded a full voice in postwar planning, it will have the desirable reaction of making other Asiatics discredit Japanese race war propaganda.

It's not too early to consider the fate of Japan after her defeat, and whatever plans are made will have to be worked out with the full approval of

China as well as Russia, her neighbors, if there's going to be any kind of real peace. No Anglo-American alliance is going to go in and run Japan in utter disregard of the wishes of the Soviet Union and the Chinese nation without inviting eventual disaster.

The problem of India also enters the equation. Here are 450,000,000 dissatisfied souls wanting self-government. The promises made them in World War I by the British were as little kept as those made to Negro Americans in World War I by this nation. A guarantee by the British now of self-government, backed by the Americans, Russians and Chinese, would not only make for unity but would remove what might become a danger in the peace to follow: the danger of Indian revolt. And there is also dissatisfaction in Africa that ought to be wiped out to insure a lasting peace.

The fact of the matter is that the world is not confined to North America and Western Europe, nor can it be successfully run from Washington and London. Most of the globe's population live elsewhere.

The last member of the Big Four is the Soviet Union, against which certain powerful and vocal forces in this nation are carrying on a war of their own. This is caused by the growing admiration of Americans for the amazing power of this great country, which had been lied about so much in the United States before World War II; the fear that Russia wants to foist her system of government upon the world, and the fact that the attitude of the "private enterprise and monopoly" democracies was to a large extent responsible for the present global conflict.

I do not include France among the Big Four, for that nation has temporarily at least lost her front rank status in the world political arena. She was eliminated by the Nazis and will have to regain her standing.

• • •

CHURCHILL OR WALLACE WORLD?: PART III
OCTOBER 7, 1943

In a recent column I stated that the mounting popular admiration for the Soviet Union, caused by that nation's stand against Nazi military might and the revelation that what we had been taught to believe about Russia was in the main false propaganda, had caused our champions of the status quo and homegrown fascists to launch new and vigorous assaults against her through the press.

So intense has been this war of vilification that the Soviet publication, *War and the Working Class*, saw fit last week to run a special article on the anti-Russian blasts of the Hearst, the Howard, and the McCormick-Patterson newspapers. The Soviet editorial was careful to point out, however, that such sentiments did not represent the feeling of the American masses which remains friendly to our Red ally.

But I want to say here and now that if the common people of America are opposed to the reactionary and isolationist voices now being raised, they've got to open their own mouths. The foes of progress are skillful fighters and well organized; they will curve our foreign policy into those channels leading toward World War III unless we who are sick of death and destruction raise our voices and tell Congress and Roosevelt that we want the kind of world cooperation and brotherhood envisioned by Henry J. Wallace and other advanced humanitarians of the day.

Currently British and American conservative and imperialistic ideas rule. Churchill dreams of an Anglo-American alliance manhandling the world; with the cooperation of our state department, fascists are allowed to continue their rule in conquered North Africa, Sicily, and Italy. Churchill wants to prop up the old kings and regimes in Greece and the Balkans, to re-create a 1930s world in eastern Europe.

But this isn't going to happen. The reason is that Russia won't allow it. What happens to the little states on her borders is of more direct concern to her than to anybody else; by being the only nation to roll up German military might on the continent of Europe she has won the right to speak with authority. Russia wants peace, but she knows she's not going to get it by allowing a return to those conditions which started a war four years ago.

The truth is, nobody wants to stumble backward along the path but the monopolists, the international financiers, the business-as-usual boys, and their satellites. They make money out of wars. Just how many hundred percent greater was the profit after taxes of our industries in 1942 as compared with the boom period of 1929?

And don't ever think that what goes on in Athens or Belgrade has nothing to do with you, brother. Somebody you know or maybe our son is in Italy or New Guinea today because we here in America, black and white, never paid the right kind of attention to what was happening in Berlin and Tokyo.

The American Negro can no more be isolated than can the American nation. What Churchill, Roosevelt and Stalin decide when they meet in Moscow will have its effect eventually on Mose Washington, illiterate sharecropper in the Mississippi backwoods. So we might as well get in our say-so now.

We might as well tell our congressmen, our senators, and Mr. Roosevelt that the approximately one million brown boys we have under arms ought to be the last this nation needs since there's no sense in having another war.

We can tell them that we are not fighting to establish Anglo-American imperialism, return of a 1930s world, the retention of fascism, or restoration of decadent dynasties to European thrones.

We can tell them we will not be satisfied until the black men of Nigeria, the yellow men of China and the white men of Czechoslovakia, the cotton picker of Georgia, the coal miner of Pennsylvania and all others in between are divorced from hunger and privation and hate and fear of their fellowmen.

We can tell them that this country has got to join with Great Britain and the Soviet Union and China in formulating a world program of international cooperation and democracy for all humans, with an end to special privilege because of color or dollar bills.

We can tell them we want this to be the century of the common man in reality, not merely a Wallace dream.

How about it? Are you willing to outtalk the imperialists, the isolationists, and the fascists: Or would you prefer World War III?

• • •

THAT AFL RESOLUTION
OCTOBER 14, 1943

Up at Boston last week, during the American Federation of Labor convention, the bruised dove of democracy was allowed to flutter around the room for a little while and then was hustled back into its cage. The two Negro delegates, A. Philip Randolph and Milton P. Webster, were shown the food of black-white labor equality in the form of a resolution condemning discrimination, but when the brothers asked for an actual helping by passage of a law expelling those affiliates which violate the federation's official anti-Jim Crow policy, they were told No, Sorry, Uh-Uh, You Ain't Gonna Eat Today.

It was, of course, ironic to find Randolph cast in the role of a man fighting for abolition of the racial barriers in AFL brotherhoods. Mr. Randolph, in case you have forgotten, heads the March on Washington movement which bars whites from membership. It is obvious that he and the anti-Negro unions have much in common. It's amazing that some delegates did not point out this embarrassing fact from the convention floor.

However, the chief of the Pullman porters merits full praise for his strong fight to heal democracy in this branch of the labor movement. It is at times a discouraging fight, but Mr. Randolph has not retreated from the battle. He listed twenty unions that bar Negroes either by their constitution or by inference and told the convention, "Until the AFL abolishes race discrimination there can be no pretense of democracy within the AFL."

Said the resolution, "The doors of our trade union movement must be open. Substantial progress has been made toward eliminating prejudice, but there still remains the obligation upon the AFL to expand the good work so that the principal of industrial equality of all men will be established."

President William Green then stated, "If I had my way, every organization in the AFL would admit Negroes to membership on the same basis of equality as whites."

Good words, but what about putting them in practice? "Only by education and understanding," said Mr. Green, "will the problem be solved." Mr. Randolph's suggestion that the AFL threaten to expel unions who violate the resolution and Green's statement are a "dangerous proposal," according to the AFL leadership. And so we end up, for all practical purposes, where we started.

The unions charged with race bios rushed their mouthpieces into action. Why, we wouldn't think of that, said John P. Frey, president of AFL metal trades. We've always protected Negro workers, asserted Charles J. MacGowan of the boilermakers, the union which under pressure admitted colored workers but segregated them into voteless Jim Crow units. Must have been a couple of other guys, in effect declared G. M. Bugniazet of the electricians, Roy Horn of the blacksmiths, and W. L. Allen of the telegraphers.

"And besides," quote President Green to the assembly, "if Negro leaders want us to organize the Negro workers and we spend our money and employ organizers to do it, why don't they line up with us? I can't prevail upon representatives of any colored organization in America to appeal to workers to join the AFL. They persistently aid the CIO. What about the prejudice against us?"

I'm glad you brought the CIO up, Mr. Green. In this we have an organization in which the president, Phil Murray, doesn't go around saying, "If I had my way." He believes black and white workers should be integrated in democratic unions and works to put this belief into practice. He doesn't stop with wishful thinking, and the Negro leaders know it. That's why there's little effort to get AFL recruits if the CIO can serve the purpose.

Frey of metal trades also accused Negroes of "abusing the union" by flocking into shipyards as strikebreakers during a work stoppage on the west coast. To anyone but a standard bearer for idiocy, the reason is obvious. Quit barring Negroes from the union and they can't be pitted against organized labor.

Lily white unions are those which best advance the cause of management as against labor. Black worker is automatically pitted against white worker to the detriment of both. The rule of divide and conquer succeeds. Keep them fighting among themselves and they'll have less time and energy to seek their rights from capital. But when they join forces and move together, it's altogether different. Ask the motor industry about the United Auto Workers' CIO.

If the AFL is really serious about making its resolutions bear weight, it will set in action a strong and vigorous educational committee for the sole purpose of showing its membership the necessity of complete democratic cooperation with Negro labor. But I fear actually that this may be the last year we hear about the matter until Randolph gets up to lambast discrimination again at the 1944 convention.

• • •

WE HAVE TWO PARTIES, HUH?

OCTOBER 15, 1943

Since we were kids in public school, we have been told of America's two party system, of the Republicans and the Democrats, and the great advantages of this kind of government. It has been taken for granted by most of us. It is probably a shock, therefore, to find that when you shake off the thin camouflage you don't uncover Republicans and Democrats underneath. What you find are Reactionaries and Progressives.

You find also that these groupings cut thickly across party lines. In most instances, you find the think-a-likes of both parties joining hands. The solid south Democrats dance a mad mazurka with certain northern Republicans. The rest of the Democrats and the rest of the Republicans generally line up side by side.

There's all the difference in the world between Democratic Senator Wagner and Democratic Senator Bilbo. You find a real spiritual kinship between Representative Stephen Day, an Illinois Republican, and Representative John Rankin, a Mississippi Democrat. President Roosevelt and Wendell Willkie are Progressives, despite their party labels; Senator Wheeler and Senator "Cotton Ed" Smith are reactionaries, despite their party labels.

That's a fact that voters who want a better deal for the common man must not overlook. The label itself means nothing. There's no way of telling definitely by the party whose togs he bears whether this candidate will be a Progressive or a Reactionary when he sits in Congress.

All this was especially stressed by the Senate action on the Soldier Vote bill. On this measure, thirteen Republicans lined up against and twelve voted for. There were also twenty-four Democrats voting against, all but five or six of them from Dixie. And it must be stressed that Rankin, a Democrat, left the House to lobby among senators against passing the bill.

Both Democratic and Republican members of the Reactionaries had their reasons for scuttling this measure. The southerners, from poll tax states, wanted nothing that would endanger the rotten system by which they have been riding into office. The northern Republicans, learning that the Gallup poll showed the members of the armed forces to be 61 percent in favor of the Roosevelt administration, wanted to keep our fighting men from giving support by ballot to the New Deal. The coalition was motivated by selfishness. And reaction is selfishness.

The old cry of "state rights" was raised. States' rights means basically the privilege, where the Negro or labor is concerned, of passing this or that discriminatory law although it may be contrary to the spirit or letter of the federal Constitution. No state which desires to do otherwise gives full citizenship and voting rights to the Negro despite the plain language of the Fourteenth and Fifteenth Amendments.

If the House follows the Senate in lead, there will be no federal control of soldiers' voting. That will be left to the discretion of each state. In other words, Georgia and Alabama will disfranchise the Negro soldiers just as they have the Negro civilian.

It is morally wrong to ask a man to give his life for you on the battle-front and then refuse to let him vote. If a gun is to be shoved in one hand, then let the other reach for a ballot. That goes for Americans of all colors and creeds. That also goes for eighteen-year-olds.

What are you going to do about it? Have you told your congressman how you feel? And have you paid attention to what your senator did when this matter came up and was defeated?

• • •

WANT A WAGE CUT?

OCTOBER 27, 1943

Say, buddy, how would you like to have a salary cut? Do you want to pay 10 percent more for that pound of pork chops or new suit? That's what will happen if Congress passes the proposed 10 percent sales tax. And if the action by the House Banking Committee in voting to kill all subsidies by January 1 is approved by the nation's lawmakers, you may for all practical purposes be handed a wage slash of 25 or maybe 50 percent of the amount you now contend is not enough to meet living costs.

You see, according to the Federal Bureau of Labor statistics, the average factory worker in June had gross weekly earnings of $43.35. In August 1939, the median salary was $23.77. I don't know how those figures hit you. But anyway, you're supposed to be making more now than previously. Uncle Sam needs ten billion dollars in new taxes. And some of the smart boys think it's a waste of cash to pay subsidies to keep food prices down and thus strive to avert inflation.

And so Congress, which voted to abolish the $25,000 wage ceiling imposed by the president, thinks it's the right thing to dip into the pocketbooks of the workers, the masses, the little guys who make $2,500 a year or less. Smash 'em, make 'em pay. This is a democracy and if everybody forks over a 10 percent sales tax, it proves our vaunted equality.

Did I hear someone say what about increasing the taxes on big business? Hush! Have you never heard of the National Association of Manufacturers? The poor, lonesome millionaires who have the say-so over what you buy and where you work, who "donated" $20,000,000 to the American Legion for a national "educational" program in "Americanism," who tell many of our senators and representatives and our state governments what to do and when?

According to the Treasury Department, the corporations this year after taxes will show an estimated $8,750,000,000 profits—most of it from government contracts for war goods that you and I have paid for. That even exceeds the net return of the fabulous year of 1929, up to that time the largest in history, and when taxes were far lower. Randolph Paul, treasury general counsel, last month estimated the three-year wartime and defense area profits of American corporations at $24,200,000 after payment of taxes.

Here are some facts of 650 corporations selected by the department of commerce for analysis of their profits, 75 percent earned as much after the high war taxes of 1942 as they did in 1939 after paying much smaller taxes, and 40 percent more than doubled their 1930 earnings after taxes. Remember, in 1939 there were no starving millionaires. But many of us who are in the lower income brackets were working on WPA that year while the corporation executives wintered in Florida mansions.

Want still more figures? Bethlehem Steel made $19,260,000 after taxes as an annual average from 1936 to 1939. For 1942 the profit after taxes was $38,188,000. Anaconda Cooper from 1936 to 1939 averaged $12,503,000. For 1942 the take was $49,785,000. U.S. Steel took $45,098,000 for those three years as compared with $96,819,000 for 1942. United Aircraft had $5,161,000 left after taxes from 1936 to 1939, while last year alone the figure zoomed to $20,994,000. These are only a few specific instances, and every one of them stands to grab a bigger pot of gravy for 1943.

As was the case during World War I, we are breeding a new crop of millionaires. I submit that making money out of the business of manufacturing implements to kill other humans is morally wrong, and if Uncle Sam wants more money from taxes, let him turn toward the monster businesses that today are realizing more profits than ever before in their history.

But the National Association of Manufacturers does not want it that way. In fact, this noble champion of Americanism has been spearheading the drive to pocket even bigger war profits by seeking repeal of the contract rene-gotiation law which curbs—yes, the word is curbs—excessive profits.

Which side are you on? A 10 percent sales tax which ruptures your budget or increased taxes on corporation profits?

The House Banking Committee members who tossed a comb into your pocketbook by voting to kill all subsidies on January 1 were Republican representatives out to sabotage Roosevelt's program. The ten Democratic members made a minority report branding this action a step toward runaway inflation and stating it would up the cost of living from ten to fifteen billion dollars, making "dollars worth a dime."

Putting this in dollars and cents, it means the cost of butter would be increased five cents a pound, an increase in ceilings on canned vegetables of enough to cover jumps of 25 to 50 percent in the cost of the raw material, a forcing of meat ceilings up to cover an increase of at least $13.75 per hundred-weight on hogs, and spiraling prices on other staples accordingly.

Do you want this? Can you afford to spend this extra money?

There is still another little matter which has already cost you plenty of cash and which, if corrected, would mean a lessening of the tax burden. It is the cost-plus-fixed fee war contracting system with War Department approval which, according to the testimony before the House Military Affairs Committee Monday by Controller-General Lindsay G. Warren, has already cost the taxpayers millions of dollars.

Warren listed 270 specific instances where War Department contracting officers approved contractors' claims which involved such items as false teeth, vitamin pills, sanitary napkins, liquor and juke boxes. One firm gobbled nearly $2,000,000 in one deal. In other words, the boys have had a field day with your and my money.

It all boils down to this: cut the fraud and waste, thus reducing the sum needed to finance the war. Stop the proposed sales tax but increase the tax on staggering corporation profits and swollen incomes. Restore the $25,000 salary ceiling. And to avoid inflation and help control the cost of living, retain food subsidies.

For three cents and five minutes of your time spent in writing a letter, you can tell the same thing to your congressman and senators.

• • •

SIGNPOSTS TO FASCISM

NOVEMBER 3, 1943

I don't like what's happening in much of America today. The signs point toward a determined effort to create fascism in areas which heretofore had some semblance of genuine democracy. It seems a desperate effort on the part of forces, now facing defeat in Europe and Asia, to split the nation and hamper our war effort, thus enabling the Nazis to stave off impending defeat and so lengthen the war that the public can be sold on a negotiated peace instead of unconditional surrender, thereby leaving the Axis strong enough to rise again in a generation.

Consider, if you will, these recent developments, some substantiated and others hard to pin down for obvious reasons:

1. A drive is underway in California to revive the Ku Klux Klan after it had been virtually non-existent there for several years. The Klan fights Jews, Negroes and Catholics. It's tieup with the German-American bund and other subversive pro-Nazi groups has long been known. California has had huge migrations from the South to work in aircraft and shipbuilding, and these southerners dislike the comparative freedom enjoyed by Negroes on the west coast.

2. Gerald L. K. Smith, notorious American fascist whose gospel of hate was a major factor in causing the recent Detroit riot, is reported moving quietly to Cleveland to stir up strife there. Cleveland is also important as a war production center, has long had decent interrace relations and has as its head Mayor Lausche, a liberal executive who is friendly to Negroes.

3. When Negroes won their victory against Jim Crow schools in Hillburn, New York, white children were withdrawn and sent to private schools. This tuition is beyond the reach of poor white families and obviously must be financed by some undercover force. Walter Winchell in a recent column said certain Hillburn residents suspect a certain summer resident was back of it. This summer resident was exposed in the book, *Under Cover*, as an enemy of the United States.

4. The American Federation of Labor is understood to be collecting funds for an all-out campaign against President Roosevelt and the New Deal

and for a coalition of reactionary Republicans and anti-Roosevelt Democrats, mainly from the South. John L. Lewis is to have returned to the AFL fold and will campaign for a national elective office, possibly as vice president of the 1944 ticket.

5. Charges have been made that an organization without a formal name, originating in New Orleans, is seeking to pressure Jewish storekeepers in the South into signing an agreement that they will help "put down" an uprising foreseen when Negro soldiers return to that section and Jim Crow after the war.

6. Efforts by the *Chicago Tribune*, second biggest daily in America, to destroy the new Abraham Lincoln school, with a mixed faculty and student body, on the ground that it is "Communist" and therefore "subversive," an "expose" of the National Maritime Union as "Communist controlled" and therefore "dangerous." This union, incidentally, received a citation during this year's Negro History Week as one of the groups that had done most to break down race discrimination in 1942.

7. Consistent efforts on the part of the McCormick-Patterson-Hearst newspaper axis and such press prostitutes as Westbrook Pegler to counteract growing American respect for the Soviet Union and hamper full collaboration by hinting of an impending peace deal between Russia and Germany and insisting on suicidal bombing bases in Siberia. In addition, some of the papers lambast Great Britain in a further effort to slit the Big Three united nations.

8. Attacks on Jews by organized gangs in Boston, first brought to public attention by the newspaper, *PM*, and attacks on Jews in Chicago by gangs of young rowdies, many of them Italian.

This list contains only a few of the more obvious developments, but they are enough to show what's going on.

Our native Nazis and Hitler-lovers are scared. Their dreams of national and world domination by a few are being shaken by allied victories in Italy and western Russia and the South Pacific. In Europe the masses in the conquered countries are determined on democracy. Here at home Vice President Wallace preaches the gospel of the century of the Common Man, while Wendell Willkie crusades for One World, and the straight thinking leaders of the CIO move determinedly forward in their attempt to unite black and white labor in a solid front.

The result is a powerful effort by the touts of the status quo, by the enemies of progress, by the die-hard reactionaries, to keep the common man under control. They have money, say-so in strategic places and they are skilled fighters. By accounting prejudices, they seek to turn parts of the masses against the rest of the masses, hoping thus to paralyze democracy and delay normal societal evolution.

Since fascism feeds on hate for minorities, it should be obvious therefore that to counteract fascism those same minority targets must join hands in a united front. Negroes, Jews, Mexicans, Catholics, Filipinos, Orientals and democratic trade unions must unite to save themselves and rescue American democracy.

There is no time to be lost. None of us can afford to sit back and hope by wishful thinking to end the danger of American fascism. Nor can we allow it to be bludgeoned abroad and grow fat here at home. And if we awaken one morning to find our native Hitlers firmly entrenched in the driver's seat, we shall have only ourselves to blame for not suffocating this monster while we still had time.

• • •

LONG OR SHORT WAR?
NOVEMBER 10, 1943

A controversy has arisen over whether it would be of most benefit to the Negro to have a short or long war. I concede immediately that those who favor a long war have an important point when they hold in the spotlight employment gains since Pearl Harbor.

It is of course a cockeyed society that grants gains to a racial group only when that society itself is in jeopardy, but that is the fact whether we like it or not. Black men and women throughout the nation are of necessity holding down jobs that would still be denied them had not military demands created a manpower shortage. Many industries out of necessity have hired Negroes to keep their production lines moving, and with the army and navy still hungry for draftees there will be even more opportunities.

It may also be argued that if the war lasts long enough, these employers and white employers who look upon the Negro worker as a temporary evil to be tolerated only until peace returns, will have their attitudes changed. When you work beside a man four or five years, you got to look upon him as fixture and the feeling of permanency walks in.

At the same time, the dusky loud mouth show-offs who can't take newly found prosperity would during the course of a long war either be weeded out or also would settle down to normalcy after their honeymoon with those new jobs. This would eliminate another damaging complaint against Negro workers in places that never hired them before.

But I do not believe this line of thought can stand against what I consider the chief reason for complete victory at the earliest possible date.

The major argument against long drawn out hostilities is in the rising tide of American fascism. It is growing stronger daily. The longer World War II lasts, the bigger this menace becomes.

It is to the advantage of our own domestic Hitler lovers to have a lengthy conflict. Slick propaganda spread among a war weary public would pave the way for a negotiated peace instead of the smashing defeat and unconditional surrender now the goal of the United Nations. This would mean that fascism abroad would be only stymied for a time instead of blasted to atoms and, after a rest period, could rise anew for another world war and perhaps victory next time.

Nobody who read the signs accurately can deny fascism is rising at home. It is a desperate effort engineered by skillful, seditionists and enemy agents or sympathizers to save Hitler. It is a determined campaign by reactionaries, by anti-labor forces to prevent an extension of gains already obtained under the New Deal. They would sound an alarm clock in the midst of Vice President Wallace's dream of the century of the common man.

The generals of fascism, like those on the battlefields, single out detached minorities to envelop with their armies, cut off from the main force, and annihilate. The campaigns and outbreaks throughout the nation against Jews, Negroes, Mexicans and others follow the fascist pattern snipped by Hitler in Nazi Germany.

Let nobody dismiss the withdrawal of white children from the Main School in Hillburn, New York, or the racial tension of the recent Detroit mayoralty campaign or the drive in California for Ku Klux Klan memberships as isolated and totally unrelated incidents. Let nobody tell you the beatings given to Jews in Boston and Chicago by organized gangs are mere hooliganism.

It is true that America had a sack of prejudices long before Hitler. But it is also true that Hitler and his agents know this. Any smart foe will strike his adversary at his weakest point. The fomenting of strife between Negroes and whites, Jews and Gentiles, is one of Hitler's strongest and most easily forged weapons, for people who can be induced to fight among themselves will have just that much less energy and unity to direct against a common foe.

Don't forget that the Klan and German American Bund held joint meetings and exchanged speakers, and that ill feeling between ethnological and cultural groups is sharpest today in those areas long known to be hotbeds of subversive activity. And don't forget that at Hillburn those poor white parents who put their children in an expensive private school didn't pick the cash for tuition from a tree in the backyard.

I don't know where trouble will crop up next, but you can be sure it will. And you can be sure it won't be something spontaneous or isolated, no matter how much it seems so on the surface. And some of fascism's chief errand boys may not realize the true nature of their roles.

All this means that the Negro has got to bend every effort to wipe out fascism as quickly as possible. The longer it exists abroad, the stronger it becomes at home. It's not going to be ended here as long as it lives elsewhere, but if it can be demolished in the rest of the world, the entire nation can then bend its efforts toward smashing fascism in America.

For his own survival, the Negro therefore must bend every effort toward a speedy victory in World War II.

• • •

WHY NOT FORM A COUNCIL AGAINST RACISM?
NOVEMBER 17, 1943

Why can't we of all shades and backgrounds unite together in a Council Against Racism whose sole purpose would be to use every weapon possible to combat prevailing myths about distinctions between humans based on the bogey of race?

The simple truth is that racism has no place in a democracy. Someone has knocked the props from under every traditional belief about color. It is up to the enlightened and understanding elements of the population to popularize the work of these scientists.

There are no inferior or superior human stocks, says anthropology. Man is the product of his environment. All advanced nations are mongrelized, that is, various primitive stocks have fused for nobody yet have been able to erect a barbed wire around sex.

A belief of racism and racial differences is a springboard to fascism. Hitler sold his followers on the idea of "Aryan superiority" to all other "races." You know the result. Here in America the Ku Klux Klan has cashed in on misconceptions about white Americans and Jewish Americans and black Americans.

The South is of course, the locality where medieval fallacies about race are strongest, but these ideas are popular through the rest of the nation. Most persons honestly believe there are fundamental differences between what are called Negroes and whites. And so long as they continue to serve this false god, so long will "white supremacy" and all its evils continue.

The fact is there an immensely greater gap between a blonde born and reared in Norway and a blonde born and reared in Greece than between a blond and a brown American born and reared in the state of Oregon. But the inclination is to accept the Norwegian and Greek and Oregonian blondes as equals and as similar because they are white, but to shove the brown Oregonian to one side as different because he is what is called a Negro and therefore he must be dissimilar.

This same faulty but dangerous racist thinking pattern resulted in the unconstitutional ousting since Pearl Harbor, of American citizens of Japanese ancestry from their homes on the Pacific coast and their incarceration in concentration camps. There was no attempt made to mete out similar treatment to Americans of German and Italian ancestry, for they belonged to the "white" race. And soft pedaled though it may be, the racial aspect of the war against Japan cannot be minimized.

And so today popular opinion has created strong racial boundary lines between groups of people. Americans call some people Negroes and since that means they don't belong to the white race, they are set apart. Similar treatment is accorded Chinese, Japanese, Filipinos, Mexicans, and to some extent, the American Indian.

Suffering from the same racial malady is the Jew. Most persons look upon the Jew as a race with distinct physical and mental characteristics. That, too, is a fallacy. There are coal black Jews from Ethiopia and blonde Jews from Sweden; there are flatnosed Jews and sharp-nosed Jews. The fact is that Judaism is a religion and a culture; there is no Jewish race.

Man has roamed this planet thousands of generations. And yet can any of you go back a mere five generations out of those thousands who produced your ancestors, and name your thirty-two foreparents of a mere five generations ago? If you can't, how do you know that you haven't got Chinese and Senegalese and Irish and Spanish and what not blood flowing through your veins? And if you have, how can you raise so much fuss about race?

It is my contention that whoever is born and reared in America or becomes naturalized should be known only as an American. Forget whether he has blue eyes or red hair or thick lips or a chocolate complexion. He is an American. And let it be remembered that the United States Constitution makes no distinction between Americans. You are either an American or you are not. Common sense dictates that Americans think likewise.

So long as persons are thought of in terms of race, just so long are the race racketeers and native Hitlers given a powerful weapon to divide Americans and promote disunity. I do not contend that elimination of racism is the sole solution to this serious problem, but I do hold that it is of major strategic and psychological importance.

It would be the duty of the Council Against Racism to use radio, press, motion pictures, schools, billboards, the lecture platform and printed matter in its crusade against the evil of race thinking, with the eventual goal of eliminating the use of words which place Americans in different categories. This can be successful if enough persons will band themselves together and set out to influence the rest of the nation.

Are you interested? Are you willing, no matter what your ethnological or known cultural background, to help get a Council Against Racism under way immediately? Let me know your reaction. Write to me, care of this newspaper or directly to Frank Marshall Davis, Associated Negro Press, 3507 South Parkway, Chicago, 15, Illinois.

• • •

LET'S TRY SOLIDARITY

NOVEMBER 24, 1943

In the quest for a way out of the labyrinth of race discrimination in which the Species Aframericans finds itself, the darker brother is the living fulfillment of Lencock's classic fiction of the man who threw himself on his horse and galloped off in all directions.

It so happens that all Negroes, from reactionaries to radicals, are seeking an exit from the nation's black ghetto. But that's about all we have in common. This leader, who has Plan A and a number of followers, looks down upon the proponents of Plan B. The result is that the disciples of Plan A spend four hours daily seeking ways of advancing their own idea and six other hours trying to sabotage Plan B to Z. As a result nobody gets very far.

I suppose this is a working hangover from the era of "rugged American individualism." We get independence, yes, but few results. And the white section of the nation refuses to think of us as individuals.

There have been attempts, of course, to combine and integrate the activities of various organizations. The National Negro Congress tried it in 1936 but has not succeeded as a coordinating agency, although it is an important force. A. Philip Randolph's March on Washington movement gained adherents and headway, but committed Hari Kari last summer at its convention by voting to become coal black. Edgar Brown's National Negro Council is largely mythical except to the McCormick-Patterson-Hearst newspaper axis.

I would be the first to admit that an honest to goodness solidarity of race advancement efforts would be hard on the professional leaders. Many who are big frogs in their individual lily ponds would be lost in a large lake. They might be forced, as a last desperate resort, to work to make a living. But it's a possibility that I believe Duskymerica could survive.

There are too many important issues now and in the future for our interracial civil war to continue. We haven't got the time to battle among ourselves, and we ought to have some sense enough to know.

There's this little matter of a global conflict now raging. It should be obvious to any but a refugee from an insane asylum that it is to our best interest to smash fascism with all our power. and when I say fascism, I mean not only that in other lands but our domestic brand. And yet there are too many of this kaleidoscopic people who secretly pray for a Japanese victory, for the conquest of America by the Nazis, and who have no intention of aiding the war effort in any way if they can avoid it. This sort of thinking needs to be eradicated by every organization working consciously and vigorously toward that end.

There is also the necessity of creating a strong band and feeling of kinship between all minority groups. There is strong anti-Jewish sentiment among many of us; white majority propaganda has taken root and made large numbers opposed to Mexicans, Chinese, Filipinos and other minorities. We need a united campaign to erase this feeling. And while we're at it, we might also try to cure the anti-Negro sentiment among Negroes.

Thanks to intelligent CIO leadership, we are today more trade union conscious than ever before and have started learning the fundamental truth that the Negro worker must ally himself with the white worker, that their interests are one and the same, that the distrust and suspicion between the two has been created consciously and skillfully by the profit grabbers who saw in this artificially created enmity the chance to grab still bigger profits while the workers fought among themselves solely for color reasons. But there's still a field for education along this line by our leaders.

What kind of America we're going to have after the war and our place in it should be of concern to every colored man in this nation. Will we retain the social gains made since the New Deal? Will we have others? Or will reaction set in? And what are we going to do about it? The answers to these and similar questions should be worked out now by all our leaders.

There's no reason under the sun why 13,000,000 people, the Negroes of America, can't agree on a workable program and walk together strongly to gain the things we want. We need this solidarity. Who'll take the lead in achieving it?

• • •

SHIFT FROM CONSERVATISM

DECEMBER 1, 1943

One of the encouraging signs of the times is the bold reality with which thinking southerners are breaking away from tradition. Speaking recently at

Hampton, Mrs. Jessie Daniel Ames, white, field director of the Commission on Interracial Cooperation, blamed racial difficulties in the South on the efforts of northern and southern industrialists to maintain their dominance of the area. Mrs. Ames pointed out that the carefully cultivated enmity between white and black has kept the South in poverty and at the mercy of political demagogues who realize that unless the schism continues, their power to exploit will be taken away.

Thomas Sancton, white, southern born managing editor of the *New Republic*, has brilliantly advocated intelligent Negro militancy short of conflict. Virginius Dabney, white Dixie "liberal" editor who has recently been discredited among thinking Duskymericans, recently amazed us all by coming out for repeal of segregation laws on public carriers.

And just a few weeks ago Professor Chivers of Morehouse College in a series of speeches in Virginia called for a change in the approach to Negro education. He asked that the school programs be made more aggressive, that the Negro's education be directed "left of center."

Boys, get prices on a good cemetery lot. It's only a matter of time before conservatism can be lowered into a hole and buried.

Probably there may have been a time when conservatism had a place in interracial relations. But that kind of attitude as a program for the best interests of those people called Negroes should have been blown out with the last gas light.

To be conservative is to be immature, to put your independence upon white paternalism which is interested only in perpetuating itself while tossing a few crumbs to the hungry black masses to keep them just a little less dissatisfied. The ordinary Negro never got a full belly under conservatism; his death by starvation was merely prolonged.

Despite the efforts of the National Association of Manufacturers, of our native semi-fascists, of the reactionary industrialists, the world—and that includes America—is not returning to the debauchery of 1929. We've done a lot of serious thinking during the Depression hangover since those drunken days, and we're going to be more temperate.

Up until a few years ago, a Negro who belonged to a union—any kind of a union, even a Jim Crow AFL local—was looked upon by Aframerica as almost a radical. But the tempo has increased; the Duskymerican who belongs to the ordinary AFL local is gazed upon almost with pity by his fellow workers.

It has taken a long time to soak in, but it is becoming widely known that the big industrialists are interested in the big industrialists. To move forward, Negroes, being for the most part members of the working class, must identify themselves with that class: organized labor with a progressive program of solidifying all workers on a common front. Capital will yield no more to labor than labor is able to demand. With labor split along racial lines, capital can play white against black to divide and exploit; but with white and black fused in a solid front, capital loses one of its most historically effective weapons.

The more of us who realize this, the more of us there are who will desert conservatism. The numbers are growing daily. And it helps us understand why those who control the nation's wealth, the real rulers of the land, frantically use every device to discredit the social gains made under the New Deal, why their mouthpieces in Congress and the daily press try to confuse and disorganize the masses by yelling Communism at every worthwhile idea that would advance the common man.

We can get nowhere by eating the crumbs of conservatism. We've got to be intelligently militant, if for no other reason than to keep pace with the progressive elements of white labor. We've got to work with all forces sincerely and intelligently interested in advancing our cause, in ending the disgrace of discrimination. And we've got to get over our fear of labels. We hurt only ourselves when we run purely because the smiling interests opposed basically to our progress sneeringly call this idea or that program Red.

Let's be sane. But let's trade our horse and buggy of conservatism for the airplane of intelligent militancy.

• • •

LET'S GO FASCIST!

DECEMBER 22, 1943

Let's turn America over to the reactionaries and the fascists. A good start has been made on the industrial front, in Congress, and among the people. Why fight against it? Let us continue to sit tight and do nothing. It's easier that way and painless. Shake our heads, if we wish, and make "tsk, tsk" sounds with our teeth, but let's not work with any democratic organizations fighting fascism, or try to guide our congressmen, or many any kind of move aimed to defeat reaction.

Take the Soldier Vote bill. Just why should the "precious boys"—praise Senator "Cotton Ed" Smith—be given the ballot? Isn't it enough that we give them a gun and the chance to lose their lives? What more could they want? Let 'em vote and they might put Roosevelt back for a fourth term, or they might ballot certain poll tax congressmen out of easy pickings in Washington. And for goodness sake, don't reduce the voting age to eighteen. Just because a kid that age can die in Italy is no sign he has a right to have a voice in the government which ordered him to die, if need be.

Why abolish the poll tax? All it does is keep ten million Negroes and whites from having a chance to vote. They don't need to vote anyway. They ought to be glad they live in America, greatest nation on earth, champion of democracy, land of plenty. That ought to satisfy anybody. Hurrah for America! Hurrah for the Constitution, especially the Fourteenth Amendment!

What we need is more fascists in Congress. Of course we do have Senator Gerald Nye of North Dakota, but there's a possibility he may not be reelected. That is tragic. Who else is better fitted to become der feuhrer of the United States? And Senator Robert Rice Reynolds of North Carolina will not run for reelection, so we who want fascism lose a strong ally. Nye, Smith, Wheeler, Bilbo and the rest can't carry the load by themselves—not even when supported by Rankin, Dies and the other reactionaries in the lower house.

Let's fight for states' rights. Dixie champions this cause, since it allows discrimination without federal intervention. Big business wants it, since no one state can control a countrywide financial empire or monopoly. And just why should we be dictated to by bureaucrats in Washington! What does the capital think this is, a nation?

Beware, in 1944, of presidential candidates. By no means must the Republicans pick Willkie. Do you know that Willkie thinks this ought to be one world, and that race discrimination ought to end? Insist on Governor Dewey, an opportunist who has come out for an Anglo-American alliance which automatically excludes China and the Soviet Union, or Governor Bricker, whose grasp of international subjects is equaled only by his inability to say anything sensible about them. Both have the kiss of big business. President Roosevelt doesn't need a fourth term, for then we'd hear still more of Eleanor running around talking and dining with Negroes. And we can't have a thing to do with Henry Wallace for vice president. Wallace thinks this is the century of the common man. The nerve of him!

There ought to be some way to nullify the effects of the Moscow, Cairo, and Teheran conferences. There's no sense in cooperating closely with our major allies for victory and a permanent peace. Don't you know that Russia won't give us Siberian bases for bombing Japan! What? You say the army doesn't want them! Now just what does the army know about running this war? And look at Great Britain! Refusing to give us permanent airfields so that we can dominate world aviation and freeze out the British!

What we need is more disunity. There's too high a regard in this country for the Soviet Union and the British. The Russians have lost ten million lives in the war against Hitler, but after all they were dirty Communists and it was their war anyway. Coventry was virtually destroyed and thousands of lives were lost in London, but look at us! Why, we can't even get all the porterhouse steaks we want. I have it. Buy all the newspapers published by the McCormick-Patterson-Hearst axis and send them to your friends.

Not only do we need more disunity between allies but also between minority groups here in America. We Negroes who really want fascism owe it to themselves to engage in Jew baiting, in bitter attacks against all other minority groups, in misbehaving in public places, and on their jobs. And for goodness sake, let's steer clear of labor unions, especially the CIO, as well as all other organizations that want to win the war and think black workers and white workers should share equally.

• • •

MORE HOME FRONT FASCISM

JANUARY 5, 1944

It is one of the innumerable paradoxes of this war that as fascism is being crushed abroad in Europe, it is flowering in America. As our allied soldiers give their lives for the four freedoms and to end the Hitlerian doctrine of superior peoples in other parts of the world, our own herrenvolk, in Congress and elsewhere, make strong war against the same ideals here at home.

I refer specifically to the campaign now under way to "get" the FEPC and Malcolm Ross, by all odds its strongest chairman. The committee survived the South's assaults after the Birmingham hearings, smothered the attempt to block the recent railroad hearings, struggled back from its WMC assignment, and bested the Controller General Warren attack.

Now it is up against its most concentrated opposition. The Smith Committee in Congress is "investigating" it with an eye to declaring FEPC unconstitutional, Rankin and Hamspock and others have blasted it from the House floor, certain Dixie railroads and unions have stated they did not intend to follow its findings, and the Dies Committee has turned loose its investigators to prove that Chairman Ross is a "Communist" and therefore "dangerous." As might be expected, the *Chicago Tribune* and similar organs of disunity have pounced on this report with drunken glee.

It is, of course, a sorry reflection upon our so-called democracy that such an organization as the FEPC ever had to be created in the first place or an executive order issued by the president to make employers hire Negro citizens in a time when every available human must work to win the war. It was issued because of fascist race theories in our country; it is being fought because of American fascism. The power of the blows against it indicates the rising and concentrating power of domestic Hitlerism.

Opponents claim the FEPC is "disrupting race relations." The charge is admitted. That is its purpose. The race relations which countenance discrimination and denial of a job purely because of the happenstance of color have got to be disrupted, if we want real democracy. To fight against giving full equality to all citizens shows a cynical disregard for our written Constitution.

The Dies Committee claim, and *Chicago Tribune* delight, that Ross is taking his strong anti-discrimination stand because he is a Communist should have the effect, among thinking Negroes, of making Communism attractive instead of reprehensible. This column has pointed out before that if those Americans who want to end race prejudice and believe that America should be America think that way purely because they are Communists, then common sense demands that every Negro appoint himself a committee of one to turn more whites into Reds.

It is significant that anti-Negro Martin Dies, whose "investigators" are shouting Communist at Ross, considers himself one of the herrenvolk and has been of invaluable service to the fascist cause in this nation. Dies has been publicly accused of working hand in glove with Joseph P. Kamp, notorious fascist and head of the subversive Constitutional Education League. Kamp himself was co-editor, along with Lawrence Dennis of the fascist publication, *The Awakener*. And Dennis was an intimate associate of Dr. Friedrich Auhagon, Nazi agent and self-styled "theoretician of American fascism." In 1938 Kemp chose Dies for his "Americanism award" and boasts that he has access to the files of Dies for use in compiling his seditious propaganda.

That picture ought to help clarify this column's oft-repeated warnings about the strength of American fascism. And when this vicious anti-Negro and anti-democratic doctrine reaches directly from Berlin to Congress it should prove the strength of the foe. And it ought to show that any war against fascism must be fought at home as well as abroad.

The FEPC needs the support of every citizen, white or black, who believes in the Four Freedoms and the rights of the common man. But a mere belief is not enough. Tell President Roosevelt and your congressman to back the FEPC and its directives. And while you're at it, you might also point out that the Dies Committee should become a dead committee and the Smith Committee should follow suit.

• • •

LET THE SOLDIERS VOTE!
JANUARY 19, 1944

There's still time to influence passage by Congress of a Soldier Vote bill with federal control over the ballot. But it requires speedy and direct action by every person and organization in America who believes that if a soldier is ordered to defend democracy, then he should have a chance to vote and thereby help shape the kind of democracy he is risking his life to defend.

You know what has happened in Georgia when the matter was left to the states after the Senate passed an anemic measure catering to the reactionary battle cry of "state's rights." The Georgia bill allows nobody to vote who ordinarily would not vote if that person were home—which means Negroes now serving the country still can't have the ballot in the lily white Democratic primary, tantamount to election in Dixie.

The Georgia law also says that relatives of the service man must apply to their election board for the ballot. Can you imagine the pappy of Private Sambo Brown asking for time off from Mr. Jim, who owns the plantation, to go to the election board in Lynchem Town and get a ballot for his boy! And even if he has the nerve to do so, just what do you think the white board will tell him before its members call up Mr. Jim and the other priests of white supremacy?

We have been asleep on this issue. Few are our Negro newspapers that have campaigned vigorously for a measure like the original Green-Lucas bill. And I am still waiting for William L. Dawson to rise in Congress and use his oratorical brilliancy to proclaim to his fellow congressmen and the world at large that only federal control will assure every member of the armed forces his constitutional right to the ballot. He can point to Georgia as proof, with the virtual certainty that Georgia has set the pattern for Dixie from whence comes the bulk of Negro servicemen.

The very fact that state control means discrimination in the South, should be enough to make every Negro back the fight for a federal bill, but there is also another angle to the matter. Fees—and they are that same unholy reactionary alliance of poll tax Democrats and anti-Roosevelt Republicans—contend the national government has no right to control the vote. They say this would abridge state's rights.

It seems to me that if Uncle Sam has the right to take a boy from Alabama and Oregon and Maine and give him a gun and send him to Italy to die, maybe, then Uncle Sam also has the right to give him a ballot.

To carry state's rights out to their logical conclusion, the drafted infantryman from Omaha stationed on the firing line in the South Pacific ought to crawl in the dark to his Japanese enemy, nudge him on the shoulder, and ask, "Say, fellow, before we carry this thing any further, are you just fighting the United States or has Nippon also declared war on Nebraska?"

Seems to me every week or two I ask you to speak your mind to Congress. I'm not stopping now. I say it is your duty as an American citizen and as a Negro who has seen his brothers disfranchised in the South because of states' rights to demand of your congressman immediately that he vote for House approval of a strong measure like the original Green-Lucas bill when the matter is thrown open for general action. A letter or a penny postcard will do the trick—and don't think your representative won't be influenced if all of you write. But it's got to be done right away.

• • •

ABOUT ROOSEVELT'S LABOR DRAFT

JANUARY 26, 1944

Some months ago I wrote that I was opposed to the Austin-Wadsworth Bill to conscript labor. I am still against it. But at the same time I am whole-heartedly in favor of Roosevelt's five point program to speed victory, which includes a labor draft, although it is obvious that certain special safeguards need to be written into any such measure to protect the interests of the Negro.

You see, I am an American. I do not consider myself a member of an internal Negro nation waging constant war with the rest of America, for that would make me one with the fascist foe abroad and would lessen my chance of getting full equality. I recognize the fact that my interests are part and parcel of those of the entire country, that what is good for the United States is automatically good for me. And I acknowledge there are white Americans who will go just as far to remove the obstacles to complete Negro citizenship as I will go.

It must be remembered that Roosevelt looks constantly toward tomorrow and formulates his program from the needs of the coming day. The record shows a long procession of correct appraisal. He sees the entire forest, not small clumps of trees as do the various special interests and segments of our population. He, along with other high government officials whose business it is to find ways to defeat the Axis with the smallest loss of life, considers a labor draft essential.

This proposal has been singled out for attack. We have the amazing spectacle of reactionaries and pro-fascists such as the *Chicago Tribune* and a number of beloved congressmen siding with many labor leaders against it. Their motives obviously are not similar, and the sooner that union heads realize they are playing into the hands of their traditional foes by refusing to go along with a program of sacrifice for the entire nation which will help hasten the century of the common man, the sooner will we be able to present that solidarity necessary for speedy victory.

But the drafting of labor is only one part of the Roosevelt program. He also asked for a stringent tax law, limitations on profits (he's the guy who tried to invoke a $25,000 wage ceiling. Remember? A billion a year in food subsidies to keep prices down and avoid inflation, and re-enactment of the 1942 Stabilization Act. Those all hang together, and call for concessions by capital, labor and farmer for a common purpose. Roosevelt has also said that unless Congress enacts all five of these measures—which includes the labor draft—he will not ask for the passage of just one.

Obviously, the Austin-Wadsworth Bill is not the answer to the labor draft section, for it contains none of the safeguards necessary to protect Negroes from our native semi-fascists.

Such a measure should contain specific provisions stating that persons must be drafted for work at only their highest skills. This would prevent prejudiced officials from assigning Negro skilled workers to jobs as common laborers, a practice all too prevalent. And such assignment should be limited only to essential industries, thus preventing southerners from drafting domestics back into their kitchens.

If the measure is to be administered by draft boards similar to those sending men to the armed forces, then the law should make it mandatory for each local board to follow the population pattern of the area it serves. This means that in any district predominantly Negro, as is the case in much of the South, most of the members should be Negroes. There should also be Negroes on appeal boards for the expressed purpose of preventing some board sending a Harlemite to a job in Mississippi if the Harlemite did not want to go because of the race situation.

With such safeguards as these, the Negro would have no more to fear than any other American. At the same time it would work to his advantage, for many firms now refusing to hire Negroes would have to take them or else, and many competent skilled workers deprived of a chance to show their ability would for the first time get the kind of jobs they merit.

Of course it looks now as if Congress will keep its hands off the whole program. But that is no reason why we cannot clarify the issue and see its advantages. If nothing else, the spectacle of an America at last united and utilizing every person to win the war would have a terrifying psychological effect upon the Axis, for look what we have done even with disunity. And if this also means that your husband or your brother or your sweetheart has his life saved by a speedier end of hostilities, wouldn't it be worth the personal inconvenience?

• • •

CHECK YOUR DAGGER, MISTER?
FEBRUARY 9, 1944

How about removing that dagger you have hidden on your person and leaving it in the checkroom for a while, Mr. Race Leader? I'm talking directly to you, A. Philip Randolph, Perry Howard, George Schuyler, William L. Patterson, Willard Townsend, Milton P. Webster, Frank Crosswaith, Edgar Brown, Max Yergan and the rest of you who are out in front fighting for a brighter day for Aframerica.

Not every one of those named goes around with his nose to the earth smelling up excuses to stick a knife between the ribs of the leaders who refuse to think as he does. Some are willing and ready to sit down right now and plan with the others for a unified program. But too many of those named seem to live only for an opportunity to sock the others. You know who you are.

The united nations demand unity in the war against the Axis. America itself must have unity to bring the conflict to an early conclusion and save lives and money. It is obvious that the Negro himself needs unity in this same battle against fascism abroad as well as against the anti-democratic front which gets stronger day by day within our borders. The very fact that we are at the bottom of the pile strengthens the need for unity if we seriously intend to better our lot.

The recent Teheran decisions between Roosevelt, Stalin and Churchill ought to set the pattern for our group thinking. If such conflicting ideologies as those of Socialist Russia, Imperialistic Great Britain, and Capitalistic America can find a common basis for cooperation not only in war but in the peace to follow, why cannot leaders of Duskymerica do likewise, particularly when all have common grievances and look toward the same goal: full citizenship for the Negro?

But instead we see the continuing and sorry spectacle of racial disharmony. Certain leaders, notably Randolph, Crosswaith and Schuyler, follow the pet Rankin and Goebbels line of Red-baiting, when even the sorriest ignoramus among us ought to know that there is no element in our population more desirous of completely eliminating fascism at home and abroad and working in harmony than are the Communists. Webster takes public potshots at Townsend, although both are labor leaders. Howard aims a blunderbuss at any and all who are not diehard Republicans, even though it may provide the opposition with valuable aid as was the case in his diatribe against the poll tax bill. Brown meanwhile wears the hand-me-down political prejudices of Colonel McCormick of the *Chicago Tribune.*

It is not necessary to mention the Democratic politicians, or the churchmen of conflicting denominations, or the northern leader vs. southern leader controversy, to underline the wide open breaches among us. Every sensible person knows they exist, and the fact weakens our fight. The energy we should be using to advance the race as a whole is dissipated squabbling and battling among ourselves.

I call upon each of you leaders to consider which is more important, your age and personal likes and prejudices, or the progress of thirteen million black folk?

And if you decide that marching forward to unqualified Negro citizenship is more important, are you willing to accelerate the pace by subordinating your own selfish attitudes to a broad and unified program that cries for the cooperation of all groups if it would be successful?

There seems to be no reason why intelligent men cannot sit down together and shape a pattern for things to come. Of course there would be clashes, but if those leaders are sincerely interested in advancing the common cause and determined to formulate a practical program, they can find a way to do it.

Specifically, I believe that Walter White and William L. Patterson and Willard Townsend and Milton P. Webster and Frank Crosswaith and Max Yergan and Lester Granger and our top Republicans and our top Democrats can sit down and plan together, if they are sincere about wanting to help black America. But if they were interested only in personal glory or advantage, such a conference would be doomed from the start.

What about it readers? What do you think, leaders?

• • •

DEFEATS OF THE HOME FRONT
FEBRUARY 23, 1944

Unity and democracy are still taking a shellacking here on the home front, despite our successes in the Marshall Islands and in Italy. Our home grown fascists continue singing the siren song of racism at the top of their voices. There is no Negro in America who does not stand to suffer.

Last week William Randolph Hearst used all of the papers under his command to stage a new defensive in his private war with the Soviet Union. In a large editorial he screamed in print that "Russia may ultimately JOIN UP with the Japanese." He printed the pictures of three Red army generals, describing them as "typically oriental," and bleated that "the Russians are orientals—as oriental as the Japanese—spiritually, morally and culturally oriental. In other words, the Russians are of a different 'race," therefore not like "the white people of America" and consequently are likely to "join with their oriental brothers, the Japanese, in fighting America."

I want also to call attention to the action of Judge A. Marshall Thompson of Pittsburgh last week in freeing five Ku Klux Klan leaders on trial for plotting to "create ill will, hatred and strife against people of this country who are of certain religious or racial classifications." To convict these Klansmen, these tools of fascism, would "abridge the right of freedom of speech," Judge Thompson said.

Meanwhile the executive board of the United Service Organizations supported its president, Chester Barnard, who banned that informative booklet, *The Races of Mankind*, from distribution at USO centers because it was "too controversial." In other words, the USO prefers to allow the continuation of fascist race theories, the kind of rot promulgated by Hearst and the Klan and Hitler, to dissemination of scientific information that gives the lie to race myths!

And let it not be forgotten that ten years ago there were only nine anti-semitic organizations in the nation. Today there are at least 115. Those who fight the Jew are also enemies of the Negro.

This picture of the rising tide of racism, of ever increasing fascism and the refusal of those in key spots to curb this evil, sickens every lover of freedom, every believer in brotherhood and justice and equality. We stand in mortal danger of losing the battle against fascism at home while our fighting forces win victories abroad against the foreign standard bearers of the same foe.

The Hearst press spewed its poison at the strategic time. We are still shocked at revelations of Jap atrocities to prisoners taken at Battan. So if the unthinking public can be sold on the idea that the Russians will join forces with the cruel Nips, it will cause widespread hostility to our glorious ally, the Soviet Union. That would help negate the effects of the Moscow and Teheran conferences by creating disunity, and at the same time take pressure off the Nazis, who have tried to sell the world on the idea that they are waging a holy war against Communism anyway. Hearst evidently will do anything to help a friend whether in Boston or Berlin.

The lie that there are distinct races and these races are inherently different, with certain ones morally and spiritually inferior, is a cornerstone of fascism. Hitler has used it successfully, handing Hearst the blueprint. Fact is, two of the generals pictured were Slavs and the other an Armenian. The Soviet Union has every type of person, from blonde to black. The Chinese are orientals. Are they, too, to join with Japan and Russia in fighting America, Mr. Hearst?

Judge Thompson's attitude is illogical. The connection between the Klan and the German American Bund, and the Klan's part in precipitating last year's Detroit race riot, are common knowledge. To follow the Pittsburgh jurist's line of reasoning to its logical conclusion, we have no right to jail any seditionist since such would be against the "right of free speech." And next time you are in a crowded theatre, get up and yell "fire." The audience may stampede and lives may be lost, but you are secure if Judge Thompson's attitude prevails. You have merely exercised your constitutional right of free speech.

What few persons realize is that absolute free speech is impossible in a democracy. An individual has the right to free speech only so long as it does not imperil the rights and freedom of others.

The position of Barnard and his USO bigwigs is absurd. They have a chance to counteract this fascist evil of racism by allowing the distribution of *Races of Mankind*. It is a matter of record that the Y.M.C.A.—not known for radicalism—distributed it and the U.S. army has purchased thousands to use in certain soldier training courses.

You ought to tell the USO what you think of its stand.

• • •

SOUTH TODAY NEEDS YOUR HELP

MARCH 1, 1944

One of the heartbreaking penalties of espousing a liberal cause is that the enemy, those who want to keep the status quo, never lets up in his efforts to make you a casualty, while those you seek to help seldom lend you real encouragement.

Is this to be the story of Lillian E. Smith and her courageous *South Today*, published in Clayton, Georgia, where the Civil War is still going on?

Lillian Smith is a white woman. She believes so seriously in the Constitution and democracy that she wants to make both work. She believes that Negroes should be treated as citizens and human beings, and is not afraid to say so. Since she lives in Georgia, that makes her a novelty.

Her publication, *South Today*, has carried the torch of equality throughout the nation. Its fight for justice has been so bold and uncompromising that she has been cited along with Pearl Buck and Eleanor Roosevelt as champions of the Negro people and the underprivileged.

Naturally, she has made enemies. The rulers of Dixie, the exploiters, consider her dangerous. Imagine a white woman taking democracy and the Constitution seriously! And so every kind of pressure has been brought to bear to silence her voice, to liquidate her efforts.

In a frank statement issued in January to subscribers, Lillian Smith told why *South Today* had not appeared in some months. She said:

"If you are one of our old and experienced subscribers you have probably guessed the truth: the issue has been delayed because of lack of office and editorial assistance and because of the time consumed—month in and month out—in outwitting those anti-democratic forces that are not pleased with the existence of a liberal magazine in the South.

"This is an old story and a never-ending one. In addition to these more familiar difficulties, are the newer problems of increased cost of paper, printing and production generally. Because we prefer to keep the price at one dollar (the same price the magazine was eight years ago when it consisted of only twenty pages), we find these increased costs of some real concern. Our magazine now is larger, consisting of from sixty-four to a hundred pages and we think it wise to keep it so.

"We have at the present time one assistant. All of the editorial and clerical work (including the answering of the thousands of letters now coming to us) is done by three of us. Most of the magazine is written by the editors themselves with only a few contributions made by others. In addition to this, the editors have to find more remunerative ways of making their own living.

They are not supported by an 'endowment fund,' nor by an 'angel,' nor in any other mysterious, convenient fashion."

Because of those difficulties, *South Today* will be published twice a year. Between issues a newsletter will be sent to subscribers, and reprints will be made of articles for which there is unusual demand. The only alternative is to discontinue the magazine under pressure. And neither the editors nor anybody else of progressive thought would want that to happen.

Now that you know the problems, you ought to help solve it. Talking will do no good, unless it is the voice of the dollar. We can't let a fighter down. We've got to back our champions.

I'm sending a dollar for a subscription to *South Today* at Clayton, Georgia. How about you?

And I'm also going to get a copy of Lillian Smith's new novel, *Strange Fruit*, (remember Billie Holiday's record?) published by Reynal and Hitchcock.

What are you going to do?

• • •

MEET THE RECORD, MR. DAWSON
MARCH 8, 1944

I really should take time off, go to Washington, and look up Congressman William Dawson of Chicago. Then I ought to grab him by the hand and lead him to the government printing office. There I should stop in the proper place and in my most formal manner say, "Mr. Dawson, I want you to become acquainted with a friend of mine. Congressman, meet the *Congressional Record*. You've been strangers too long."

It's unfortunate, but it's a fact. Mr. Dawson and the *Congressional Record* seem purposely to shun each other, as if one had the smallpox and the other was in deathly fear of becoming diseased. I am at a loss to understand why since I think a good thick friendship would be beneficial to both.

It seems to me that the first Negro Democrat ever elected to the House is muffing one opportunity after another to make both his voice and the sentiments of Negroes heard in a place where it would do a lot of good. The lower house rings with the raucous ravings of Mississippi's RanKKKin, the divisionist speeches of Clare Hoffman of Michigan, Smith of Virginia, Dies of Texas and a host of others. The silence of Dawson almost splits the eardrums.

If the cat has Bill Dawson's tongue, then I favor forming a posse to hunt down the cat and return this essential organ of speech to its rightful owner. A congressman without a voice may get into Ripley's cartoon strip, but there's no virtue in being a curiosity for curiosity's sake.

RanKKKin habitually howls about the race question. His is the loudest voice of fascism in the lower house. He engages in a constant crusade against Negroes. He seeks to hogtie progressive legislation. He fought the federal soldier vote bill—with the aid of Republicans. And he repeatedly refers to Walter Winchell with the epithet of "kike"—equivalent to calling you or me a "nigger"—while his colleagues applaud and then come around later to shake his hand.

It seems to me that Dawson should take the lead in combating the Mississippian's fascism where it gets full play, right on the floor of the House. Dawson has the right, the privilege and the duty of answering all such charges and attitudes as soon as they are aired. The same people who get the poison should be administered the antidote.

Dawson has enough background, knows enough history, and is well enough acquainted with the fundamental issues of this global war to refute the white supremacy doctrines and divisionist tactics of the congressional reactionaries. He should lose no opportunity to point to the need for unity between Negro and white, between capital and labor, between all groups and individuals who want to win this war and secure the peace. And in addition to having his say, and thus contributing vocally to progress, his words would go down in the *Congressional Record* to be read by the same people who see what the obstructionists have to say.

The irony is that Dawson is a sort of spokesman without voice. The speeches he ought to make in Congress are delivered on the outside. The Negro must look to Vito Marcantonio of New York, young Will Rogers of California and a half dozen so others for the kind of leadership he ought to expect from his own ethnic kind.

I say those things without belittling Dawson's value, for value he does have. Dawson is a supporter of President Roosevelt all down the line, and every intelligent voter ought to know that Roosevelt is as brilliant and farsighted a leader as this nation has ever had. Any representative or senator who stands back of Roosevelt in a day when Congress as a whole seems bent on wrecking the win the war program is to be commended. But I say that Dawson could give added support to the president's program by rising in Congress to air his pro-Roosevelt views.

To make matters worse, Dawson's support of the chief executive makes it unwise for Chicagoans to replace him at this critical time. He undoubtedly will win the Democratic nomination again in the April 12 primaries in his own district. Opposing him next November will be either Earl B. Dickerson, ex-Democrat now running as an independent Republican, or William E. King, GOP machine candidate. Dickerson could be far more vocal than Dawson, but by wearing the Republican logo he would automatically be opposed to the president. King, most likely to be Dawson's foe in the fall, would be a standard bearer in the Taft-Dewey-Bricker backward looking coalition.

• • •

SOME FASCISTS ARE BLACK
MARCH 1944

Let no one think that the white brother has a corner on fascism. This prehistoric myth of superiority and inferiority, from which all Negroes suffer, has its disciples even among its victims. The statement that some fascists are black is not a revelation, but it is seldom that they parade their ignorance before the public in the open and unashamed way they are now doing in Chicago.

Restrictive residential covenants have walled-in black Chicago, giving the Southside a population density greater even than that of Calcutta. Expansion in the Negro ghetto proper is almost out of the question. But several miles farther south there has for some decades been a dusky settlement known as Lilydale. In recent years wealthier Negroes suddenly "discovered" this area and began building as fine homes as their dollars would allow on the eastern end of Lilydale.

The newcomers, the boys with the bucks, did not choose to be identified with the common people who already lived here. So they called their part of the community West Chester, and it was safer to dance with a blue eyed blonde in Meridian, Mississippi, than to refer to a resident of West Chester as an inhabitant of Lilydale. That should have been the tip-off.

Not long ago the Chicago Housing Authority, determined to relieve the ever-increasing housing shortage (The Chicago Urban League estimates 70,000 Negroes have come since 1940 to an already overcrowded Chicago with virtually no increase in living space), decided to erect a war housing project. Thousands of Negroes work in the South Chicago industrial area. They needed homes within reasonable proximity to their jobs. The West Chester-Lilydale area was ideal. So the CHA picked a site and announced construction.

That was the signal for our black fascists to slide and slither into the light from their hiding places under the stones of economic snobbery.

A group calling itself a citizens' committee met and passed a resolution against the housing project. Those homes, said our fine black citizens, would bring an "undesirable element" into the community. They would "depreciate property values." Their stuff sounded as if it had been written by the real estate board of Mobile, Alabama, with the assistance of Goebbels and the Ku Klux Klan. The housing authority was asked to take its project and stick it—somewhere else.

The only bright spot is that a small group, calling itself the West Chester Improvement Association, took an opposite view and invited the project in. But this group represented only a small minority, and since its stand was made public, most of its officers have had to resign because many of the membership went over to the fascist side.

The sundown Hitlers include those who have been traditionally looked up to as leaders. They are doctors, dentists, lawyers, school teachers, with a high school principal as the reported ringleader. This principal, Mrs. Maudelle Bousfield, is the only Negro high school head in Chicago and is in charge of Wendell Phillips High. The Negroes she seeks to block are those undoubtedly who rejoiced loudest at a racial achievement when she won her appointment a few years ago.

These are the people who have made their piles from the pennies of the striving poor. And the public which gave them prestige ought to take it away. They are also the people who sigh over Brahms and Bach and proclaim scorn for the blues and boogie woogie, who sing hallelujahs to Hoover and razz the Roosevelts, who are sorry they were born black and who try to get as far away from their group as they know now. They are festering sores in the midnight skin of Duskymerica.

I cannot stomach the superior attitudes of our inferior leaders. Being one of the common people—and proud of it—I am with the common people.

I am ashamed, not of our workers and masses, but of those who get their bread and beans from the plain people and then fancy themselves above us. This Chicago situation throws in bold relief the bankruptcy of much of our so-called leadership. It indicates that our champions have got to be those who have strong roots in labor and the masses.

It is to the credit of a number of West Chester professional people and teachers that they have vigorously opposed the action of the sundown Hitlers, and have gone on record as favoring the construction in their front yards, if need be, of modern dwellings that will ease the race's burden of squalor and overcrowding and disease.

We who are fighting fascism can stop at neither geographical nor racial lines. The fascists have got to go, whether in Berlin or Birmingham, whether white or black.

• • •

REPUBLICANS, WHAT OF FEPC?
MARCH 22, 1944

Republican members of Congress, who consistently join with poll tax and anti-Roosevelt southerners to defeat important legislation, will soon have another chance to show their colors. But since this new action, which involves the fate of the FEPC, will take place closer to election, Negroes are more likely to remember who voted which way and why.

This means simply that since the Republicans hold the balance of power in both House and Senate between white supremacy southern Democrats, who vote as a bloc, and progressive northern Pro-Roosevelt Democrats, who also vote as a bloc, the fate of the FEPC is in the hands of the Republicans. They can kill it or save it.

There will, of course, be a disposition to play politics on the issue. Since the FEPC was created by Roosevelt, its death would be another defeat of a Roosevelt measure, a further extension of the party policy of criticize and obstruct. And there is no doubt that slick politicians would find some way of twisting facts to make the gullible black voter believe that the Democrats were responsible.

It is the duty of realistic Republican Negro leaders to demand that their party members of Congress support not only the Marcantonio and Dawson-Scanlon Bills to create a permanent FEPC, but that they also back the budget appropriation recently requested. The rank and file voters of each political persuasion must do likewise.

Concentrated efforts are being made to abolish the FEPC and all it stands for. The opposition of the white supremacy southerners is to be expected. Senator Russell of Georgia will do his best to block the requested $585,000 appropriation. Representative Smith, another foe, is head of a House committee seeking to knock out the committee. The attitude of those and other southerners was foreordained.

Its support, therefore, must come from the north and east and west where Negroes have a say-so in the election, where people are a bit closer to civilization. And, if we judge the future by the past, most of the Democrats from these sections will stand back of FEPC.

Certain Republicans have already joined hands with anti-Roosevelt Democrats from Dixie in sniping at the committee. Representative Clare Hoffman of Michigan is such a one. Representative Taber of New York, ranking GOP member of the House Appropriations Committee and therefore in a strategic position, said in Congress:

"The FEPC hasn't made a very good reputation for itself. I am suspicious of it."

These straws show definitely which way the wind is blowing. And if you want to know what the Republicans did lately in their blind zeal to discredit Roosevelt, take a good look at the Senate vote on the federal Soldier Vote Bill. This emaciated hybrid, which guarantees states' right and the denial of the ballot to Negro servicemen in Dixie, was supported by twenty-three Democrats (all but five of them from the South) and twenty-four Republicans, all from the North.

Against this worthless compromise bill were twenty-four Democrats, all but four of them from the north, and six Republicans and one Progressive. The conclusion is obvious that more Democrats backed the administration's desire for a genuine federal ballot than were opposed. The count also shows the Republicans were almost solidly against it. In their fanaticism, they thought nothing at all of the Negro and gladly sacrificed our soldiers' and sailors' chance to vote in the South on the altar of Roosevelt hate.

Nobody contends that the FEPC is perfect, but no sensible person can deny that it represents a huge step forward. Many firms have hired Negroes and other minorities solely because the FEPC so directed, believing it would be better to change their policy than face the unfavorable publicity, or because they had been made to see that such attitudes were impractical and un-American.

Unfortunately, certain black Republican politicians have closed their eyes and joined with southern opponents in blasting the committee. Some have charged the FEPC has received "little support" from the president. Of them I would ask: "Who created FEPC? Who has authorized changes intended to strengthen it? Who issued an order negating Comptroller General Warren's effort to wreck it? And who just submitted the recent formal request to Congress for $585,000 to finance it?

Getting back to my original premise, the fate of the FEPC is up to the Republicans. If they cannot be importuned to drop their unholy alliance with Negro hating southern Democrats and support this important committee, then you know what to do in November.

• • •

DON'T BLAME DIXIE ALONE
MARCH 29, 1944

It's simple and convenient to blame the South solely for race prejudice and the pattern of race relations prevailing there. But that is basically as fallacious as putting the whole blame on the hand when a theft is committed. The truth is that the financial centers along Wall Street in New York and LaSalle Street in Chicago must share the guilt for the maintenance of white supremacy just as the brain must be held responsible for the indiscretions of the hand.

Speaking recently against poll terms before the Georgia Electoral Reform League in Atlanta, Professor Glenn W. Rainey of Georgia Tech had these significant words to say:

"In the case of the South—and notably of Georgia—the percentage of voting is so low that elections can easily be carried by rings or machines, controlling a disproportionately large part of the vote through office holders and through money supplied by selfish interests."

Let nobody be so naive as to believe that big business has no interest in who goes to Congress. It is to the advantage of the corporations and
monopolies to have friendly senators and representatives who will introduce
or support legislation giving them special privilege, or block bills that would
reduce their power. Northern capital has millions invested in southern agriculture and industry. Because fewer people vote in Dixie, it is less expensive
to control an election. Naturally, they are going to be opposed to anything
permitting greater enfranchisement and their undercover Charlie McCarthys
will do all they can to maintain the status quo. It's bread and butter to them.

You might take a look at the records of some of the southern congressmen on non-racial legislation. Drew Pearson, the syndicated columnist, has
done a lot to expose the connections between Senator George of Georgia and
others on measures of economic importance to all the nation. Some of the
bitterest opposition to federal food subsidies came from southern salons—
purely because powerful agricultural combines were against subsidies. And it
is no secret that most of the richest and wealthiest Dixie farmland is owned
by northern capital, with thousands of additional acres controlled through
mortgages, etc.

The majority of southern mills and factories are likewise the investment
of Wall Street and LaSalle. Industry has been moving south, not because of
any altruistic desire to help that section, but for the very practical reason that
race prejudice helps return bigger profits.

Race prejudice has an economic basis and will pay dividends to investors
as long as it continues to exist. Black worker and white worker have refused,
except in a pitifully few instances, to plan and act together for the common
good. They are jealous rivals for jobs. This competition threatens both and
keeps wages low. So the industrialists have gone South to build plants because
of the cheapness of labor, with the resultant increase in profits.

It is obvious that a coalition between white and black labor, an end to
this foolish and suicidal civil war, would result in the creation of strong unions
which would then be in a position to demand a larger share of the profits in
the form of increased wages. That, of course, would lessen the "take" of the
boys in Wall Street and LaSalle. It is to their financial interest, therefore, that
race prejudice continue strong, that the southern patterns remain basically
unchanged, and—by all means—that the dangerous CIO with its interracial
program be fought in every way possible.

That explains also why the management of southern industries, with few exceptions, maintain the thought patterns of the community. Protesting does little good; the good executives are there to maintain the status quo. It is also perfectly obvious that if race discrimination and inequality were not satisfactory to the northern financiers, they would order their hirelings in Dixie to break away from tradition and move intelligently to educate the southern public away from prevailing attitudes.

The hard truth is that big business is out to make money and cares little about democracy no matter what platitudes are mouthed at certain times. If race prejudice means more money, then keep it, don't kill it.

So let's not blame Dixie alone for its attitudes on color. Give a goodly share of the shame to Wall Street and LaSalle. And since little help in the fight against race discrimination is coming from the financiers, it becomes doubly important to remember that the common people themselves have got to be taught that prejudice keeps the poor people poor and helps the rich get richer, that their only hope for economic advancement is to work together.

• • •

AYD FIGHTS ARMY JIM CROW

APRIL 4, 1944

That now forward looking interracial organization, American Youth for Democracy, has just launched a national campaign to end Jim Crow in the armed services. Since this is of primary interest to Negroes, it behooves all of us to back this drive in every way we know how, from lip service to cash.

Perhaps you want to know something about this group, known as AYD for brevity's sake. Formed last October, it numbers a young colored woman, Winifred Norman, among its six national officers. She is vice chairman. A Negro girl is editor of the official publication, *Spotlight*. This is the same organization, incidentally, which sponsored Sunday night's tribute to Fats Waller in New York in which the nation's outstanding stage and orchestra stars participated. Andy Razaf, the songwriter and buddy of the late pianist, is contributing a share of all royalties from his new composition, "Big Boy," to AYD.

It is rather obvious that there are no clear lines in this organization. Members take democracy seriously, believing it should be a reality instead of a slogan. For that reason the reactionary enemies of everything progressive, those who fear the unity of the people, have smeared AYD as "Communist." Fact is, its membership rolls are open to young people of all shades of political and religious belief. Republicans, Democrats, Catholics, Protestants, Jews, Gentiles, Negroes, Caucasians are equally welcome.

But its members must be actively opposed to fascism in all its phases, must be vigorous proponents of democracy. They must be pro-labor, they must be willing to fight Hitlerism at all times, they must strive to become good citizens of the United States.

As for the Negro, here is the official policy:

"We recognize that we have a common bond and a special duty to the Negro youth, who have so proudly risen above humiliation and injustice to take up arms in the nation's cause. We will work in the interests of victory, democracy and a united nation, for full integration of Negro youth in the life of our country, for full and unconditional equality for the Negro people in the armed services, the factories and every phase of social and political life. We will work for an end to all forms of Jim-Crowism, discrimination and segregation and for unity among Negroes and white."

That's straight stuff. And the current campaign against Jim Crow in the armed forces underlines this hard hitting policy.

AYD now has positions out all over the nation in addition to a special four page tabloid telling of segregation and discrimination in the armed forces. Signatures totaling 500,000 names are sought. These are to be presented to Navy Secretary Knox and War Secretary Stimson by a special committee. Arrangements for the conference, tentatively scheduled for near the first of May, are now being made. The petition reads:

"We, the undersigned, petition you to establish the policy of military equality for Negro servicemen and women in all units of our armed forces. The existence of officers' candidate schools, where Negro and white officers are trained on an equal basis with excellent results, proves the feasibility and desirability of the complete extension of such a policy.

"To carry out this policy, we ask that every man and woman wearing a uniform in our nation's service be accorded the full dignity and complete equality of American citizenship in training, promotion and assignment to active combat duty. Punishment must be meted out for all acts of violence and discrimination against Americans in uniform.

"The establishment of this policy of military equality will raise morale, unify and strengthen all forces on the home and battle fronts and increase our prestige among our allies. It will give to our fighting forces greater striking power in the impending offensive for the speediest, complete defeat of the Axis:

"Let us be true to the American spirit of 'one nation indivisible, with liberty and justice for all.'"

Do you agree with this stand? Then how about you signing this petition and getting your friends to do likewise? Copies may be obtained by writing to American Youth for Democracy, 13 Astor Place, New York, S., New York.

And if you are under thirty years old, why not join this magnificent new organization? Branches are being formed everywhere. There are high school and college chapters in addition to those for young persons not in school. This is an excellent opportunity for interracial cooperation, for furthering educational, social, cultural and artistic programs. You ought to work with those who are bending every effort to help you.

And even if you are over thirty, you can still help. Organize and sponsor new chapters. Work with these young people. And contribute funds to either your local or the national office. Your dollars can work for you in helping make democracy real. Think about it, then act.

• • •

WILLKIE HELPS ROOSEVELT

April 12, 1944

Withdrawal of Wendell Willkie from the race for the Republican presidential nomination should prove of immeasurable benefit to President Roosevelt if the latter can be induced to run for the fourth term.

In the first place, it widens the gulf between progress and reaction. There is no Republican candidate not in the running who has the awareness of Willkie, his approach to world problems, his savvy of the necessity of world cooperation and unity to win the war and the peace. Dewey, whose nomination now seems assured, has nothing at all to recommend him to those who look ahead, not back to 1929.

Although Willkie, frankly, is far below the ideological stature of Roosevelt and borrows from our president instead of creating ideas of his own, he nevertheless found support among certain sizeable elements of the population who wanted to vote both Republican and liberal at the same time. As the Republican nominee, in November, he might have chopped away enough Roosevelt support to give the White House a new tenant.

It is obvious, now, that those who put nation above party will have to vote for Roosevelt. There is no alternative.

As for Negroes, they can have no reason at all to support the Republicans in November. Willkie's pronouncements on the race question, his verbal lashings of Jim Crow and discrimination won for him many supporters from the black masses. Thousands were ready to desert the Roosevelt banner to vote for the former Indianian.

No self respecting Negro can support Dewey. He did win friends by naming Judge Francis E. Rivers to his post. But this was only a temporary appointment. Rivers was elected last November, not by Dewey's Republican machine, but by a coalition of Republicans, Democrats, Communists and the American Labor Party. Let that not be forgotten.

Since then Dewey has undone what advantage his support of Rivers gave him. He came out in favor of states' rights in the federal soldier bill fiasco, thus throwing the weight of his office against letting our Negro service man from Dixie use the ballot. Then recently, in a broad bid for southern anti-Negro support, he sabotaged the work of his own committee which sought state anti-discrimination statues.

These are special Negro arguments why we don't want Dewey. They are merely added parts of the whole picture in which the colored voter should be just as deeply interested. The New York governor has no known postwar program for America except a return to the outmoded policies of cartels and monopolies and unemployment, masquerading under the catch phrase of "unrestricted free enterprise"; he has spoken out on the world situation only once and then to ask for a British-American coalition which would pave the way for a new world war by throwing the Soviet Union, China and all the other peoples of the world into an alliance against us.

And that makes Dewey a good man for McCormick and Pew and all the other reactionaries. Even Gerald L. K. Smith, the professional race hater, has given Dewey a pat on the back. And the governor waited until after the Wisconsin primary, when he had been given the advantage of Smith's support, to repudiate this demagogue.

The Republicans obviously do not want a man. They prefer a puppet. The party leaders were confused and befuddled when Willkie slipped in during 1940, and they promised not to let that happen again. Wendell can't be handled. He refuses to be next in line in the long procession of second and third rate Charlie McCarthys which the party has supported and gotten elected since Lincoln. In fact, there has been only one first rate Republican president since the Civil War, and that was Theodore Roosevelt. But it was no fault of the party; he was to be buried as vice president under McKinley and the bosses had no way of knowing McKinley would be assassinated.

Conversely, no second rater has been able to win for the Democrats. Grover Cleveland, Woodrow Wilson and Franklin Roosevelt have been Grade A. To go with this list, the Republicans can offer only Teddy Roosevelt.

And so the atmosphere is cleared. The battle lines are being drawn. With Willkie out of the picture, you have to support Roosevelt if you care anything at all about Negroes and eventual equality and brotherhood and peace.

• • •

YOUR VOTE, SUH!

APRIL 26, 1944

Gather round, dear Dixie kiddies, and we shall all trip lightly to the polls and vote, for has not the Supreme Court voided the white primary in the famous Texas case?

What? You doubt me? And did you mention something about a poll tax? Why, don't you know Congress is going to knock that out of the ring, maybe this week, this month, this year—or this century?

I am afraid, dear Dixie kiddies, that you don't believe in Santa Claus! After all you know the average white southerner, and he is not going to yield his supremacy without the dirtiest and trickiest kind of fight.

There are still plenty of barriers, despite the abolition of the white primary and the possible ending of the poll tax. Special laws and bald intimidation will be used; the best brains of the Negrophobes are now studying ways and means to deny full citizenship to darker fellow Americans.

There is still the "literacy" test in which a black holder of a doctor of philosophy degree may be barred from registration because he can't "interpret" the Constitution to the satisfaction of a registration clerk who may have had trouble finishing the third grade. The validity of those trick educational requirements has not been tested in the Supreme Court, and indeed it will be most difficult to obtain a bombproof decision should the high tribunal be confronted with the issue.

One new proposal is that, since color and race cannot be used to bar a citizen from the polls, then geography be leaned upon. The Supreme Court has of course not passed on this question. Accordingly, some southern states may insert clauses limiting participation in the Democratic primary only to those persons whose ancestors did not come from Africa. A good anthropologist and a smart lawyer could make this embarrassing even to Rankin and Talmadge, since virtually nobody can name his eighty-four ancestors of even a mere six generations ago. But it takes time to get Supreme Court action, and the bar would probably prove effective until then.

Property ownership is a prerequisite to voting in some states. One scheme is that the phrase "and of good character" be inserted after the requirement of land possession. The implications are of course tremendous. Dixie being what it is, the constabulary could be directed to arrest for disorderly conduct or worse a Negro property owner who wanted to vote, and the judge could give him a fine. The registrars would often be able to say that the applicant was not of "good character" because he had a police record!

These are some of the more subtle approaches. Down in the backwoods districts, the local rednecks would merely dare the darker brother to come up to the polling place. Nothing fancy, just the plain old knock 'em down and drag 'em out tactics.

It should be obvious that the powers now in control of the party and the South will resist every effort at change for their own self-preservation. They fatten at the tax troughs; they have no desire to stand on the outside and look hungrily in.

The only workable solution lies within the common people. Black worker and white worker have been taught to hate and fear each other; the already wealthy ruling classes got richer and wealthier by encouraging this civil war between plain persons who, by every right of logic, should join forces and battle for the common good.

Frankly, I have more faith in the CIO, as long as it continues its militant program of organizing workers interracially, than in any Supreme Court decision or act of Congress itself. The South has consistently found ways and means of getting around the Constitution and Supreme Court decisions; seven years later how many states provide full and equal training within their borders for Negroes, despite the *Lloyd Gaines* decision?

Let the CIO continue to educate the masses and to weld labor together in the South and there will be no way possible for the divisionist, anti-Negro tactics of the Dixie politicians to continue, and no Supreme Court decision need be placed in the equation.

• • •

CHICAGO TRIBUNE WANTS RACE RIOT!
MAY 3, 1944

Chicago has had no major race strife since 1919. But that is not the fault of the *Chicago Tribune*, the huge pro-fascist daily owned by Colonel McCormick which is carrying on a private war against President Roosevelt, the Soviet Union and Great Britain in the order named. The *Chicago Tribune* circulation, 925,000 daily, has a big backlog of hate ready to be hurled at all times against any person who favors the president or thinks the United States ought to work with other nations to secure a peaceful postwar world.

Singled out for special hate are *Time* and *Life*, published by Henry R. Luce. A week ago Sunday two white photographers and Earl Brown, reporter, were assigned to cover a meeting of "We, the Mothers, Mobilize for America," an organization described in the amazing book, *Under Cover*, and by many officials, as openly subversive. Trouble followed, ending in the courts when the press trio was freed and two belligerent members of the opposition drew fines for disorderly conduct.

The *Tribune*, of course, is angry. All last week it played up the case, seeking to make martyrs of We, the Mothers, while other Chicago dailies forgot the incident. The climax Friday in a long editorial entitled "Provoking a Race Riot" in which that newspaper slyly sought to arouse racial antagonisms by the bold and slick stratagem of accusing Time-Life of doing so.

Said the editorial, in part:

"The principal actor in this bit of hoodlumism was the reporter. He was Negro, and he was sent here from New York for this particular job. The reason Luce and his gang sent a Negro all the way to Chicago to cover a meeting of white women should be apparent to anyone who has read thus far and has paid attention to the tactics these alleged newspapermen used to get into the hall. Luce was trying to start a race riot for exploitation by his irresponsible and scandalmongering publications.

"Most of the members of this particular organization are excitable women and all of them have been subjected to most scurrilous abuse in Luce's publications. It was a natural place for violence, fanned by high emotions and bitter feelings to start, and what the Luce gang did was to furnish the Negro as a starter. Nobody will be willing to believe they were so stupid they did not know what they were doing."

This is the same device used by such anti-Negro papers as the Jackson, Mississippi, *Daily News* to fan the flames of prejudice. Outsiders are accused of coming in, by white supremacy Dixie spokesmen, to cause race trouble. Thus, by innuendo, race strife is suggested to the populace along with erection of the defense of "foreign agitation."

What the *Tribune* really means is that if Brown, while in Chicago, is assigned to write about any other McCormick beloved, anti-American organization, then let the members remember Brown is a Negro. Beat him up, start a race riot if you want to, my white friends. My *Tribune* and I are back of you, just rearin' to blame it on that louse, Luce.

The attitude of the *Tribune* fits into a pattern. That pattern is to discredit Roosevelt in every way and split the pro-administration support in the hope that a Republican can win the fall election. No device is too low for this gang of hybrid Hitlers, not even a race riot if it can be twisted to blast Roosevelt and cause resentment against the president. Remember this in the stormy months ahead. It may happen in your town.

One of those fined in the *We, the Mothers* controversy was the Republican congressional candidate from the sixth district. Charles J. Anderson, Jr., loudmouthed anti-Semitic and hatemonger. To the *Tribune*, Anderson was a martyr and the Mothers were angels. This is at least consistent. McCormick's paper has defended the thirty accused seditionists on trial in Washington, calling them victims of persecution, and has all but begged a public defense fund for Liz Dilling. These are the people, mind you, who have openly and loudly praised Hitler and his attitudes toward Negroes, Jews and other minorities.

The *Tribune*, which first rode Willkie and then Dewey and Joe Martin out of the Republican Party for advocating any kind of postwar cooperation with our allies, and which would like to see the European war stopped so that Japan alone could be crushed, is a kind of glorified handbill for the ravings of Rankin, Clare Hoffman of Michigan and anybody else who dislikes Roosevelt. Let Rankin castigate the president or the administration for any act favorable to Negroes and he can get columns. McCormick, incidentally, has not had one word to say editorially about the Texas primary decision and campaigned vigorously against a federal soldier vote bill.

Such publications are dangerous. They are enemies to America and to the progress of racial relationships, to the future of the common man. They spew poison under the guise of "free speech"; a nation at war is doomed to reap a painful harvest unless we stay on our guard and understand clearly what makes them click.

• • •

IF IT'S RED IT'S DANGEROUS
MAY 10, 1944

Seeking to justify the stand by Representative May of Kentucky against army use of that factual and important booklet, *The Races of Mankind*, a House Military Affairs subcommittee last week denounced the pamphlet as "inaccurate" and "filled with techniques of Communist propaganda." The learned scientist who heads this subcommittee is Representative Carl T. (shouldn't it be Karl von?) Durham of North Carolina.

Congressman Durham, who would probably have to consult a dictionary even to spell anthropology, nevertheless is a greater authority than Dr. Ruth Benedict and Professor Gene Weltfish of Columbia University, writers of the book and world renowned in their field. Durham is an authority because he is in Congress, has power, and is able to kick science in the teeth when it disputes white supremacy. Ergo, the work is inaccurate. And, if necessary, the earth is flat and has four corners if teaching otherwise disturbs the Dixie pattern of race relations.

The claim that *Races of Mankind* is filled with "techniques of Communist propaganda" is intended as the final blow, the knockout punch. Durham and his fellows evidently believe that some persons might question their decision if based solely upon the scientific judgment of the subcommittee. But let it be labeled "Red" and the opposition would run for cover.

The idea that if a thing smacks of Communism it is dangerous, that if it is what the Reds believe or want or practice then Americans should do it, has interesting possibilities if carried to its logical conclusion.

Take, for instance, the whole war. The Red army is fighting the Nazis, killing fascists by the hundreds of thousands. The Reds are united for the death of Hitlerism. Therefore America's duty is plain. The United States must not battle with the Nazis, according to Representative Durham's logic, must not slay the fascists, must keep Hitlerism alive. And, in all fairness, that is precisely the attitude of certain segments of the population, of Colonel McCormick of the *Chicago Tribune*, of William Randolph Hearst, of the Peace Now movement, of the thirty seditionists on trial in Washington and their followers. Is that also the real attitude of the House Military Affairs subcommittee?

I think it all boils down to this: after the mighty battle put up by the Soviet Union, which has saved us and the rest of the world from the Nazi menace, with the general realization that most of what had been said in the past about the Reds was wholesale lying, with generally increasing knowledge of the truth about the Soviet system, can the majority of the nation still be stampeded because some selfish political mountebank raises the wolf cry of "Red"?

It seems to me that this sort of thing is soon going to have an effect exactly opposite from that intended. It should be obvious to Negroes as well as fair-minded whites, that if the ideas on race as expressed in the Benedict-Weltfish booklet are "Communistic," then the Communists must be followed to bring enlightenment to our nation.

The same goes for labor unions. Only the most democratic, those fighting most vigorously to erase color lines, are dubbed Red. Who calls them Red? The supporters of white supremacy, the pro-fascists, the reactionaries, the apostles of special privilege and vested interest, the anti-Negro, anti-labor sections of the nation. They are the enemies of progress, of real democracy.

You ought to be able to reason it out from there.

• • •

WATCH HOME FRONT D-DAY
MAY 21, 1944

With summer almost here and the resultant greatly increased contact between whites and Negroes who will spend more time out in the open, the time will be ripe for a new series of race riots unless cooler heads of both races begin taking steps to avoid this bloody and senseless battle to the death between fellow-Americans.

There is a belief among responsible Chicagoans that efforts will be made to stage a race riot immediately before or during the Democratic National Convention in July, when large numbers of southerners will flock to this comparatively liberal community. It is no secret that Detroiters fear a recurrence of last year's disgrace; anything may happen in Texas on or around the annual Juneteenth observance; many other communities in all sections of the nation are listed as danger areas.

Let us answer this question: who would gain by bloodshed, by civil strife between black and white?

Let us remember that this nation is at war against the Axis. The successful prosecution of this war and the complete destruction of fascism and all it stands for demands unity and solidarity between all forces that believe in genuine democracy and brotherly love and who are opposed to the Nazi doctrine of inferior and superior peoples.

If disunity can be created internally inside a major ally, if there can be developed battles between groups who should be using their united strength to blast the Axis, then that major ally is weakened in its effort in proportion to the seriousness of its domestic strife. An America in which there rages a civil war between black and white cannot throw the same strength at Hitler and Hirohito as an America without race rioting. The Axis is therefore aided, and that today looms as complete defeat could under those circumstances be salvaged by world fascism as a stalemate in the battle of Europe, which would give Hitler a breathing spell and perhaps a chance to eventually come back.

Those so-called Americans who sympathize with Hitler would therefore win a major victory if race strife could be induced. They know also it would not be too difficult to ignite friction between Negroes and whites who substitute passion and prejudice for clear thinking, emotion for mind. The Hitler lovers are everywhere, from Congress on down. The thirty on trial for sedition are only a small fraction of their actual strength in this nation.

At the same time President Roosevelt today is the leader of the nation's win the war forces, and these forces include Democrats and Republicans, Negroes and whites. All these persons friendly toward the Nazis and the Japs are bitter enemies of the president. And by "persons" I include a number of our leading daily newspapers whose editorials and cartoons are used by Herr Goebbels in his pro-Nazi propaganda activities. They do not want Roosevelt reelected, and will stop at nothing to gain this objective.

Those enemies within will do anything to discredit Roosevelt. They realize he has the support of the masses, both black and white. They know also that race riots would not only stunt the growing unity between Negro and white but could be used skilfully to smear the president and perhaps be the difference between defeat and victory in the November elections. Most effective of all politically would be a race riot in Chicago in July which could be blamed on the southern Democrats.

This should be understood by our leaders of both races and hammered home to the masses, so that the unthinking gullible will not become dupes of our nation's enemies.

It seems to me that every community should be on the alert. Both white and Negro editors should confer frequently and evolve a campaign tending to create interracial harmony, at the same time soft-pedaling all news items tending to stir up friction, and smoking out fake rumors such as the Eleanor club and Bumpus club myths.

The police departments should get special attention. Their attitude can often foment or halt a riot. They cannot show favoritism and expect peace.

You know what happened in Detroit, how most of the Negro victims were slain by cops. Police officers with the right kind of attitude would have nipped this clash in its infancy.

In other words, a home front D-Day does not have to happen. It can be avoided by intelligent cooperation between the races, and it is to your personal interest that you do all you can to bring about this cooperation.

• • •

WE NEED WALLACE

JULY 19, 1944

National unity and the growing world crusade on behalf of the plain people of this planet will receive a serious setback if the Democratic convention meeting this week in Chicago fails to re-nominate Vice President Henry Agard Wallace as the running mate of Franklin Delano Roosevelt.

The issue of Wallace's re-nomination transcends party politics. It strikes at the heart of democracy. For the forces which have waged better warfare to sidetrack the vice president are the same forces which shoved Wendell Willkie out of the Republican picture. They are in the reactionaries, the America Firsters, the labor baiters, and the Negro haters.

These, the handmaidens of fascism, took complete possession of the Republican Party. Governor Tom Dewey is the stooge of Herbert Hoover, the high priest of monopoly and big business and skybusting profits and breadlines. Governor John Bricker is worse. He is the darling of Colonel McCormick and William Randolph Hearst, the Herr Goebbels twins of America. They carry the ball for national reaction.

Having locked up the Republican Party, the same powerful anti-democratic interests turned to the Democrats. It is no secret that the recent revolt in Texas was plotted and financed by certain northern Republican industrialists. They formed the same kind of coalition with anti-Roosevelt Democrats that has consistently blocked the president's program in Congress.

Although this unholy alliance has met success in Texas, South Carolina, and Mississippi and is a potential danger in the electoral college, it has been unable to block the re-nomination of Roosevelt, because the majority of Democrats realize Roosevelt is their lone hope in November. The campaign against Wallace has met with infinitely better success, and in an effort to split Roosevelt and Wallace and thus score a victory for reaction in the Democratic Party, it has been made known that the revolt against the president would end if he would drop Wallace.

The reasons why big business, the union busters and Negro haters don't like Wallace are the reasons that should make all trade unionists, Negroes and the common people demand his re-nomination.

Wallace is right on the race question. Publicly and fearlessly he has lambasted the silly myths of race differences and inferiority. He has battled cartels and monopolies and uncontrolled profits. He wants peace and security and equality for all human beings. He has sung the hymn of humankind when Roosevelt himself found it politically inadvisable to speak, because of the plot against him in Congress.

There is no other known prospective running mate for Roosevelt who can compare with Wallace. None other has the respect and confidence of labor and the Negro. Despite the president's personal record, a southern nominee would lose both labor and Negro votes and provide readymade propaganda for the Republican Negro ballyhoo experts.

The reactionaries are playing it close. If they win and nominate a conservative, they will have overwhelming odds of three to one in their favor: the two Republican nominees and the Democratic vice presidential candidate. That would leave only Roosevelt standing alone as the champion of human progress.

It is a matter of personal and practical necessity for Negroes to unite with other democratic groups and make a last ditch stand for Wallace.

The vice president will likely be nominated Friday. Roosevelt is known to favor Wallace. You barely have time to wire the president urging that he stand by Wallace and pledging your support, and to telegraph Chairman Robert Hannegan as well as delegates from your state at the national convention in Chicago demanding that Wallace be re-nominated.

Will you do this immediately?

DEMOCRACY, HAWAIIAN STYLE

Why Davis left Chicago for the Territory of Hawaii in December 1948 is still the source of some speculation. But the planned vacation, which evolved into a permanent relocation, did little to dampen his fervor for racial and labor politics. Over a four-month period in 1949, he maintained his connection with the Associated Negro Press by writing a series of articles under the collective title "Democracy: Hawaiian Style." As the name of this series suggests, Davis used this opportunity to probe the nuances and peculiarities of Hawaii's version of the American creed and its practice. Ultimately, his observations would be fleshed out in a number of poems written about this island territory and its history, including "This Is Paradise," "Pacific Invasion," "Tale of Two Dogs," "Horizontal Cameos: 37 Portraits," among others. This news writing proffered here is partly autobiographical, social, political, and cultural. The function in each of these genres can be best described as didactic, in that his purpose was to instruct mainlanders about a way of life unfamiliar to most of them and to show how a pluralistic culture can point the direction toward true racial integration.

The beginning of this instructional process required an understanding of the complexities of the islanders' ethnic make-up. The proliferation of Filipinos, Samoans, Koreans, Japanese, Chinese, Puerto Ricans, Portuguese, full-blooded Hawaiians, and, from the mainland, African Americans and whites forced Davis to view Hawaii as "a land of ethnic hash." As with any tourist or newcomer ("malihini" in Hawaiian), Davis was at first "unable to distinguish the good from the bad by island standards" (January 5, 1949). His confession reveals more than just a newcomer's lack of familiarity; it reports that he experienced no personal acts of racial discrimination. The reason for his unusually generous reception was that Davis benefited from his celebrity as reporter and poet and islanders in his presence were on their best behavior, since they also knew of his intention to write a series of his observations on Hawaiian life and culture. However, by the time he wrote his second installment in this series, entitled "Land of Ethnic Hash" (January 12, 1949), Davis had discovered the existence of prejudices, which were "more complex than those on the mainland where feeling is directed primarily against Negroes and Jews."

The prejudice Davis observed subverted the intentions of "democracy." Democracy usually signified the citizenship guarantees of "life, liberty, and the pursuit of happiness," as well as the philosophical concepts of value tolerance and cultural pluralism. As a result of his observations, Davis takes a wry, ironic, or even satirical attitude about the meaning of democracy practiced in Hawaii. Instead of a land teeming with tolerance for difference and thus rendering the conventional modes of racial discrimination inoperable, Davis perceived the subtle persistence of ethnic tensions. Many of these feelings were directed toward the two largest groups: whites and Japanese. The strong economic position enjoyed by the Japanese elicited from other groups an anti-Japanese bias. Anti-white feelings were precipitated by the influx of "'foreign' customs and ideas, by the Caucasians' economic strength, and by the contempt with which they so often show for non-Caucasians" (January 12, 1949).

This imbalance of power made the usual "rules" governing Jim Crow even more confusing. African Americans, for example, experienced discrimination but not because of their racial background; instead, the contempt was based on the fact they were "malihinis." They were shown the same contempt expressed toward white "malihinis." Or, among the Japanese, those of Okinawan descent were considered by their fellow countrymen as inferiors, in much the same way, Davis said, as southern whites regarded Negroes. Even the University of Hawaii contributed to a kind of disinformation campaign by refusing data listing the student population by ethnic group to the Social Science Department. The administration feared that because most of the students were Japanese, the school would become known as "Little Nippon," resulting in an escalation of the number of white students returning to the mainland for college. On occasion, Davis reported, Chinese and Koreans might leave a Christian church if too many Japanese began attending. Although Davis reduced this migratory pattern to the status of "clannishness," he found something good to report. Despite whatever impediment it posed to the struggle of all people of color for equality, these intergroup tensions did little to prevent the formation of a united front against "haoles" or whites. In his focus on the possibilities of intergroup cooperation and tolerance of difference, Davis found "a tremendously effective argument for miscegenation" (February 2, 1949). The struggle for racial equality must be fought collectively by those who suffer the ill effects of discrimination.

Davis's challenge was to educate a mainland African American readership unfamiliar with Hawaiian customs and mores. This series was written expressly for distribution by the Associated Negro Press to its subscribing member newspapers. What purpose could be served by reporting, as he did in "Hawaiian Habits" (January 19, 1949), on dress, speech, food, and music? It is one thing to report on the persistence of barbecued ribs, fried chicken, and blackeyed peas on the islands; it is quite another to tout poi, laulau, kalua pig, limu, and coconut pudding as island delicacies. Cuisine and other cultural practices act as a portal or gateway into the lives of a people. Such an introduction opens the door to a way of knowing by connecting groups unfamiliar with each other. In effect, Davis uses poi and other delicacies to foster intercultural understanding and knowledge. His quest to eradicate white supremacy must be viewed as an engagement by all people of color. If mainlanders knew something about the cultural practices of Hawaiians, then the struggle for equality could be seen as a collective undertaking among people of color, who have a shared, vested interest in eliminating white oppression and fascism.

By pointing specifically to the United States military based on the islands, Davis sets forth another part of his strategy for educating mainland African American readers about Hawaiian life and culture. In "Armed Forces Democracy" (February 16, 1949), he writes: "You can depend upon the armed forces to act as bold defenders of Americanism wherever they may go. Only it's too often the Rankin brand." Davis thus makes the claim that southern-style racial discrimination only seriously infected the territory of Hawaii after World War II, when the Navy and Army's presence became much more pronounced. People of color, for example, seldom held supervisory positions in the naval yard and never supervised whites. In periods of retrenchment, people of color, always the last hired, were the first to be fired. Thus Davis uses this denial of equal opportunity to demonstrate to mainland African Americans a shared civil rights problem.

In discussing the internal problems of the Honolulu NAACP branch, Davis again attempts to educate mainland readers. Although the "Red scare" had splintered the branch into factionalism, many members were unified in their determination to see a civil rights bill passed by the territorial legislature. "Civil War in NAACP" (February 13, 1949) effectively demonstrated how the internal wrangling over leadership prevented the organization from being an effective voice in achieving equality. Without specifically addressing the issue, this column also points to the major opposition to statehood being granted to Hawaii. U.S. senators and congressmen from the South would later campaign against Hawaiian statehood on the grounds that a racially diverse state would provide leadership in undermining racial segregation. For this reason, the internal strife of the Honolulu NAACP held tremendous importance for southern members of Congress.

This series is significant for a number of reasons, not the least of which is that it summarizes many of the concerns in Davis's news writing and anticipates issues discursively presented in his poetry. In *Livin' the Blues*, Davis rhetorically poses the question, "Are you with me in my determination to wipe out white supremacy?" The column "Democracy: Hawaiian Style" functions, in part, as a recruitment poster, that is, as a means for enlisting volunteers in a civil rights campaign. It both broadens the scope of the conflict against Jim Crow and creates an informed group of participants in the struggle to dismantle this form of American apartheid.

• • •

THERE'S JIM CROW, BUT—

JANUARY 5, 1949

Yes, there's Jim Crow in Honolulu. Most of the one thousand Negro civilians and the two thousand members of the armed forces will agree to that. They can be bitter about the increasing discrimination which has been the heritage of World War II. And after they have had their say, they will then tell you:

"Hawaii is still the best place under the American flag. We get better treatment here than at any place back on the mainland."

Boiled down, this means that even the "best," as exemplified by these islands, is still far short of what democracy is supposed to be. What our nation so glowingly sells to the world is considerably different from the product as it really is.

I say this after two weeks in Honolulu which, the people here insist, "is not the real Hawaii." They tell my wife and me that we must leave Oahu, the island on which overcrowded, sprawling but beautiful Honolulu is located, and go to the unspoiled "outer islands" where life is more leisurely, the people more friendly and the scenery more lovely.

But thus far, we have few complaints with Honolulu other than high prices and the housing shortage. Still, we're mere "malihinis" (the Hawaiian word for newcomers) and as yet unable to distinguish the good from the bad by island standards. However, judged by Chicago or New York, this place is pretty terrific. We've had experiences that just simply couldn't occur anywhere on the Mainland.

We arrived in the morning by plane. Hubert White, the Associated Negro Press correspondent, somehow had the idea we were getting in that night. So we read in the morning paper that the "Negro editor and his wife" were due to arrive that evening. That night, I later learned, White took a battery of cameramen and reporters from the two daily papers and both the Associated Press and United Press to the airport. Naturally, we weren't aboard the plane from California. Next morning the paper headlined its story, "Negro Editor Fails to Arrive."

At this point our travel agent, a huge and friendly native Hawaiian with an unpronounceable middle name, who had got us reservations at the ritzy Willard Inn, a half block from famed Waikiki beach, called Mr. White and told him we had been in Honolulu for a whole day.

So that afternoon's paper explained that we had arrived "quietly" and had gone into seclusion for a slight "rest" after our trip before meeting the press. It also made the radio news bulletins that night.

It would have been all right with us had the Willard also considered us as arriving a day later. It's a beautiful place, with private cottages in the midst of a tall coconut grove, but it's a tourist trap and it costs you ten bucks a day. But anybody who wishes can stay here and the treatment will be extremely courteous. This is true of all the other leading Honolulu hotels as well as most of the second and third rate hostelries.

Five days later, a press conference was held at the Willard. The reporters were white or "haole" as they are called here. One photographer was Japanese, the other Chinese. Both dailies gave prominent space to the interviews and used two column pictures of my wife and me. Her picture was carried alone on the society page of the afternoon paper. Altogether, there have been some eight news articles about us in our two weeks here, and the daily papers have dealt with us as they would anybody else whom they considered newsworthy. I know of no place on the Mainland where we would receive like treatment.

And it seems that an amazing number of the 275,000 people of all colors and descriptions who make up Honolulu read the papers. Since the pictures appeared, I have been stopped on the street by haoles who wanted to chat; while waiting for a bus, people have stopped their cars and offered to drive us wherever we wanted to go; store clerks recognize us; strangers have called by telephone to arrange to talk with me about the colored problem here. It makes me feel like "Somebody Important" and I am just sucker enough to love it.

We have left the Willard for the Pleasanton, a hotel more in keeping with the economic status of a reporter. The neighbors on our floor are Korean, Japanese, Chinese, Filipino and a few Mainland haoles. The maids are Portuguese.

With the wide variety of peoples here ranging from black to blonde, nobody pays much attention to color—on the surface. It's too dangerous. About the only persons wanting to make an issue of race are haole newcomers, mainly from Dixie. And they don't get too far, generally speaking. But in specific instances, they have been amazingly successful, such as in some taverns, restaurants and the like.

Thus far, I have not personally experienced Jim Crow here. But most Negroes, liberal whites and Orientals tell me of its existence and have many examples. However, my chances of meeting with discrimination, they say, are much less than those of the average Negro because (1) the daily papers stated I was going to write about conditions in the islands (2) I am considered a "superior Negro" because I am a poet and reporter, and (3) the old residents (called "kamaainas") both haole and oriental are embarrassed by the rising tide of anti-Negro feeling and want to keep down bad publicity which would make the islands less the "paradise" they are supposed to be.

But I'll tell more than Jim Crow and its rise here later. I'm still enjoying a "winter" where people swim every day and many kids and adults never wear shoes or coats, where the mercury drops down to 66 at night and gets up to 77 in the day; where live the most beautiful people I have ever seen, and where even the slum shacks have banana trees and mangoes and orchids.

• • •

LAND OF ETHNIC HASH
JANUARY 12, 1949

You soon learn that in Hawaii you can't tell an individual's ethnic origin by looking. Put most of the full-blooded Hawaiians and many of the part-Hawaiians on 47th Street in Chicago, Lenox Avenue in Harlem or Auburn Avenue in Atlanta and you'd bet your last dollar they were Negroes.

The same goes for other peoples here including many Filipinos, some Samoans, and even a few mixed Japanese and Chinese who are aware of no African ancestry. And of course there's no doubt about the dark Puerto Ricans. Even a smattering of Portuguese will fool you.

In this rainbow land of beautiful color mixtures, it isn't always diplomatic to inquire about one's ancestry. But if you go ahead and ask anyway, you're likely to be told, "I'm one third Chinese, one sixth Hawaiian, one sixth French, one sixth Portuguese and one sixth Puerto Rican." Sometimes it makes you wish you hadn't asked.

And yet, despite this amazing and wonderful ethnic hash found here in the "crossroads of the Pacific," there are prejudices. These are much more complex than those on the mainland where feeling is directed primarily against Negroes and Jews. Out here many dark Puerto Ricans are insulted if they are mistaken for Japanese; the Portuguese bitterly resent being called "haole" or mainland white; many Koreans will let you know right away that they are not Chinese. Recently I met the son of a white father and a Japanese mother who hates both haoles and Japanese.

There is sizeable prejudice against both Japanese and mainland whites. Until the census estimate last year, the Japanese were the largest single group in these islands. Now, for the first time, they are outnumbered by whites as a result of World War II. Of the estimated 525,000 population, haoles now total about 173,000 with 170,000 Japanese and around 75,000 Chinese. Full blooded Hawaiians are today only about 10,000 in number with part-Hawaiians totaling 65,000. The rest of the sizeable groupings include Koreans, Filipinos, Puerto Ricans (both light and dark) and Portuguese. U.S. Negroes number only about 1,000. The population is predominantly Oriental and Polynesian, thus making Caucasians a minority in the overall picture.

Anti-Japanese prejudice seems based mainly on a strong economic position. Anti-white feeling is caused by Caucasian migration here, bringing "foreign" customs and ideas, by the Caucasians economic strength and by the contempt which they so often show for non-Caucasians. Even the groups that dislike Japanese will often join with Japanese against mainland whites or haoles.

The fact that many white men have married Oriental or Hawaiian women for "convenience," then mistreated or deserted them when they returned to the mainland has not created a feeling of deep love and affection for haoles.

Hawaii's Negroes have a shifting place in this complex mosaic of prejudice. As the last to arrive, they have yet to "prove" themselves as have other peoples. Further, haoles had spread their usual propaganda to the effect that Negroes were "no good," then when black underworld characters showed up on the scene, they were pointed to as proof. They also used the fable that "all Negroes have tails" as one young colored woman, graduate of a California University, found out personally to her utter amazement.

And yet the anti-Negro prejudice is not status by mainland standards. It is flexible and, for that reason, can be eliminated or allowed to crystallize largely by the efforts of Negroes themselves. As one young white labor union organizer, a keen student of the color situation here, told me, prejudice against Negroes exists not primarily because they are Negroes but because they are for the most part "malihinis," or newcomers, and often are looked upon with the same contempt shown white malihinis from the mainland. In other words, we have the strange paradox of Negroes and haoles being classed together!

This seems likely. I do not know that many Negroes who have been here for long periods of time and who mingle with other peoples are fully accepted. There was anger when one Negro man who had made friends all around married a white girl.

His Oriental pals thought it disgraceful, wanting to know why he "didn't marry some nice Chinese or Japanese or Hawaiian girl instead of that damned Haole." However, his wife has since come to be accepted as "one of them" and she is no longer referred to as a "haole." Still another Negro man has lived with a Chinese family since coming here nine years ago and goes along to every function to which the family is invited.

As for the Hawaiians, many of them feel quite close to the Negro. They vary in size as much as Negroes do, coming both huge and little. (Most Orientals here are small in stature).

Shortly after arriving, I went to a dance given by a CIO union and almost on entering the hall, an elderly dark Hawaiian insisted on buying me both drinks and island food. He explained in his broken English, "You black, me black, you my friend. We black people got to stick together, huh?"

Hawaiians have a private term of endearment corresponding roughly to both "brother" and "nigger," so often used by Negroes. They can call each other "kanaka" but if anybody else calls them that, it means a fight. They call an outsider "kanaka" only when they are ready to accept him into their charmed inner circle.

Christmas eve at a cafe, a young Hawaiian came up to me, threw his arms around my shoulders and said, "You're kanaka, you. If any haole jump on you, you call me and I fight him. Mo' better I fight for my kanaka, huh?"

Yes, Hawaii is an amazing place.

• • •

HAWAIIAN HABITS

JANUARY 19, 1949

You are not here long before you start adopting Hawaiian habits. That goes for everybody, including Negroes, although some of them hang on tenaciously to certain customs that are a part of living in the mainland Harlems.

These habits are mainly Oriental and Polynesian, although since World War II and the great influx of whites or haoles, there have been certain changes.

However, it is still customary to remove your shoes at the door of most homes. This saves wear and tear on rugs and floors, but it does require good sox or none at all. Yet in most Negro homes, you keep your shoes on.

You soon get used to seeing barefooted adults on the streets. Even many whites follow suit. Some dining rooms refuse to admits guests without shoes, and a few of the schools are trying to get all students above the seventh grade to cover their feet. When it rains a lot, men and women will take off their shoes on the theory that it is easier to wash their feet than clean their footgear. And yet, despite our folk humor about going barefoot for so long, I have seen few Negroes without shoes except at the beaches.

Out here the idea is to dress comfortably and casually. Most men wear loud aloha shirts, and they are acceptable almost everywhere. Some don't own a coat. A man wearing a jacket, particularly in the day, is considered to be a professional, a clerk or office worker or a "malihini" (newcomer). At one dinner our host wore nothing but a pair of shorts.

This casualness of dress is accepted generally by Negroes except those who attend affairs given by the top sepia social set. Then you come togged as you would for a comparative informal function in Harlem or Chicago's South Side. The men may get out of their jackets after a few highballs and some jitterbugging (be-bop dancing hasn't reached Hawaii, yet) but they'll start out in sharp drapes with collars and ties. Maybe it's to satisfy their wives who thus recreate that old "back home" atmosphere.

But they've latched on to the other habits, particularly speech, food and music.

Out here there's a special way of saying things. The talk is a mixture of straight English, pidgin English and Hawaiian with some Oriental thrown in. There's also an island inflection. You notice it particularly when somebody asks a question. On the mainland the last word of a question has a rising inflection. For instance, you might ask, "Do you sell eggs?" The first three words would be in the same tone, with "eggs" pitched higher to show it is a question.

They do it differently in Hawaii. "Do you" would be in a medium tone, "sell" would get the highest pitch, and "eggs" would be midway between the two. It gives a sort of lazy casualness entirely apart from the implied urgency of mainland questions. Similarly, a positive statement is often followed by "huh," as a question, such as "I'm going to work now, huh?" This has to be heard to be believed.

Negroes have slipped into the speech habits so easily that they are amazed when it is pointed out to them by a newcomer. And if you want to hear something for the books, listen to a combination of pidgin, Hawaiian and Dixie rattled off by a brown brother from the deep South.

Old standbys such as barbecued ribs, fried chicken and blackeyed peas continue strong but many have developed a liking for poi, the starchy Hawaiian staple that tastes like old wallpaper paste. Abalone, a sliced raw shellfish, is popular and many go for raw tuna and seaweed, another island delicacy. A few daring souls have had marvelous results blending New Orleans cookery with the many Chinese and Japanese dishes.

The soft Hawaiian music has its dusky fans. You're likely to hear "Lovely Hula Hands" mixed in with platters by Ellington and Basie and Gillespie on the home record players. It also works the other way. Some of the Hawaiian and Oriental boys are learning how to shout the low down blues accompanied by steel guitars and ukeleles.

As a matter of fact, Trummy Young, the trombonist who rose to fame with Jimmie Lunceford and Benny Goodman, has developed some marvelous young hot musicians during his fourteen months in Honolulu. He has three bright Filipino stars—a bass player, a tenor and an alto saxist—who are capable of holding down jobs any place on the mainland.

Many Negro women go in for the hula. They take lessons from some of the many professional teachers, buy the outfits, and then sit around waiting for a chance to show what they have learned. You don't have to coax them to dance; often you have to persuade them to stop. You'll find out for yourself if and when they get back to St. Louis or Washington.

• • •

HONOLULU'S HARLEM
JANUARY 26, 1949

Most of Honolulu's Negroes shake their heads in disgust when they mention Smith Street. That small section, they contend, is responsible for the rise of Jim Crow in this "Paradise of the Pacific," a land which knew little or no anti-Negro feeling prior to World War II.

The Negro area of Smith Street is not impressive, as such places go. Located in downtown Honolulu, it consists of a couple of taverns, a pool hall known as a "recreation center," a restaurant, a barbershop, and a few shoe shine parlors. But what it lacks in size, it makes up for in impact upon the whole community.

For it is here in Honolulu's Harlem that the rowdy and twilight element makes itself felt. Here are the smart guys with the $5,000 Cadillacs and no visible means of support; here is where you can arrange for fun or get into a fight on a moment's notice; here the blues blaring jukeboxes and the raw, raucous shouts of the boys from "down home" cut curious cacaphonic capers in the comparative calm of the predominantly Oriental and Polynesian atmosphere.

The reputation is such that if a man and woman tarry here, they are immediately tagged as pimp and prostitute. Those Negroes generally described as "the more respectable element"—in this case mainly civilian employees of Uncle Sam—complain that the entire city judges the group by what is seen on Smith Street, that Smith Street confirms what prejudiced "haoles" (mainland whites) have said about Negroes.

Smith Street is a survival of World War II. Prior to Pearl Harbor, the tiny dusky civilian population was pretty well absorbed throughout Honolulu. Then during the big conflict, a brownskin veteran who had long been stationed here died. His widow opened a small cafe on Smith Street serving such Dixie viands as black-eyed peas and cornbread.

This clicked immediately with the increasing numbers of Negro soldiers, tired of army rations and unaccustomed to island cooking. They ate it up, literally and figuratively. Other enterprises sprouted in the area, including a rooming house with all the "conveniences."

Desperately in need of civilian workers, Uncle Sam was soon forced to lower his standards and bring out anybody who said he could do the job. To Hawaii came many persons, black and white, who were anxious to get from where they were to somewhere else. Some were from the Deep South, untrained to do the kind of work for which they had signed. Naturally, they brought along their folkways and attitudes.

Before long, many were fired. Some lacked the fare to get back to the mainland. Others came out here actually to work their rackets. To those from deep Dixie, it was the first time that most had been thrown into an environment free from the restrictions that handicap a Negro's life in the South.

For too many, freedom meant license. The sociologists and psychologists can explain it, but most people don't understand the reasons.

Meanwhile, both the fired southern whites who remained, as well as others who came over as soldiers and civilian workers, were poisoning the minds of islanders who had previously experienced little or no contact with Negroes. They said that Negroes were vile and low; they were drunkards and gamblers and thieves and rapists; they were sub-human creatures with tails; they were uncivilized; their women could be bought by any man with a few dollars.

So whenever Negroes were arrested for fighting or gambling or pandering or prostitution, as would inevitably be the case, the prejudiced whites would triumphantly shout to the islanders, "See, what did I tell you." It did not matter that mainland whites were jailed for similar offenses. Consequently, Hawaii began judging all Negroes by the activities on Smith Street, where this way of living was concentrated.

As a result, many places previously open to Negroes have withdrawn the welcome sign. Certain taverns and restaurants have suggested to Negro patrons that they might be happier if they went to their "own" places on Smith Street. Also, many businesses are owned by mainland whites who maintain their prejudices, and others are patronized by white soldiers or by recently arrived white civilians who want to keep the familiar patterns.

In opposition is the fact that many Oriental and Polynesian people have overcome this newly found, white-induced prejudice by actual contact with individual Negroes. Still others, particularly the working class and trade union members, stand ready to join forces with Negroes here in a joint assault on discrimination which often victimizes them too, particularly in housing, where many desirable districts bar non-white residents; and in employment, where the top jobs are reserved on a caste basis for Caucasians and where there is generally a dual wage system if both whites and Orientals do exactly the same kind of work.

But there has been little disposition on the part of the "more respectable element" to utilize this potential good will. They will complain about the Smith Street influence, but few are active in the local NAACP branch or the recently formed Hawaii Civil Liberties Committee. Instead of mingling with the other groups in the city, most seem content to go to their civilian jobs for the armed forces then come home at night to their segregated section of the government-maintained housing project a few miles from Honolulu proper. There their social contacts revolve, in the main, about other Negroes. Consequently the rest of Honolulu does not see too much of the Negroes who, by their conduct, could easily minimize the bad effects of Smith Street.

Many of these Negroes would like to see Smith Street wiped out, without realizing the lasting solution is elimination of the conditions which make Smith Street possible; they wish to halt the rise of Jim Crow but are unwilling to do more than talk about it at their social affairs. To make matters worse, some tremble at the great Red bogey, fearing loss of their federal jobs if they are too active in militant organizations that might include Communists. That, then, is the picture and it is not too pretty.

• • •

HAWAIIAN STUDENTS STUDY THE NEGRO
FEBRUARY 2, 1949

People here are interested in the Negro. Last week I talked before a sociology class of some one hundred students at the University of Hawaii who, all semester, have concentrated on the pattern of Negro-white relations on the mainland. Such books as Myrdal's *American Dilemma* and the Cayton-Drake *Black Metropolis* were required reading.

It is not that there are enough Negroes here to constitute a problem. Only two or three of the one thousand Duskymerican civilians attend the university. But since the majority of people in these islands are non-Caucasian, the white attitude toward people of other colors is of primary importance.

These young people wanted to know whether Truman's civil rights program would be passed, about the inequalities of education in the South, about denial of the ballot, the influence of the Negro press and the attitude of organized labor. They were as alert as other students their age, and seemed genuinely glad to hear about these problems directly from a Negro rather than from a book.

In return, I added to my education the complexities of inter-group relations in these islands.

For instance, even the social science department is not permitted to learn the ethnic composition of the university. The administration refuses, even in the interests of science, to let anybody know just how many Japanese, Chinese, Koreans, etc., are in attendance. The reason is that most of the students are Japanese, and the powers that be live in mortal fear of having the school referred to as "Little Nippon." Many whites already send their sons and daughters back to the mainland for education; this would be the finishing touch.

This also highlights a peculiarity of island thinking. If, for instance, large numbers of Japanese begin attending a specific Christian church, the Chinese and Koreans will leave and go elsewhere. This clannishness has undoubtedly hampered the struggle of all the colored peoples here for complete equality. But the one good thing is that, despite these tensions between colored groups, they tend to join together to present something of a united front against the attitude of whites or "haoles."

In fact, haole is often a word of contempt. The Portuguese, who have been here a long time working on the plantations, resent being called haoles. One reason is that originally, haole meant any foreigner and only more recently has it been limited to whites, particularly those from the mainland. Today the haoles are blamed—and justly—for most of the bad phases of island living.

Getting back to the university, virtually all the professors and instructors, except the teachers of oriental languages, are haole. There are capable, even brilliant, non-Caucasians either teaching or otherwise employed in the States, but efforts to get the administration to hire them are fruitless. They will employ clerks and assistants and general personnel, but the top jobs are reserved for whites. That, incidentally, is a pattern that exists throughout the islands, but I'll have more to say on this subject later.

I learned also that few haole girls attend the university, most being sent back to the mainland for college if at all possible. The reason is a practical one with their pale faces, they don't stand a chance in competition with the yellow and brown girls on the campus. They look washed out and unhealthy beside the dusky and sensuous beauty of the Oriental and Polynesian co-eds. A Caucasian girl has to be sensationally beautiful to get a play even from the white boys.

After you see some of these girls, you understand why. The Japanese are tiny and delicate as little brown dolls. The mixtures of many peoples are generally larger. Their lush loveliness is a tremendously effective argument for miscegenation. Further, the open living, the sunshine and activity possible in this wonderful climate the year round gives a wondrous healthy glow to the complexion and an aliveness to carriage and actions not generally found among the ordinary mortals born and reared on the mainland. It's something you can't fully appreciate until you see it for yourself.

• • •

ARMED FORCES DEMOCRACY
FEBRUARY 16, 1949

You can depend upon the armed forces to act as bold defenders of Americanism wherever they may go. Only it's too often the Rankin brand. It's prevalent at the navy installations at Pearl Harbor, and in the army.

It's still white supremacy, even in Honolulu where the majority of the population is non-Caucasian and which knew little of color prejudice prior to World War II. That was when mainland patterns were grafted upon this territory by the armed forces who at one time in the recent conflict outnumbered Hawaiian civilians.

Most of the one thousand Negro civilians work for Uncle Sam. They are here because they can get higher ratings and better pay than back in the States. In that way, they're happy to be in Hawaii. But even this improved treatment is still discriminatory and far less than a citizen has a right to expect in a nation that preaches equality of opportunity.

I have talked with Negroes employed in the navy yard who have wide reputations for mastery of their jobs. One, an excellent mechanic, has trained white workers who now are in supervisory capacities while he maintains the same old rating. There are truck drivers who seem unable to become anything else. Some have been treated fairly and have ratings commensurate with their ability, but these are the exceptions.

In all fairness, it is not official naval policy to maintain a color caste system. The trouble comes from prejudiced individuals in key positions. Some have no bias, and there are instances of workers being able to get transfers to such supervisors and being thoroughly satisfied; but there are others whose sole aim in life seems to be frustration of non-white employees. And they retain their posts despite complaints.

Negroes are not the only victims of prejudice. This discriminatory treatment also extends to other dark peoples such as Filipinos, many Puerto Ricans and even native Hawaiians. The Chinese, being lighter, and the Japanese, because of their sheer weight of numbers and economic importance, fare considerably better.

Between now and July 1, the color caste system will be brought into even sharper focus. By that date, the number of civilian navy workers, must be greatly reduced, in keeping with the official policy of retrenchment in the whole Pacific area. Some Negroes will get the axe. Others are likely to be changed to unpleasant jobs.

Such an attempt has been made in the case of a woman whose name cannot be revealed for obvious reasons. She was the only Negro left in a naval base office from which all others had been systematically removed. The personnel director was known to have a strong color complex.

Two weeks ago, orders came through to abolish her department. She was assigned to a pier as storekeeper checker, even though official orders had been handed down that no women were to be sent to this dirty job. When she refused, she was asked to resign. Only by going to higher officials was she given another job. A similar effort was made to ease out a Hawaiian girl. Meanwhile the lighter-skinned girls in this office, some with less seniority, had been placed at once.

Many of these federal workers also live in a civilian naval housing project, known as CHA-3. Here they are segregated. Although it is possible for Negroes to live in the hotels and most of the residential sections throughout the islands, Uncle Sam insists on Jim Crow. At this government project, they are confined to a separate area set aside for Negroes.

That's democracy in Hawaii, armed forces version.

• • •

CIVIL WAR IN NAACP
FEBRUARY 23, 1949

I doubt if, anywhere else in the world, there is an NAACP branch similar to the one in Honolulu. And for the sake of Negro advancement, I hope not.

On the books are, roughly, two hundred members. Naturally the bulk of the membership is Negro. There is but a smattering of Orientals, for by custom "colored" means Negro and I have noticed no great effort here to have the term embrace all non-white residents. Also included are a sizeable number of Caucasians, and it is among some of them that the difficulties have originated.

Like the rest of America, Hawaii is going through a Red scare. The Communist bogey has been strong enough to divide the chapter into two bitter factions. So heated is this miniature civil war that the fight for the advancement of colored people has come to a temporary halt while the rival groups fight for control. For two consecutive months, the battle for the presidency has resulted in a tie vote.

Heading the right wingers is a white woman, secretary of the Republican club, who blandly told me there is no prejudice against Negroes "as a group," and who insists that individual Negroes must "prove their worth." She does not favor enactment of a civil rights law for the territory. That is the official Republican position here, for the party swears there is no Jim Crow—while more and more cafes and taverns bar Negro patronage.

Working with her are several Catholic leaders, a disgruntled lawyer and quite a few Negroes, including the faction's candidate for the presidency. He, like most of the Negro members, works for Uncle Sam and is therefore especially susceptible to the Red bogey, what with Truman's loyalty order and all!

The left wing whites are primarily from the ranks of organized labor. This means they come mainly from the Harry Bridges CIO union, the International Longshoremen's and Warehousemen's Union which is constantly called "Communist dominated." The ILWU, with thirty thousand members, is far and away the biggest and strongest union in Hawaii. Also identified with the left are the brilliant labor lawyers who have made history here during the past few years, Harriet Bouslog and Myer Symonds, who have developed wide reputations as fighters for the underdog.

This group is backing another Negro for the presidency, a Negro who also works for Uncle Sam, but who understands the cry of Communism is often used to scare off minority groups who wage militant fights for their rights. He has the support of others who have been angered by the attacks against the National Alliance of Postal Employees and some NAACP branch executives who were charged with disloyalty purely because they battled aggressively for equality.

Another important factor is that this group wants a civil rights bill passed by the territorial legislature. Organized labor here is Democratic. The conservative forces are Republican. This means that right wing control of the chapter presidency would hardly find support for a civil rights bill, no matter how urgently needed.

The vote at the annual election in December, after several hours of wrangling, name-calling and lost tempers was thirty-one to thirty-one. The problem was placed in the lap of national headquarters in New York, only to be sent back to Honolulu. So in January they did it all over again. The vote was thirty to thirty after two leftwingers had been disqualified on questionable technicalities. Now they will try it a third time this month.

Many came out to cast their ballots but left in disgust. They remarked that if as much time was spent in fighting for the rights of colored people as in fighting each other for control, the local NAACP would be tremendously powerful.

There are Negroes here who don't want the NAACP anyway, contending such an organization in a place like "democratic Hawaii" is "self segregation." Naturally, many whites don't want it. But if it does exist, they want it powerless. Could that be the reason for the intense interest taken in its internal affairs by some Honolulu Republicans?

• • •

THEY'RE DIFFERENT HERE

[UNDATED]

There is often considerable difference in the way white Americans behave toward Negroes at home and away from the mainland. This obviously is not an original observation, but until recently I never had this experience.

Last week I went over to the "big island" of Hawaii about two hundred miles south of the island of Oahu on which Honolulu is located. I wanted to see the eruption taking place in the crater of Mauna Loa, the great volcano which rises almost fourteen thousand feet from the ocean.

I had misgivings. I would be the only Negro in a large party of tourists from all over the U.S. And if there is any animal which considers itself the lord of all creation, it is the white American tourist in a different land. Three days and two nights with such a group could be difficult.

For this kind of trip, you make arrangements with a travel bureau. Cost of air transportation, automobile, guide, meals and hotel accommodations are paid for in a flat package rate. Head of the best agency here is a big brown Hawaiian, Howard K. Morris, who, perhaps for ethnic reasons, seems to have taken a special delight in making the stay here pleasant.

We landed at the Hilo airport and were being assigned to autos for the tour before it dawned upon the others that I was in the same party. But except for a few curious glances, they took it in stride. In our car were an Irish woman from Seattle who is a newspaper writer, a Purdue graduate from Hammond, Indiana, studying island agriculture; a red-haired navy officer from downstate Illinois who has lived out here seven years and has no intention of returning to the States; a couple who owns a resort camp in California; our guide and driver of mixed Chinese-Portuguese ancestry, and the director of the trip, Hiram Morris, son of Howard K., who hopped from car to car during the three days.

Color was ignored. The seven regulars in our car and Hiram ate breakfast together in Hilo. By the time we had driven through the giant fern forest to famed Volcano House some 4,000 feet up on the rim of Kilauea, Hawaii's other active volcano, and had looked deep into the steaming lava pits, we sat down to luncheon calling each other by our first names.

On this tour, you stop two nights at the Kona Inn a luxury hotel almost on the lap of the sea in the fabulous and dreamy Kona coast, an area so lushly beautiful that Honoluluans want to go there when they retire. When we arrived in early evening after driving through the great Kau desert of old lava flows and cactus detouring for a stop at a black sand beach, and halting many times for breathtaking panoramas of ocean and sloping mountain side, not only tourists in the other cars but guests at the Kona Inn were wondering who I was.

Hiram had been well briefed by his father. He put it on strong. I was not only an editor who wrote for papers "all over the mainland," I was a "famous poet," a "great photographer," I was gathering material "for a book on the islands," and had come to Hawaii to "consider investing in some land on the Kona coast."

That did it. During the rest of the trip men who back home would probably be insulted if a Negro visited in the block where they lived were offering
me highballs and introducing me to their wives and daughters: I suppose that
from now on, when the occasion arises, they will point to this as proof of how
democratic they really are!

Yet, there is another factor which seems important. Although Hawaii
prides itself on being as American as Boston or Kansas City, the huge, almost
64 percent Oriental and Polynesian population makes many Caucasians feel
strength even in Honolulu. On the big island there are fewer white faces.
Foreign languages and pidgin English are heard constantly. Since inter-mixing
here is not taboo, is it not possible that there is a tendency for whites in such a
situation to more readily accept any person, no matter what his color, who is
readily identified with mainland cultural patterns?

I think too, that many sense the basic hostility that non-whites may have
toward "haoles" or mainland whites. There may be courteous service, professional smiles, etc., but underneath, many of the Orientals and Polynesians
have the same bitterness that you often find among Pullman porters and wait-
ers. Get them out of earshot of haoles and they'll open up.

But no matter what Hiram Morris thinks, he has a way with the tourists.
He is a graduate of the University of Hawaii and was a captain in the war. Now
just twenty-five, he is handsome and one of the most likeable persons I ever
met. He kids everybody, and does it in such a way that the women go wild over
him and the men show no resentment when he comes up and places a brown
arm soothingly around a pale shoulder.

In a way, Hiram is getting even. A native Hawaiian, he took officers'
training at Fort Benning and spent some time in New York. He has had first
hand experience with American color prejudice. But out there he told me, he
is king. As leader of these touring parties, he has almost complete control over
their actions for a few days. Those who treat him right as a man and as an
equal get utmost consideration. But those with the usual mainland ideas on
race will have a most miserable trip. It's up to the individual.

P.S. I didn't see the eruption. Too many clouds around the top of Mauna
Loa but with so many other amazing bits of scenery on the islands, why worry
about a little thing like molten lava shooting five hundred feet in the air and
hissing down the mountain side.

• • •

DEL MONTE'S NEGRO FOREMAN

MARCH 16, 1949

Next time you get Del Monte pineapple, you will be buying a canned product for which a mainland Negro is in large responsible.

He is California-born Lucius F. Jenkins, general foreman of both the processing and syrup recovery plants at the huge California Packing Company factory here where Del Monte pineapple is processed. His position gives him the responsibility of seeing that the standard flavor of this well-known brand is maintained.

Jenkins has worked for this company since a year after graduation in 1934 from the University of Hawaii. That was also the year he married Rose Cupchey, a gracious and friendly woman three-fourths Chinese and one fourth Hawaiian, who is a registered nurse. She finished her training at Queen's hospital here.

Jenkins, who says he wouldn't trade one square foot of Hawaii "for a square mile on the mainland," is the only mainland Negro among the two thousand employees at the canning factory. The other Negroes are not Negroes for they come from Puerto Rico. Out here, that merely makes them "dark Puerto Ricans." Of course it's screwy but, for that matter, so is the whole prevailing conception of race.

Los Angeles was Jenkins' birthplace some forty-one years ago, and he still has parents, sisters and other relatives in California. He had spent a year in Sacramento Junior college before coming to Honolulu in 1931. In the eighteen years since then, he has returned only twice to the mainland and then just for short visits. There are too many unpleasant and bitter memories of Jim Crow and discrimination for him to have any nostalgia for the States.

When he finished the University of Hawaii with a degree in civil engineering, after having starred as a track man in the high jump and weights, he went into the pineapple cannery in 1935 as an assistant foreman in the processing department. There was some grumbling on the part of whites or "haoles" over a Negro getting such an important job. There is still some resentment, but he chooses to ignore it.

In 1939, he became a full foreman of his department and in 1943 he was also named foreman for the syrup recovery plant. His training as a civil engineer has been most valuable, for he installed much of the present beverage juice plant, boilers, and redesigned equipment. For a while he did much of the factory's civil engineering, cutting down on this activity only since the end of World War II when the company set up a separate engineering department.

Under his direct supervision at the peak season are some two hundred workers, the majority Oriental. As assistant foreman he has one haole and one Japanese. Naturally, the ordinary employees are not white, for the caste system of mainland "white supremacy" maintained here opposes the hiring of a haole in a menial capacity.

Jenkins gets along well with his fellow workers, no matter what their ethnic origin. He has found the non-haoles friendly and willing to meet others half way. There's no denying the fact that the Oriental and Polynesian workers feel a common bond with Negroes. Credit much of this to the educational program of the International Longshoremen's and Warehousemen's Union, CIO, which has a strong local at Del Monte.

Jenkins is well satisfied with his job, with his family—there are seven children from fourteen down to one year—and with Hawaii itself. He calls himself, after eighteen years here, a "kamaaina" (Hawaiian word for old resident) and has no intention of changing his status.

• • •

NEGROES, OKINAWANS HAVE SIMILAR REACTION
APRIL 6, 1949

Minority groups, facing similar patterns of discrimination, develop similar reactions. Close your eyes, listen to the thoughts expressed in serious discussion by Okinawan Japanese, and you can imagine you're in Harlem.

If you've been used to thinking of Japanese as Japanese and nothing else, this will come as a surprise. The Japanese people, those of Okinawan extraction, occupy the same inferior status as the Negro in America. They are looked down upon and discriminated against.

There are cases in which parents threatened suicide if their sons or daughters married Okinawans. Some refuse to permit them inside their homes. Association and contact are kept to a minimum. Sounds sort of familiar, doesn't it?

Okinawans are also supposed to possess different group characteristics. They are "crude and uncultured," they are "loud and vulgar." Also, they are "darker," have "coarser features," are "more talkative and laugh more," and if all else fails, they can be identified by "different kinds of names." That's also familiar, isn't it?

I learned these things recently when I talked before a Japanese club of some four hundred members, all of whom are young Okinawans. I told them of the struggle of Negroes and other minority peoples for full equality on the mainland. After the meeting was over, several told me privately they felt a strong bond of kinship with me as a Negro because of the fight they faced to get equality, not only with white America but with other Japanese.

The question period shaped up as it might in Atlanta or Chicago or any other community where serious young colored Americans were trying to find answers to group problems. I was asked if I thought a club composed exclusively of Okinawans might not be "self-segregation"; why was it that when there was no enforced segregation members of a group tended to gravitate together; if cultural traditions were maintained would it not hamper their being accepted as full Americans.

I was also asked if members of a group that suffered discrimination didn't often look for trouble when none was intended, and if inter-group contact and education would really be of much help in breaking down prejudice. One young man, a graduate of a mainland university, told me he had become so frustrated in beating his head against the stone wall of discrimination that he felt like withdrawing into his own group and not even trying to fight anymore.

You can see that I felt completely at home. To make it even more so, I talked with one young physician who during the war had studied one quarter at the medical school of Howard University. Still others who had attended college on the mainland had been in Dixie where they saw for themselves the patterns of color prejudice.

Since then I have also learned that Okinawans lead other Japanese proportionately in the trade unions and progressive activities in general, just as on the mainland Negroes lead other groups proportionately in the fights for civil rights and full democracy. The reason in both instances is the same: those who suffer most are most anxious to correct the situation.

• • •

HAWAIIAN LUAU IS LIKE COUNTRY PICNIC, EVEN TO FIGHTS; BUT FOOD IS DIFFERENT

[UNDATED]

If you like the good old-fashioned country picnic and social, you'd have the time of your life at a luau (pronounced loo-ow), the Hawaiian feast. The food is different, but otherwise it's like down home, even to the fights.

A first class luau is an expensive proposition, the cost of food being what it is plus the number of uninvited guests. If you invite fifty, it is best to prepare for at least eighty; if your invitations total three hundred, you'll probably have five hundred. Hawaiian hospitality is such that a complete stranger may chance to pass by, see the crowd, join in, and get the same eats and drinks as anybody else.

For this reason, many persons hold luaus not only to entertain socially but also in the hopes of maybe showing a small profit. Nothing is charged, but guests are supposed to make voluntary contributions in support of the event for which the luau is being held. Time was when you were asked outright for donations, but police put a stop to that; then open pots were left suggestively in obvious places but the cops also called a halt to that. The procedure nowadays is to put from two dollars upward per person in an envelope and hand it to your host.

If it's a luau celebrating the arrival or first birthday of a baby, the envelope is addressed to the child and carries the name of the donor. If it's a housewarming or birthday of an older person, the same procedure is followed unless one wants to bring a nice gift. Since such donations are made purely on an honor basis, your host keeps his fingers crossed and hopes that, when the expenses of the luau are balanced against the "take," he will come out ahead.

Luaus are generally held in the yard, with the guests eating at long tables under gaily decorated canvas canopies. To one side is the makeshift bar. The guests are limited in their consumption of food and drink only by the available supplies and their own consciences. There have been instances of well-stocked luaus lasting two or three days.

The liquor is the same as in Seattle or Miami but the food is different. Here it's strictly Hawaiian cookery and dishes. Some dainty souls use a spoon, but it's the custom to use your hands and fingers and lick them clean.

The major item at a luau is called kalua pig. It's a Hawaiian version of Dixie barbecue. An imu (oven) is dug in the ground. Actual cooking is done with hot stones. A tender young pig is seasoned with spices wrapped in large ti leaves and baked. The trick is knowing precisely when to take it out and how to handle the meat which is so tender it almost falls apart.

You will also have raw fish. Don't get squeamish, because it's good. There's what they call lomi salmon and its quite appetizing. Perhaps there will be pieces of ahi, a dark native fish, or slices of abalone or dried octopus. Along with this you may have limu, a tender and tasty seaweed also served raw.

Even if you're determined not to like any of these "foreign foods," you'll probably break down on laulau. It consists of pork, salmon, and chicken embedded in young ti leaves, (they taste a little like spinach) with taro leaves on the outside. It's served steaming hot.

With these sharply flavored and highly spiced foods, you need something bland for contrast. That's where poi comes in. It may take some time to get used to poi, but one day you may suddenly discover that you like it. Poi is eaten in place of bread. Served in a bowl, it is a kind of brownish gray and looks like a close relative of the glue family. You dip one or two fingers into the stuff and rush the paste to your mouth before it drips. But it doesn't pay to get too fond of poi if you want to preserve your waistline. Although it is one of the most healthful foods known to medical science (babies thrive on it), poi is also one of the most fattening. But that suits the native Hawaiians. Men and women alike, they're proud of their big "poi bellies."

Topping it off may be a dish of fresh cocoanut pudding, and it's truly delicious. Of course, there are fresh pineapples, bananas, papaya, and mango (in season), but these are so common why bother with them at a festival such as a luau?

Last Sunday we attended a birthday luau given for the youngest child in a Hawaiian-Chinese family who was baptized at the start of festivities. Paper hats and tin whistles for the adults and candy canes and balloons for the many children added to the gaiety. There were two small Hawaiian bands alternating, with impromptu singing and hulas by the guests.

When the child's mother, a hefty brown woman in a long tight-fitting dress danced for the people, the boys in the band shouted "Shake that thing now," "Get hot, baby," and similar expressions emanating from the Harlems of America. There really must be a close relationship between Hawaiians and Negroes other than color.

It was a real ethnic cocktail, with members of every group [from all the] islands in attendance. Some two hundred fifty invitations have been put out and four hundred dollars spent on the affair. The take was $783, giving the hosts a nice profit of $383 for their pains.

It looked as though this would be one luau without a fight. It began at noon, but it wasn't until nearly midnight, when only a half dozen guests were left, that the host family staged a battle of its own with the father of the child attacking the grandfather and the wife and other in-laws pitching in with their fists. It took four squads of police, who thoughtfully brought along an ambulance, to quell the little domestic riot. But by the next evening the damage had been patched up, and everybody was happy again—probably until the next luau.

GLOSSARY

Abraham Lincoln School: Located in Chicago, this school was the site of Davis's course in the history of jazz, one of the first to be taught in the nation. Its various activities were described by Attorney General Tom Clark in 1947 as Communist-inspired. The school was therefore placed on the list of subversive organizations.

Algren, Nelson (1909–1981): In *Livin' the Blues*, Davis says this of Algren: "I worked actively with the Chicago chapter of the League of American Writers . . . and became personally acquainted with such writers as Nelson Algren, Stuart Engstrand and Meyer Levin. . . . These were all socially conscious 'proletarian writers,' painfully aware of economic inequalities which brought on the Depression and determined to help change the world."

Allen, Henry "Red" (1908–1967): Trumpet player Henry "Red" Allen, Jr., left New Orleans in 1926 to play with Sidney Desvigne's Southern Syncopators on the riverboat *Island Queen* which ran between St. Louis and Cincinnati. From there his career saw him play with such luminaries as Duke Ellington, Fletcher Henderson, Coleman Hawkins, and Louis Armstrong.

American Youth for Democracy: In 1943, the American Youth for Democracy organization succeeded the Young Communist League, which had operated as the youth wing of the Communist Party. After the succession of American Youth for Democracy, party youth sections grew but did not especially flourish; what youth activity took place in the immediate postwar years centered around the revival of fraternal movements such as the Jewish people's Fraternal Order, friendship work with the Soviet Union, coalitions joined to the broader liberal movement, and Henry Wallace's Progressive Party campaign for the presidency.

AMGOT: Allied Military Government of Occupied Territory was established during World War II, with the entry of the United States into the war and the invasion of Italy and Sicily. AMGOT consisted of a number of British, American, and Canadian officers who had received special training in civil administration. By the time the armistice with Italy had been signed and its name shortened to Allied Military Government (AMG), the organization had become an efficient and respected component of the Allied Armies in Italy.

Apex: Located at 330 East 35th Street in Chicago, the Apex Club hosted, among others, Dave Nelson, Johnny Wells, Earl Hines, and Jimmy Noone.

Aptheker, Dr. Herbert (1915–2003): A prolific writer whose work deals primarily with African American and working people's history, Aptheker wrote *The Documentary History of the Negro People in the United States*, *Anti-Racism in U.S. History*, and *American Negro Slave Revolts*. He also edited many collections of Du Bois's works, including *The Correspondence of W. E. B. Du Bois*.

Armstrong, Louis (1900–1971): Daniel Louis "Satchmo" Armstrong was an American jazz trumpet virtuoso, singer, band leader, and actor. His early playing was noted for its improvisation and his reputation as a vocalist was quickly established. Armstrong was a major influence on the melodic development of jazz in the 1920s; because of him, solo performance attained a position of great importance in jazz music.

Associates in Negro Folk Education: In the 1930s, Dr. Alain Locke established the Associates in Negro Folk Education, a loosely defined collection of scholars who were dedicated to publishing scholarly books on African American subjects geared toward interested adult learners.

Auburn Avenue: The street in Atlanta where Martin Luther King, Jr., was born. Auburn Avenue was dubbed "Sweet Auburn" by early civil rights leader John Wesley Dobbs because of the opportunities it afforded blacks even under strict segregation laws. In the 1930s and 1940s, the two-mile street offered black-owned nightclubs where musical greats such as Cab Calloway and Duke Ellington performed.

Auhagon, Friedrich: A paid Nazi agent, Dr. Friedrich Auhagon was a former second lieutenant in the Kaiser's army and had come from Germany to America in 1923 as a member of the German Intelligence. Together with Nazi agent George Sylvester Viereck, Auhagon edited the magazine *Today's Challenge*, to which Dennis Lawrence also contributed articles. *Today's*

Challenge was a Nazi conspiracy to initiate a highly important campaign of psychological sabotage in the United States.

Austin-Wadsworth Bill (1943): Also known as the Civilian Service Act, this bill was an attempt to provide an adequate supply of workers in war industries, agriculture, and other occupations, and to maintain a balance between these workers and the armed forces. It sought to make all civilians, both men and women, liable to contribute to the war effort in a noncombatant capacity.

Bailey, Buster (1902–1967): Bailey was a brilliant clarinetist who, although known for his smooth and quiet playing with John Kirby's sextet, occasionally cut loose with some wild solos (including on a recording called "Man with a Horn Goes Berserk"). One of the most technically skilled of the clarinetists to emerge during the 1920s, Bailey never modernized his style or became a leader, but he contributed his talents and occasional wit to a countless number of rewarding and important recordings.

Baker, Lavern (1929–1997): A gutsy vocalist capable of blending blues and jazz styles. During her time with Atlantic Records (1953–1962), she recorded half a dozen singles that rose to high positions on the pop and R&B charts, including "Tweedle Dee," "Jim Dandy," and "I Cry a Tear."

Bandung: Representatives of twenty-nine African and Asian nations met at Bandung, Indonesia, in 1955 with the aim of promoting economic and cultural cooperation and opposing colonialism. The conference ultimately led to the establishment of the Non Aligned Movement in 1961. In later years, conflicts between the Non Aligned nations eroded the solidarity expressed at Bandung.

Bear, Mr. (Teddy McRae) (1908–1999): Teddy McRae switched to music from pursuing a medical degree after hearing a recording of Louis Armstrong. He went on to distinguish himself as musical director, arranger, song writer, producer, and saxophonist for some of the great names in the field, including Louis Armstrong, Artie Shaw, and Lionel Hampton.

Benedict, Ruth (1887–1948): One of the first female anthropologists, Dr. Ruth Benedict was an important figure in the then emerging fields of anthropology and cultural anthropology. She wrote several books including *Tales of the Cochiti Indians* (1931), *Zuñi Mythology* (1935), and the bestseller *Patterns of Culture* (1934). Her final assignment was the study of Japan, and her classic work *The Chrysanthemum and the Sword: Patterns of Japanese Culture* (1946) also became a bestseller.

Bethune, Mrs. (1875–1955): An educator, organizer, and political activist, Mary Macleod Bethune's many contributions to American society include the establishment of one of the nation's first schools for African American girls in Daytona Beach, Florida. She also served as advisor to four U.S. presidents.

Big Broadcast of 1937: A musical starring Jack Benny, George Burns, and Gracie Allen. The musical stars included Benny Goodman and His Orchestra, Gene Krupa, Larry Adler, and Leopold Stokowski.

Bigard, Barney (1906–1980): First known as a tenor-saxophonist, Bigard played with several groups in New Orleans before moving to Chicago to play with King Oliver from 1925 until 1927. However, he found his niche with Duke Ellington's orchestra, where he almost exclusively played clarinet.

Bilbo, Theodore Gilmore (1877–1947): Bilbo served as U.S. senator from Mississippi from 1935 to 1947. His reputation for being a demagogue and arch-segregationist made him one of the most feared opponents of black racial causes.

Black Bottom: The Black Bottom was a solo challenge dance, predominately danced on the off beat and was the prototype for modern tap dance phrasing. The dance featured the slapping of the backside while hopping forward and backward, stamping the feet and gyrating the torso while moving the arms with an occasional heel-toe scoop. In 1926 the Black Bottom became the rage and replaced the Charleston as the nation's most popular dance.

Bolden, Buddy (1877–1931): Born Charles Joseph, cornetist and bandleader Bolden was the first of the New Orleans so-called cornet "kings." Bolden's rise to fame coincided with the emergence of Storyville—a New Orleans district of dives, honky tonks, and brothels—where he soon became a local celebrity.

Bontemps, Arna (1902–1973): The son of Creole parents, Bontemps published his first book, *God Sends Sunday*, in 1931. He grew frustrated at trying to reach his own generation and decided to write to younger readers, "not yet insensitive to man's inhumanity to man." For the remaining forty years of his life, Bontemps wrote biographies, children's fiction, and black history, and compiled literary anthologies, often in collaboration with his close friends Langston Hughes and Jack Conroy.

Bousfield, Maudelle: Educator and educational reformer, Maudelle Bousfield was the first African American principal of a Chicago public school.

Bouslog, Harriet (1913–1998): With her law partner, Myer Symonds, Bouslog defended striking longshore, sugar, and pineapple workers organized by the International Longshoremen's and Warehousemen's Union (ILWU) in the post–World War II years, at a time when the union was battling the Big Five companies that dominated Hawaii's economy. Bouslog and Symonds also represented ILWU officials before hearings of the U.S. House Un-American Activities Committee and the "Hawaii Seven" charged under the Smith Act with conspiring to advocate the overthrow of the government.

Bricker, John (1893–1986): Bricker was a staunch member of the Republican Party, serving from 1946 to 1959 as U.S. senator from Ohio.

Bridges, Harry (1901–1990): In 1937, Bridges set up the International Longshoremen's and Warehousemen's Union (ILWU) and became West Coast director of the Congress of Industrial Organizations (CIO). Proceedings in 1939 to deport him back to Australia as a Communist alien ended when he was officially absolved of Communist affiliation.

Brown, Earl: Brown was a reporter who often wrote insightful analyses for *Life Magazine*.

Brown, Edgar Allan (1888–1975): In *Livin' the Blues*, Davis likens Brown, a daring spokesman against racism in the 1930s and 1940s, to an early Stokely Carmichael.

Brown, Ruth (b. 1928): Ruth Brown took her stage name from her marriage to trumpeter Jimmy Brown, whom she later divorced. In a career that saw periods of genuine success followed by times when she had to work as a domestic, she recorded "Mambo Baby," which has proven to be an enduring indication of her achievement.

Buck, Pearl Sydenstricker (1892–1973): In 1938, Buck won the Nobel Prize for literature, the first American woman to do so. In addition to being an acclaimed writer (by the time of her death she had published over seventy novels), she was active in American civil rights and women's rights activities.

Bugniazet, G. M.: Bugniazet was the seventh secretary of the International Brotherhood of Electrical Workers, 1925–1947.

Calloway, "Cab" (1907–1994): Cabell "Cab" Calloway will always be remembered for his outrageous stage antics and wild lyrics (including scat singing, or vocalizing the song either wordlessly or with nonsense words and syllables) in the 1930s and 1940s.

Campbell, E. Simms (1908–1971): Campbell contributed cartoons, illustrations, and other art work to *Esquire, Cosmopolitan, Red Book,* the *New Yorker, Colliers,* the *Saturday Evening Post, College Humor, Playboy, Opportunity,* and *Life.*

Casa Loma: Known as the first swing band, the Casa Loma Orchestra in 1929 began playing the mixture of hot jazz and sweet ballads that Benny Goodman would later popularize and that would dominate the music industry in the late 1930s and early 1940s.

Celestin, Oscar "Papa" (1884–1954): Papa Celestin, one of the most popular of New Orleans cornetists, was considered a major player in the development of jazz. In 1910, Celestin founded the Original Tuxedo Jazz Orchestra which would become one of the most enduring bands of the era.

CHA: Civilian Housing Authority

Charleston: The Charleston is characterized by outward heel kicks combined with up-and-down steps that are thought to have originated with blacks. Movement is achieved by bending and straightening the knees in time to the syncopated 4/4 rhythm of ragtime jazz.

Chess label: Leonard and Phil Chess, two Polish-Jewish immigrants, bought the Aristocrat label in 1947, and renamed it Chess in 1950. The brothers' interest in Mississippi Delta blues led them to embark upon a career recording blues artists, which eventually gave way to rhythm and blues.

Chivers, Professor Walter: One of the most distinguished sociologists in the U.S., Professor Chivers was the author of many scholarly studies and magazine articles as well as a stimulating speaker and writer. As instructor to Martin Luther King, Jr., he remained one of the major influences on King's thinking and communicative style in King's early years as an undergraduate student at Morehouse College.

Clayton, Buck (1911–1991): A valued member of a variety of classic big bands, he was versatile enough to thrive as both bandleader, session man extraordinaire, and trumpet soloist par excellence. He worked with various artists including Duke Ellington, Benny Goodman, Teddy Wilson, Eddie Condon, Sidney Bechet, and Humphrey Littleton.

Commission on Interracial Cooperation: After World War I, returning black soldiers in the South were expected to resume their place as second-class citizens. Resentment grew and violent race riots resulted in several southern cities. The Commission on Interracial Cooperation (CIC) was formed in 1919 in response to these civil disturbances.

Condon, Eddie (1905–1973): A guitar and banjo player who worked with Red Nichols's Five Pennies and Red McKenzie's Mound City Blues Blowers.

Congo Square: An important site in New Orleans's antebellum slave culture. Africans, both enslaved and free, used this space to market goods, socialize, and participate in drumming, music-making, and dance. The activities in Congo Square helped maintain a musical heritage and social cohesion among Africans in America which also formed the foundation for creating jazz.

Congress of Industrial Organizations (CIO): The CIO was a body of unions formed in 1935 to organize mass production industries. From the beginning, the CIO made it clear that it sought to organize workers regardless of race, and in its early campaigns, it made a special appeal to African Americans. The CIO merged with the American Federation of Labor in 1955 to form the AFL-CIO, which became the most powerful labor organization in the United States.

Crosby, Bob (1913–1993): Bob Crosby's greatest claim to fame, besides being Bing's younger brother, was the Dixieland band that bore his name—the Bob Crosby Orchestra. It was actually led by sax player Gil Rodin. Crosby himself was merely the front man.

Crosswaith, Frank (1892–1965): A lifelong labor union organizer, editor, and socialist candidate for several New York State offices, Crosswaith was one of the most effective organizers of black workers in New York City. He was also one of the organizers of the original March on Washington Movement in 1941, under A. Philip Randolph.

Dabney, Virginius (1901–1995): A white southern liberal newspaperman, Dabney campaigned against racial intolerance in the South. Though not a hard-core opponent of Supreme Court decisions against racial discrimination, Dabney was a middle-of-the-road southern liberal who believed in justice for blacks, but insisted that the proponents of change still had to recognize the racial sensitivities of the vast majority of white southerners.

Davis, Benjamin J., Jr. (1903–1964): Davis was considered one of the most influential leaders of the Communist Party in the United States. Although his success with African Americans and the Communist Party was short-lived, he maintained the view that it was the best political alternative for blacks in the United States.

Dawson, William Levi (1886–1970): An African American lawyer and politician, Dawson was elected congressional representative from Illinois in 1942, holding his seat until his death in 1970. Dawson spoke out against the poll tax, and was credited with defeating the Winstead Amendment, which would have allowed military personnel to choose whether or not they would serve in integrated units.

Day, Stephen Albion (1882–1950): A representative from Illinois, Day was elected as a Republican to the Seventy-seventh and Seventy-eighth Congresses from January 1941 to January 1945. After his unsuccessful run for reelection to the Seventy-ninth Congress, he resumed the practice of law in Evanston, Illinois, where he died in 1950.

Dean, Captain Harry Foster (1864–1935): An advocate of international shipping, Dean was a black sea captain who attempted to control land in South Africa for the ultimate reestablishment of a black nation. The name of the shipping vessel he purchased, *Pedro Gorino*, also provided the title for his 1929 autobiography, which he wrote with the assistance of Sterling North.

Detroit Riot of 1943: At the height of World War II, the city of Detroit gradually felt heightened racial tensions caused by bigotry in the work force, housing shortages for blacks, and shortages occasioned by the rationing of goods. Following a skirmish on Belle Isle between two hundred blacks and whites on June 20, rumors began to fly. A crowd of blacks was told that a black woman and her baby had been thrown from the Belle Isle Bridge. Whites were made angry by reports that a white woman had been raped and murdered by blacks on the same bridge. In the ensuing riot, thirty-four lives were lost, twenty-five of whom were black; and more than 1,800 were arrested for looting and other incidents, the vast majority black.

Dewey, Thomas E. (1902–1971): The Republican challenger to President Roosevelt in the 1944 presidential election. In 1948 the *Chicago Daily Tribune* prematurely projected his victory over Harry S. Truman in that election.

Dickerson, Earl B. (1891–1986): African American attorney, teacher, and businessman, Dickerson was the first general counsel of the Supreme Life Insurance Company of America, one of the nation's largest black-owned insurance companies. Known as "The Dean of Chicago's Black Lawyers," he also helped organize the NAACP Legal Defense and Education Fund in 1939 and later became president and chairman of the board. In 1939, he represented the father of Chicago playwright Lorraine Hansberry in the case of *Hansberry v. Lee* and successfully argued before the Supreme Court for an end to restrictive real estate covenants.

Dies, Martin (1900–1972): During the 1930s and 1940s Dies was notorious for his persecution and "red-baiting" of socialists and prolabor advocates. Under his leadership, the House Committee on Un-American Activities became the prototype of the inquisitorial committees found in the legislative branches of national and state governments during the McCarthy era.

Dorsey, Jimmy (1904–1957): Brother of Tommy Dorsey, and though not quite as famous, Jimmy had a considerable following that included Charlie Parker, who was an admirer of the tone quality of his alto sax.

Dorsey, Tommy (1905–1956): A trumpet and trombone player, who, with his brother Jimmy, formed the Dorsey Brothers Orchestra, a popular group in the early 1930s.

Drake, St. Clair (1911–1990): Educator and social anthropologist, Drake studied social life in the Caribbean, West Africa, and the black communities of Chicago and Great Britain, from the 1930s to the 1980s. His major study of blacks in Chicago, *Black Metropolis*, written in collaboration with Horace Clayton, was published in 1945.

DuPree, Champion Jack (1909–1992): Born William Thomas Dupree, Dupree was the embodiment of the New Orleans blues and boogie-woogie pianist. As a young man, he was always playing the piano, but then he met Joe Louis who encouraged him to be a boxer. He ultimately fought in 107 bouts and won several championships, picking up the nickname Champion Jack which he used for the rest of his life. At age thirty, he returned to music, and in a remarkably productive period, recorded twenty-six titles from 1953 to 1955, including "Walkin' the Blues," a duet with Teddy "Mr. Bear" McRae.

Durham, Carl T. (1892–1974): A representative from North Carolina, Durham was elected as a Democrat to the Seventy-sixth and to the ten succeeding Congresses (January 3, 1939–January 3, 1961). He also served as chairman, Joint Committee on Atomic Energy.

Duskymericans: Davis combines "dusky" and "American" to create this nonce phrase describing African Americans. He follows in the wake of writers like James Weldon Johnson and George Schuyler, who both used "Aframericans."

Edwards, Eddie (1891–1963): With Nick LaRocca and Henry Ragas, Edwin Brandford Edwards founded the Original Dixieland Jass Band (later Jazz) in 1916.

Ellington, Edward Kennedy "Duke" (1899–1974): Recognized in his lifetime as one of the greatest jazz composers and performers, he became indelibly associated with the finest creations in big band and vocal jazz.

Europe, Lieutenant Jim (1881–1919): An early black music pioneer, Jim Europe did not live long enough to play jazz but his large orchestra utilized jazz instruments (including a full banjo section) and performed ragtime, marches, and dance music of the 1912–1919 period. During the war, he toured Europe with his huge military band and seemed poised to repeat his success in the U.S. in 1919, when he was stabbed to death by an irate musician.

Fair Employment Practices Commission: Franklin Delano Roosevelt, in 1942, issued Executive Order 8802 to end discrimination against blacks in the defense industry; its committee was charged with dealing with accusations of differential treatment. In five years, it investigated more than fourteen thousand complaints: 80 percent based on race, 14 percent on national origin, and the remaining 6 percent on creed or religion.

Ford, Tennessee Ernie (1919–1991): His engaging personality made him a great entertainer, and he was best known for his song "Sixteen Tons."

Four Freedoms: Roosevelt announced these worldwide social and political objectives in the State of the Union message he delivered to Congress on January 6, 1941. Roosevelt declared that all people should have the freedom of speech and expression, the freedom to worship God independently, the freedom from want, and the freedom from fear. He called for the latter through "a world-wide reduction of armaments to such a point and in such a thorough fashion that no nation will be in a position to commit an act of aggression against any neighbor anywhere in the world."

47th Street: A street that establishes the boundaries of inner city Chicago.

Frey, John P.: *The Nation*, in 1937, characterized Frey as the "chief backbiter of the American labor movement." He denounced the laborers' sit-down strike strategy as "made in Moscow." He used his influence to rescind endorsements of the CIO, referring to this labor organization as "outlaws." In short, he was seen by some as one who was invaluable in aiding labor's enemies.

Gates, J. M. (1885–1941?): The first successful "recording preacher," Rev. J. M. Gates, a Baptist preacher, holds a special place in the history of gospel music. He initially based the texts for his recordings on biblical events, stories, and parables, but by 1927, he increasingly utilized secular, contemporary, and topical issues. Beginning in 1930, he employed satire and humor in his recorded sermons, attacking the prevalent attitudes and morals of the day.

George, Walter (1878–1957): A political leader who represented Georgia in the U.S. Senate for thirty-four years, beginning in 1922. George often opposed President Franklin Roosevelt, particularly the latter's plan to "pack" the Supreme Court. Roosevelt fought unsuccessfully to prevent George's reelection to the Senate in 1938.

Gershwin, George (1898–1937): Gershwin started his career as a pianist by working in New York's Tin Pan Alley as a "song plugger." After his first hit song "Swanee" (1919), popularized by Al Jolson, he wrote a series of well-known show tunes and symphonies, including the folk opera *Porgy and Bess* (1935), based on the novel by DuBose Heyward.

Gibbs, Georgia (b. 1920): A singer with a mellow pop and rhythm and blues singing style. She had fifteen top forty hits in the mid-1950s, including "If I Knew You Were Coming I'd Have Baked a Cake" and "Kiss of Fire."

Gillespie, "Dizzy" (1917–1993): The career of John Birks "Dizzy" Gillespie, composer, bandleader and innovative trumpet player, spanned nearly sixty years. In the early 1940s, along with the alto saxophonist Charlie "Yardbird" Parker, he created be-bop, a sleek, intense, high speed, revolutionary style. Initially, Davis was opposed to bop on the grounds that it was an exercise in technical skill, which had little connection to what he perceived to be the emotional origins of "real" jazz. He later recanted because, as he said, he could see bop's anchor in the blues.

Goodman, Benny (1909–1986): Dubbed "The King of Swing," clarinetist and composer Goodman's popular emergence marked the beginning of the Swing Era in 1936. During this period, the Benny Goodman Trio featured Gene Krupa (drums) and Teddy Wilson (piano), who was the first black musician to tour with a white band. As time went on the Trio picked up other jazz masters, like Lionel Hampton (vibraphone) and Charlie Christian (guitar). These hires promoted racial integration in the band and provided the music a more "authentic" feel and sound.

Green-Lucas Bill (also known as the Soldier Vote Bill): In the first week of December 1943, the U.S. Senate had before it a bill sponsored by two Democrats—Theodore F. Green of Rhode Island, chairman of the Elections Committee, and Scott W. Lucas of Illinois. Under the Green-Lucas measure, blank ballots would go to soldiers in the field well in advance of the election. The soldiers would mark their ballots just as other citizens would have done. The Bill promised to be one of the most explosive issues of the Seventy-eighth Congress. The southern Democrats feared the loss of the poll tax and literacy test, which kept blacks from voting throughout the South. The northern Republicans simply feared the re-election of Roosevelt but discussed it as an issue of censorship of political material received overseas by service members.

Green Pastures: Marc Connelly's Pulitzer Prize–winning 1929 play occupies an important, even if controversial, place in American cultural history. Connelly, who was white, based the story of *The Green Pastures* on *Ol' Man Adam an' his Chillun* (1928), a book of tales by another white writer, Roark Bradford. Bradford's tales and the play that ultimately became *The Green Pastures* provided a black folk version of the first five books of the Bible, with a focus on the complex and evolving relationship between God and his human subjects.

Green, William (1870–1952): Green served as president of the American Federation of Labor from 1924 to 1952, through some of the most tumultuous times in American labor history. A prolific speaker and writer, he also served as editor of the AFL publication, *American Federationist* for over twenty-eight years.

Hammon, Jupiter (1711–1806): Jupiter Hammon is considered to be the first black writer in America to have his works published. His poems were like his sermons: religious exhortations that dealt thematically with race, slavery, and the alienation of slaves.

Hampton, Lionel (1908–2002): Hampton's extroverted showmanship, including dancing on his drums and attacking the piano with two fingers, mallet-style, has dismayed purists and critics, but his skill as a swinging improviser has never been in doubt. Beginning as a drummer, Hampton later switched to the vibraphone and helped pioneer the racial integration of jazz, following Teddy Wilson in Benny Goodman's quartet in 1936.

Handy, William Christopher (1873–1958): As the first musician to publish the folk blues, W. C. Handy is regarded the "Father of the Blues." However, he himself humbly acknowledged that he did not invent the blues but merely transcribed and presented them to a worldwide audience.

Hayakawa, S. I. (1906–1992): Samuel Ichiye Hayakawa, scholar, university president, and U.S. Senator (R-CA), is best known for his popular writings on general semantics and for his career as president of San Francisco State College. Here Davis acknowledges Hayakawa's renown as a jazz authority and as a columnist on jazz for the *Chicago Defender*.

Hearst newspaper: Newspaper published by William Randolph Hearst, which raised sensational journalism to unprecedented heights.

Henderson, Fletcher (1897–1952): As bandleader, arranger, and pianist, Henderson led the most important of the pioneering big bands and helped set the pattern for most later big jazz bands that played arranged music.

Herndon, Eugene Angelo Braxton: Born in Wyoming, Ohio, in 1913, Herndon latched onto Communism as a young adult. In 1930, he was arrested under Georgia's insurrection law for trying to organize workers at a mine. At this time he formally joined the party and became the chief organizer for an Unemployed Council's demonstration in Atlanta on June 30, 1932. He was arrested eleven days later. The Communist Party's International Labor Defense (ILD) made his case nationally known; five years later, after two appeals to the U.S. Supreme Court, the conviction was overturned on the grounds that the Georgia insurrection law violated the Fourteenth Amendment to the Constitution.

Herskovits, Melville J. (1895–1963): A well-known and controversial anthropologist, Herskovits argued early in his career that if any cultural differences existed between Harlem blacks and the white culture surrounding them, it was "merely a remnant from the peasant days in the South. *Of the African culture, not a trace.*" But the work for which he is most noted, *The Myth of the Negro Past* (1941), radically revised these conclusions.

Hickory House: A jazz club located on 52nd Street in Harlem.

Hines, Earl "Fatha" (1903–1983): Hines played piano in Chicago clubs in the 1920s, first as a soloist and later as a bandleader. Known for his great technique and talent for improvisation, his horn-like phrasing and rhythm influenced popular jazz through the Swing Era and into be-bop.

Hit Parade: After it debuted on April 20, 1935, *Your Hit Parade* went on to become one of the longest running shows in radio history; in 1950, it made the transition to television.

Hoefer, George: Writer for *Down Beat*, a jazz-focused music magazine.

Hoffman, Clare Eugene (1875–1967): U.S. Representative from Michigan from 1935 to 1963. In 1941, Hoffman demanded the impeachment of President Roosevelt for leading the country into war by "deception." On January 27, 1942, he delivered an address entitled, "Don't Haul Down the Stars and Stripes, or Roosevelt Is a Judas."

Holiday, Billie (1915–1959): Born Eleanora Fagan Cough, Billie Holiday took the stage name from film star Billie Dove. Assisted by Benny Goodman in her first recording session in 1933, Holiday went on to record over two hundred cuts of jazz and swing music over the next eleven years. However by the mid-1940s, she was addicted to heroin and died prematurely in July 1959.

Honolulu Star-Bulletin: The oldest and largest circulating daily in Hawaii, the *Star-Bulletin* was founded in 1912 with the merger of the *Bulletin* and *Star*. The *Star-Bulletin* played a major role in demanding better education for all citizens and equal rights, eventually leading to statehood for Hawaii.

Hottentots: A tribe from southern Africa; however, today, "Khoisan" is the appropriate term, as "Hottentot" is considered pejorative.

Howard Newspaper: Davis is probably referring to the tabloid paper *News*. Jack Howard was the New York-based editor for Scripps-Howard, the newspaper conglomerate that had acquired the *News* in 1926.

Howard University: One of the premiere institutions of higher education for African Americans. Located in Washington, D.C., its motto is "the capstone of Negro education."

Hughes, Langston (1902–1967): Hughes was one of the most important writers and thinkers of the New Negro Renaissance. Through his poetry, novels, plays, essays, and children's books, he helped shape American literature and even politics. Although *The First Book of Jazz* is intended as an introduction to this musical genre, his expertise in jazz was admirably demonstrated in his collection of poems entitled *Ask Your Mama.*

Hull, Cordell (1871–1955): Hull was elected to Congress from the Fourth Tennessee District in 1907 and served as a U.S. Representative until 1931, interrupted only by two years as chairman of the Democratic National Committee. He soon became a recognized expert in commercial and fiscal policies. Elected U.S. Senator for the 1931–1937 term, he resigned upon his appointment as secretary of state by President Franklin D. Roosevelt on March 4, 1933.

International Longshoremen's and Warehousemen's Union (ILWU): The International Longshoremen and Warehousemen's Union came about largely through the efforts of its first president, Harry Bridges. Charters were issued to longshoremen in Hawaii and the ILWU became dedicated to the idea of democratic unionism. The union's activism earned it a subversive designation by the FBI and other government agencies charged with ferreting out Communism in the late forties and early fifties.

James, Etta: Born Jamesette Hawkins in Los Angeles in 1938, she has been described as the greatest of all modern blues singers, the undisputed Earth Mother. Her raw, unharnessed vocals and hot-blooded eroticism has made disciples of singers ranging from Janis Joplin to Bonnie Raitt.

Johnson, Otis (b. 1910): A trumpeter, Johnson performed with many greats such as Luis Russell (1929–1930), Benny Carter, Don Redman (1936–1937), and Louis Armstrong (1938–1939).

Julius Rosenwald Fellowship: The Rosenwald Fund was created by Julius Rosenwald, founder and president of Sears, Roebuck and Company. The Fund awarded fellowships for social, educational, and cultural purposes, without regard for race, creed, and nationality.

Juneteenth: One of the oldest celebrations commemorating the end of slavery. Oral history says that the word about "freedom" came late to Texas, about June 19, 1865. Thus the name "Juneteenth." This unofficial holiday is also celebrated as Emancipation Day.

Kamp, Joseph, Lawrence Dennis, the *Awakener*: Of the myriad antidemocratic agencies that sprang up in the United States following the advent of Nazism in Germany, few carried on more widespread and intensive propaganda activities than the Constitutional Educational League. According to the League's director, Joseph P. Kamp, his organization disposed of 2,200,000 copies of a single booklet entitled *Join the CIO—and help get a SOVIET AMERICA*. Much of the league's literature was written by Kamp himself. Kamp was formerly the editor and publisher of a pro-fascist magazine called the *Awakener*, which included on its editorial board Lawrence Dennis, author of the book, *The Coming American Fascism*. In July 1942, Kamp's Constitutional Educational League was named in a federal indictment as an agency which had been used in a conspiracy to "impair and influence the loyalty, morale and discipline of the military and naval forces of the United States."

Kanaka: A slang term for native Hawaiians, taken from *kanaka maoli*, the name of the original inhabitants of the Hawaiian islands.

Kaneohe: City just north of Honolulu.

Keckley, Elizabeth (1818–1907): A close friend of Mary Todd Lincoln, Keckley worked in the White House as the First Lady's dressmaker and personal maid from 1861 to 1865. After President Lincoln's assassination, her book, *Behind the Scenes; or, Thirty Years a Slave, and Four Years in the White House*, was considered a betrayal by Mrs. Lincoln, who broke off her relationship with Keckley.

Keppard, Freddie (1890–1933): An important musician who succeeded Buddy Bolden as "king" of the cornet players in New Orleans. Like so many New Orleans musicians, he settled in Chicago in the early 1920s and worked with several bands in the city including those of Erskine Tate and Ollie Powers. He also worked with Charles Elgar's Creole Orchestra at the Savoy Ballroom.

Knight, Marie (b. 1925): Knight enjoyed a varied career as a gospel, pop-soul, jump-blues, and doo wop-flavored R&B singer.

Knox, William Franklin (1874–1944): In the summer of 1940, Knox was named Secretary of the Navy, as one of two Republicans appointed by President Roosevelt in an effort to form a coalition cabinet. Charged with creating a strong two-ocean navy, he was instrumental in making the U.S. fleet the most powerful in history.

Kona Inn: Built in 1928 by the Inter-Island Steam Navigation Company, Kona Inn offered wealthy residents the amenities of a country club with its saltwater swimming pool, tennis courts, and cocktail lounge.

Laine, Jack (1873–1966): Jack "Papa" Laine is often credited with being the first white jazz musician. A drummer and saxophonist, Laine formed a brass band in 1888 and performed ragtime and marching music. He went on to lead the Reliance Brass Band, which at one time or another, featured many early New Orleans white jazz musicians including members of the Original Dixieland Jazz Band.

LaRocca, Nick (1889–1961): Nick LaRocca claimed to have invented jazz and often complained that African American musicians had been given too much credit for its birth. Because of his complaints, many people tend to overlook the important contributions he made to music and the role of the Original Dixieland Jass Band in popularizing jazz around the world.

LaSalle Street: Location of the Chicago Stock Exchange.

Lausche, Mayor Frank J. (1895–1990): Governor Lausche made political history in Ohio by becoming the first four-term governor in Ohio's 150 years of statehood. Elected with a total vote of 2,019,029, he was the first Ohioan ever to receive as many as two million votes for any office in the state.

Lee, George (1896–1958): In 1927, George E. Lee's Novelty Singing Orchestra was first recorded by the Winston Holmes Music Company's Merrit label. Lee's showmanship gave them an edge over their Kansas City rival, Bennie Moten's band, and in 1929, the Brunswick label recorded the band's major hits "If I Could Be with You" and "Paseo Street." During 1933–1934, the Bennie Moten and George Lee bands were briefly merged.

Lencock's classical fiction: Davis is referring to Canadian humorist Stephen Leacock's 1911 book, *Nonsense Novels*. The quote is as follows: "Lord Ronald said nothing; he flung himself from the room, flung himself upon his horse and rode madly off in all directions."

Lenox Avenue: Street in Harlem which was home to jazz clubs, including The Savoy and The Cotton Club.

Lewis, George (1900–1968): George Lewis probably did more to keep New Orleans jazz going during the 1940s and 1950s than anyone else. His "temporary emergency musicians," as Bunk Johnson labeled them, made many classic recordings which enabled Johnson to take New York by storm and enjoy several years of relative fame after a lifetime of neglect. A 1950 *Look* magazine article described him as one of the most popular figures of the Dixieland revival of the 1950s and 1960s.

***Lloyd Gaines* Decision**: In 1935, Lloyd Gaines, an African American, graduated from Lincoln University in Missouri and was refused admission to the law school at the University of Missouri. The Missouri Supreme

Court upheld the position that it was lawful for the state to deny black residents the legal education provided by the state and to require them to obtain a comparable education at Missouri's expense in an adjacent state. In *Gaines v. Missouri*, decided on December 12, 1938, the U.S. Supreme Court overturned the lower court's decision on the grounds that sending black students to another state was a denial of their equal protection under the law and that payment of their out-of-state tuition did not remove the discrimination.

Locke, Alain (1886–1954): In 1925, Locke published *The New Negro*, an anthology of writings by various African American authors which catapulted him into national prominence as a spokesperson for the New Negro Renaissance. Although he was known for his leadership of this cultural movement, he was also a leading figure in the adult education movement of the 1930s. Locke's degrees were from Harvard, and he was the first African American Rhodes Scholar, in 1907.

L'Ouverture, Toussaint (c. 1744–1803): Born in Saint Dominique (later to be known as Haiti), Toussaint became the leader of a slave rebellion when the French revolutionaries retracted their promise to free slaves. Henceforth known as Toussaint L'Ouverture ("the one who finds an opening"), he successfully led his rag-tag army against the French, prompting the end of slavery in the French colonies. However, Napoleon soon came to power and reinstated slavery, once again plunging Haiti into war. In 1803, Napoleon agreed to recognize Haitian independence and Toussaint agreed to retire from public life. However, when Toussaint arrived for a meeting, Napolean arrested and placed him in a prison dungeon where he soon faced starvation and death. Later, Napoleon abandoned Haiti and sold the French territory in North America to the United States in the Louisiana Purchase.

"Lovely Hula Hands": Song written by R. Alex Anderson. Watching a hula dancer at a party, the composer heard someone say "Aren't her hands lovely." This was the inspiration for his most popular composition, written in 1939 and later identified with hula artist, Aggie Auld.

Luce, Henry R. (1898–1967): Editor in chief of Time Inc. publications, including *Time, Fortune, Life,* and *Sports Illustrated.* Luce was a pioneer whose contributions to journalism extended far beyond business reporting. He aimed to correct what he saw as woeful business reporting: an honest analysis of business was regarded as vulgar or communistic or both.

Lunceford, Jimmy (1902–1947): Unlike many big bands of the 1930s, Lunceford's group was noted less for its soloists than for its ensemble work. This and its practiced showmanship were widely imitated by other groups, but the groups seldom achieved the polish and good humor that marked so many of Lunceford's performances.

Mabon, Willie (1925–1985): Self-taught pianist and blues styled vocalist Willie Mabon signed with Chess Records in 1950. Beginning with "I Don't Know," he had several hits over the next few years including "I'm Mad," "Poison Ivy," and "Seventh Son."

MacGowan, Charles J.: Charles J. MacGowan became vice president of the International Brotherhood of Boilermakers in 1936. He became international president in 1944 and retired in 1954.

Marcantonio, Vito (1902–1954): Radical left-wing activist and congressman, Marcantonio was an active member of the Republican Party and was elected to Congress in 1935 from East Harlem's Twentieth District. An outspoken politician, Marcantonio was not re-selected as a candidate for the next election. In 1938, however, he stood as an American Labor Party (ALP) candidate, won his seat back, and maintained an open relationship with the Communist Party which he insisted worked for the best interests of the American working class. He served as legal counsel for Communist and civil rights activist W. E. B. Du Bois and collaborated with Paul Robeson. In Congress he was one of the strongest opponents of Senator Joseph McCarthy and the House Un-American Activities Committee (HUAC).

Marsala, Joe (1907–1978): Marsala was one of the first band leaders to form a racially mixed band which included Henry "Red" Allen. During the 1940s, Marsala's big bands included not only Swing Era veterans, but also younger musicians making the transition to be-bop and mainstream jazz.

Martin, Joseph William, Jr. (1884–1968): A representative from Massachusetts, Martin was elected as a Republican to the Sixty-ninth and to the twenty succeeding Congresses (1925–1967). Although he served as chairman on various committees, he was an unsuccessful candidate for renomination in 1966.

May, Andrew Jackson (1875–1959): A representative from Kentucky, May was elected to the Seventy-second and to seven succeeding Congresses (March 1931–1947).

McCormick-Patterson newspaper: The *Tribune* was owned by the joint alliance of cousins Robert McCormick and Joseph Patterson.

Miller, Paul Edward: Author of *Down Beat's Yearbook of Swing*.

Millinder, Lucky (Lucius Venable) (1900–1966): Millinder's band, formed in 1940, was partly responsible for the popularization of rhythm and blues. Although unable to read music, Millinder was an exceptional conductor, and composed many of his band's hits, including "Ride, Red, Ride" which he wrote in collaboration with Irving Mills.

Monk, Thelonius (1917–1982): Although a major contributor to the new style called bop, Monk's unusual technique led many to believe he was an inferior pianist. His compositions were so advanced that the lazier be-bop players (although not Dizzy Gillespie and Charlie Parker) assumed that he was crazy. However, his recording of a more accessible music and the 1956 album *Brilliant Corners* led jazz critics and the public to acknowledge and celebrate his greatness.

Morse, Ella Mae (1924–1999): Ella Mae Morse got her big break with the Jimmy Dorsey Orchestra when she was a teenager. Her hit "Cow Cow Boogie" led a list of records that sold well throughout her career, although she never found a large following.

Morton, Benny (1907–1985): Called by one jazz historian as "one of the most sophisticated trombonists of the Swing Era," Morton worked with many greats of the day, including Fletcher Henderson, Don Redman, and Count Basie.

Moten, Bennie (1894–1935): With the help of the Blue Devils, whom he recruited in the late twenties, Moten established and defined Kansas City jazz style. In 1932, he recorded "Moten's Swing," one of the first recordings to use a riff, the foundation of Kansas City jazz. The following year, Moten merged with George E. Lee, completing the formation of his fifteen-piece orchestra.

Murray, Phil: Murray was a coal miner from Pennsylvania who rose to high distinction in the American labor movement. During his lifetime he served as vice president of the United Mine Workers of America (UMWA), president of the United Steelworkers of America (USWA), and president of the CIO.

Musso, Vido (William) (1913–1982): Tenor saxophonist Musso was known for his exuberant and uncomplicated improvisations and gruff and aggressive style which made him extremely popular.

Myrdal, Gunnar (1898–1987): In 1938, the Carnegie Corporation of New York commissioned Gunnar Myrdal to direct a study of the problems faced by American Negroes. The material which he collected and interpreted was published in 1944 as *An American Dilemma: The Negro Problem and Modern Democracy.*

National Alliance of Postal Employees: Since the Railway Mail Association excluded blacks from its membership, black workers did not have the benefit of an industrial organization to appeal to for their defense. In October 1913, black employees convened in Chattanooga, Tennessee, to combat the discrimination they were encountering, and thus was born the National Alliance of Postal Employees. The major concerns were to provide a beneficiary department and an insurance department to enable black railway clerks to make suitable provisions for their families, to launch a national journal dedicated to the interests of black railway mail clerks, and to establish means to present their grievances and petitions to the Post Office Department effectively.

National Association for the Advancement of Colored People (NAACP): The NAACP was created in 1909 out of the foundation laid by the Niagara Movement, an organization of black and white intellectuals fighting for political, civil, and social rights for black Americans, under the leadership especially of W. E. B. Du Bois.

National Negro Congress: Organized in 1936, the National Negro Congress elected A. Philip Randolph as president and John R. Davis as executive secretary. A national coalition of church, labor, and civil rights organizations that would coordinate protest action in the face of deteriorating economic conditions for blacks, it was independent of the Communist Party but not unfriendly to it. The association of the group's founders with the Communist Party and the NNC's attempts to unite black labor organizations brought it under FBI surveillance from the 1930s through the 1950s.

Nelson, "Big Eye" Louis (1902–1990): Nelson was active in the New Orleans jazz scene of the 1920s, working with Kid Rena, the Original Tuxedo Orchestra, and Sidney Desvigne's big band. He was also closely associated with Kid Thomas Valentine and George Lewis.

Nixon case: In 1938, Richard Wright became deeply interested in the Robert Nixon case, involving an eighteen-year-old black man accused of murdering a white woman. He fictionalized details from this case for his novel *Native Son* (1940).

Noone, Jimmy (1895–1944): Considered one of the best clarinetists of the 1920s, Noone was a major influence on the swing music of the 1930s and 1940s. His style differed from the other great clarinet players, Johnny Dodds and Sidney Bechet, because of his smoother, more romantic tone.

Nye, Gerald (1892–1971): The Nye Committee (1934–1936), headed by U.S. Senator Gerald Nye (R-ND), investigated and exposed the role of U.S. banks and corporations in financing World War I and in supporting the Allies even before the U.S. became formally involved; their findings deepened public opinion against further involvement in European conflicts.

Okeh Records: Okeh began its music history in 1918 in New York. Two years later, it launched the first black music recording with the release of Mamie Smith's "Crazy Blues," a song that propelled the blues into instant popularity.

Oliver, King (1885–1938): Critics considered cornetist Joe "King" Oliver the biggest single influence on jazz until Louis Armstrong's ascendancy. Armstrong, his greatest disciple, referred to Oliver as "Papa Joe." He maintained that "had it not been for Joe Oliver, jazz would not be what it is today," and called him the strongest and most creative cornetist to play the horn.

Opportunity Magazine: The official journal of the National Urban League. Founded by Dr. Charles S. Johnson (1893–1956) in 1923, it played a crucial role in launching the New Negro Renaissance. In addition to exploring such phenomena as the Great Migration, its cultural mission was to bring younger black writers before the public.

Original Dixieland Jazz Band: The Original Dixieland Jazz Band, who billed themselves the originators of jazz, have long been dismissed as the white guys who copied African American music, "sweetened" it, and called it their own. They released the world's first jazz record on February 26, 1917. "Livery Stable Blues" coupled with "Dixie Jass Band One Step" signaled the commodification of jazz and the beginning of the wild, exuberant era known as the Roaring Twenties.

Parker, Charlie (1920–1955): In his short turbulent career, Charles Christopher "Yardbird" Parker became recognized as one of the most creative musicians in the history of jazz. Although he played basic chords and harmonies with the other musicians, Parker began to experiment with higher intervals of chords to produce the tunes that filled his imagination.

This sound, which became known as be-bop, took form in the 1940s and became the trademark that separated African American musicians from other swing bands.

Paul, Randolph: A lawyer, Paul was general counsel for the Treasury Department, acting secretary in charge of foreign funds control, and later, special assistant to President Truman.

Pearson, Drew: In 1932, journalists Pearson and Robert Allen launched a syndicated column called "The Washington Merry-Go-Round" (the two had co-authored a book by the same name). The column (which Allen left in 1942) became notorious for its muckraking and incurred the wrath of several presidents. An outspoken and influential critic of many leading political figures, notably Senator Joseph McCarthy, Pearson's allegations against Thomas Dodd prompted the formation of the Senate Ethics Committee.

Pegler, James Westbrook: Westbrook Pegler was among the top three columnists of his day (the others were Drew Pearson and Walter Winchell). Very outspoken and often controversial, he openly expressed right-wing views.

Pickens, Dean William (1881–1954): Pickens worked with the National Association for the Advancement of Colored People. His essays, editorials, manuscripts, clippings, and lectures cover a variety of subjects including Marcus Garvey, the Ku Klux Klan, lynching, and the Scottsboro Case. He served as dean of Morgan College from 1918 to 1919, a title that essentially became his given name.

Powell, A. Clayton (1865–1953): Clergyman and author, Rev. Powell was one of the most famous African American churchmen of his time. A charismatic preacher belonging to the Abyssinian Baptist Church, Powell was actively involved in the struggle against racism, and lectured on race relations at Colgate University, City College of New York, and Union Theological Seminary. His son, Adam Clayton Powell, Jr., later succeeded him and used the pulpit to get elected to the U.S. House of Representatives.

Pupule, J. Akuhead (1917–1983): Until his death in 1983, the disc jockey Hal "Aku" Lewis was a radio fixture for thirty-six years, most of that time as the most talked-about and most listened-to broadcaster in Hawaii on station KOU. He spun controversy as often as he spun records, chiding his listeners all the time. Lewis was reported to be the world's highest paid disc jockey, bringing in six thousand dollars per week when he died at age sixty-six.

Ragas, Henry (1890–1919): After working as a solo pianist from 1910 to 1913, he joined Johnny Stein's band and moved with it to Chicago in 1916. A few months later, Ragas, Nick LaRocca, and Eddie Edwards left Stein to form the Original Dixieland Jass band. Ragas composed "Bluin' the Blues" which was recorded by the band in 1918.

Rainey, Glenn W.: Rainey, an alumnus of Emory University, was a professor of English at the Georgia Institute of Technology in Atlanta from 1932 until 1974, and was involved in many political, social, civic, and professional organizations, including the Georgia Commission on Interracial Cooperation, the Committee for Georgia of the Southern Conference for Human Welfare, and the Southern Regional Council.

Rainey, Gertrude "Ma" (1886–1939): Along with Bessie Smith, Ma Rainey is regarded the best of the 1920s classic blues singers. In his *Livin' the Blues*, Davis describes her this way: "She commanded a big, deep, fat-meat-and-greens voice, rich as pure chocolate, and her words told of common group experiences. It was like everybody shaking out his heart. Way, way low down it was and hurting good."

Randolph, A. Philip (1889–1979): Asa Philip Randolph's attitude toward labor unions, his antiwar stand, and a political position aimed at economic change reflected his socialist ideas. With a firm belief in a movement based on workers as the main force, he was committed to the idea that a democratic redistribution of wealth was the first step toward greater freedom for all, whether black or white.

Rankin, John Elliott (1882–1960): Rankin of Mississippi served in the U.S. House of Representatives from 1921 to 1953. A committed segregationist and states' rights advocate, he often used unfounded conspiracy theories to attack racial integration.

Redman, Don (1900–1964): Known as the "the Little Giant," Redman was an orchestra leader, arranger and saxophonist. One of the architects of early big band music, his band was among the great black jazz organizations of the 1930s.

Reuss, Allen (b. 1915): Reuss was an excellent big-band rhythm guitarist and was known for his sophisticated chordal melodies, which are often compared with those of his mentor Van Eps.

Reynolds, Robert Rice (1884–1963): After visiting Europe late in 1938, Senator Reynolds made comments that convinced many that he was actually pro-Nazi. In his second term as senator, Reynolds broke with the New Deal and became identified with isolationism, ethnocentrism, and fascism. As a genuine isolationist, Reynolds broke with Roosevelt over foreign policy in 1939.

Rivers, Governor (1895–1967): Politician Eurith Dickinson "Ed" Rivers was elected to the Georgia House of Representatives in 1924. In 1936, Rivers was elected governor over Eugene Talmadge, with Rivers running on a platform of support for and involvement in the New Deal, calling his program Georgia's "Little New Deal." Under his leadership, Georgia invested heavily in New Deal Programs, with spending increasing from a hundred thousand to one million dollars in his first term alone.

Robinson, J. Russell (1892–1963): Russell performed as pianist with the New Orleans Jazz Band in Chicago in 1918 and with the Original Dixieland Jazz band in New York in 1919 and London, England. He was also part of the revived Original Dixieland Jazz band of 1936.

Rogers, William Vann, Jr. (1911–1993): A representative from California, Rogers was elected as a Democrat to the Seventy-eighth Congress and served from January 1943 till his resignation in May 1944 to return to the United States Army. He later became a writer, active in radio and television programs.

Ross, Malcolm: Chairman of the Fair Employment Practice Committee. In his book *Take Your Choice: Separation or Mongrelization*, Theodore G. Bilbo wrote that "the white people who have battled against barriers of prejudice on behalf of the Negro include Malcolm Ross, Chairman of the Fair Employment Practice Committee . . . and Eleanor Roosevelt and Wendell Willkie. These eleven men and women have, in their own ways, aided in the campaign for racial equality in the United States. . . . Without a single exception, they are professional anti-Southerners. They are the people who would destroy the civilization of the South, and set up in its stead a mongrelized people."

Ruggles, David (1810–1849): Ruggles became America's first African American bookseller when he opened a bookstore in New York near Broadway in 1834. Author of several antislavery pamphlets including *Extinguisher, Extinguished* (1834) and *Abrogation of the Seventh Commandment by the*

American Churches (1835), Ruggles worked as a conductor on the Underground Railroad (1835–1838) and was among those who helped Frederick Douglass when he arrived in New York.

Sbarbaro, Tony (1897–1969): In 1916, Sbarbaro joined the Original Dixieland Jazz band as drummer and was the only original member of the group to remain with it until its final dissolution in 1956. His showy technique and exuberant improvisatory style are rooted in the ragtime playing of such drummers as James Lent, Buddy Gilmour, and John Lucas.

Schuyler, George S. (1895–1977): An ultraconservative African American writer and often sardonic satirist, Schuyler wrote for the *Pittsburg Courier* from 1944 to 1964. In addition to his newspaper work, he distinguished himself by writing *Black No More* (1931), *Slaves Today: A Story of Liberia* (1931), and an autobiography, *Black and Conservative* (1966). During World War II, Schuyler criticized President Franklin D. Roosevelt for arguing that the United States was fighting for freedom and democracy, pointing out that Adolf Hitler and the Nazi Party had been profoundly influenced by the racial policies of the Deep South.

Scott, Raymond (1908–1994): Raymond Scott is best remembered for his eccentric compositions in the late 1930s. In 1936 CBS granted him his own band: a six-piece "quintet." His quirky, screwy, pseudo-jazz numbers quickly became popular with the public.

Shaw, Artie (1910–2004): Bandleader, composer, and arranger, Artie Shaw was a leading Swing Era figure and top-flight clarinetist who demonstrated a great jazz facility when playing either up tempo numbers or ballads. Along with rival Benny Goodman, he was known for racially integrating his bands in the 1940s, utilizing the talents of Billie Holliday and Roy Eldridge, among others.

Shields, Larry (1893–1953): Clarinetist for the Original Dixieland Jazz Band.

Smith, Bessie (1894–1937): Known as the "Empress of the Blues," Smith was one of the most successful female blues singers of the 1920s with her impeccable rhythmic sense and ability to improvise around the structural confines of the blues. Throughout this decade, she recorded with many of the great jazz musicians of that era, including Fletcher Henderson and Louis Armstrong.

Smith, Clarence "Pine Top" (1904–1929): Born in Alabama, Clarence "Pine Top" Smith is often considered to be the founder of the boogie-woogie style of playing the piano.

Smith, Ellison D. "Cotton Ed" (1864–1944): In 1908, Smith won a seat in the U.S. Senate from South Carolina where he remained for the next three and a half decades. He often remarked that civilization rested on white supremacy, but day-to-day life depended on cotton agriculture. As he defined it, the job of a southern senator was to defend states' rights and make sure that the federal government stayed out of southern affairs.

Smith, Gerald Lyman Kenneth (1898–1976): A national spokesman for isolationism and anti-Semitism, Smith reached an audience of millions in the guise of a Christian crusader for national supremacy with his organizational and oratorical skills. He carried on a lifelong campaign for an isolationist America, to be led exclusively by evangelical Christians.

Smith, Lillian E. (1897–1966): American writer and champion of racial equality, who is best known for *Strange Fruit* (1944), a controversial novel dealing with the tragic outcome of an interracial love affair in the Deep South. With Paula Snelling, she edited *Pseudopodia* (1936), which became the *North Georgia Review* (1937–41), which, in turn, became *South Today* (1942–45). Her active support of the Civil Rights Movement evoked racist anger: her papers were destroyed by arson in 1955. Two novella manuscripts were lost; *One Hour* (1959) was her only published novel other than *Strange Fruit*. Her nonfiction books include *Killers of the Dream* (1949), *The Journey* (1954), *Now Is the Time* (1955) and *Our Faces, Our Words* (1964).

Smith, Mamie (1883–1946): Mamie Smith was the first artist to record blues songs with her version of Perry Bradford's "Crazy Blues" (1920). Bradford had to convince Okeh Records of its viability. Okeh's daring was rewarded because estimates indicate this one song sold over a million copies.

Smith, Trixie (1895–1943): Smith is best remembered today for the excellent jazz bands that accompanied her on her records, notably Fletcher Henderson and his orchestra. When her career as a blues singer waned, Smith returned to her theatrical roots and worked in musical revues, Broadway shows, and film.

South Side: Chicago is famous for its division between North and South, both in the city and in the suburbs. The North is known for money and class; the south, where most African Americans were concentrated, for poverty and decay.

Stimson, Henry Lewis (1867–1950): Although a Republican, Stimson was chosen by President Roosevelt as Secretary of War (1940–1945). In order to carry forward strong measures, Stimson had urged aid to Great Britain.

He supervised the mobilization and training of the U.S. armed forces and general war operations throughout World War II. Serving as chief presidential advisor on atomic policy, he made the ultimate recommendation to President Harry S. Truman to drop the atomic bomb on Japanese cities of military importance.

Story Magazine: Founded in 1931 by Martha Foley and Whit Burnett, the magazine would publish original works for a fee of twenty-five dollars. It proved to be a launching pad for many emerging writers, including Richard Wright, Norman Mailer, Truman Capote, and J. D. Salinger.

Sweatman, Wilbur (1881–1961): Sweatman is remembered less as a jazz musician and more as a great showman famous for playing two then three clarinets at once. He released dozens of records in the 1910s and 1920s, the most famous being "Down Home Rag."

Taber, John (1880–1965): A Republican Representative from New York, Taber was elected to Congress in March 1923 and successively after that until January 1963.

Taft, Robert (1889–1953): Taft was commonly referred to as "Mr. Republican" and "Mr. Conservative." He was most famous for his opposition to Franklin Delano Roosevelt's New Deal policies and for co-sponsoring the Taft-Hartley Labor Relations Act of 1947.

Talmadge, Herman Eugene (1913–2001): Former governor and U.S. senator who directed Georgia's most potent political machine for more than thirty years, Talmadge skillfully rode the tide of southern racial politics, evolving from a staunch segregationist to a powerful committee chairman who championed economic development in appealing to both black and white voters. He served six years as governor and twenty-four years in the Senate.

Tharpe, Rosetta (1915–1973): Sister Rosetta Tharpe was an active singer of gospel and folk music in the 1930s and 1940s. Later, she performed with such jazz artists as Cab Calloway, Lucky Millinder, and the Chris Barber Jazz Band.

Thornton, "Big Mama" (1926–1984): Willie Mae "Big Mama" Thornton is best remembered as the first artist to record "Hound Dog," the song Elvis Presley made into a million-selling rock and roll hit in 1956.

Till, Emmett: On August 27, 1955, fourteen-year-old Emmett Till was beaten and shot to death by two white men who threw the boy's mutilated body into the Tallahatchie River near Money, Mississippi. Till was murdered because he talked to and perhaps even whistled at a white woman at a local grocery store. Against the instructions of the coroner, his mother held an "open casket" funeral, enabling, as she said, all the world to see what had happened to her son. *Jet Magazine* published a picture of his brutalized body, thus jump-starting, along with Rosa Parks's refusal to give up her bus seat, the modern day civil rights movement.

Tin Pan Alley: A nickname for the popular songwriting and sheet music publishing district centered in New York from the 1890s until the 1940s. The term came to be applied to the general type of song purveyed by the industry. Suggesting the tinny sound of the overworked upright pianos used by songwriters, the term evolved into a pejorative description of commercialized and thus cheaply made music.

Townsend, Willard (b. 1895): U.S. Representative from Illinois. Served in Congress from 1940 to 1948.

Turner, Big Joe (1911–1985): One of the best blues shouters and a critical link between rhythm and blues and rock and roll. He was blessed with a big husky voice that he projected with amazing power and clarity. After successfully helping to kick off the boogie-woogie craze that swept the country in the late 1930s and early 1940s, Turner made the transition to rhythm and blues with remarkable ease. His most famous hit, "Shake, Rattle and Roll," released in 1954, made it to number one on the hit charts; a subsequent recording by Bill Haley and the Comets played to a wider audience and overshadowed Turner's popularity.

Vendome Theatre: Located at 3145 South State Street in Chicago, the Vendome hosted, among others, Louis Armstrong, Erskine Tate and the Vendome Theater Symphony Orchestra, Earl Hines, Fats Waller, and Clarence Jones.

Wagner, Robert F., Sr. (1877–1953): Wagner served in the U.S. Senate from 1927 to 1949 and was author of the landmark National Labor Relations Act (1935) and a prime sponsor of the Social Security Act.

Walker, Margaret (1915–1998): Walker's *For My People* (1942) won the Yale University Younger Poet's Award the year it was published. Decades later, she would finally publish her impressive novel of the Civil War, *Jubilee* (1966). In the late 1930s, she participated in the acclaimed South Side Writers' Group, where she met, among others, fictionist Richard Wright. She recounts their conflicted relationship in her bio-critical study *Richard*

Wright, Daemonic Genius: A Portrait of the Man, a Critical Look at His Work (1988), a work many consider jaded.

Wallace, Beulah "Sippie" (1898–1986): Married to Matt Wallace in 1917, Beulah "Sippie" Thomas was unique among the classic blues singers in that she wrote a great deal of her own material, often with her brothers supplying the music.

Wallace, Henry Agard (1888–1965): Wallace was elected vice president of the United States in 1940 during Roosevelt's third term in office. A speech made by Wallace on September 12, 1946, attacking the administration's firm policy toward the Soviet Union led to his resignation by presidential request. In 1948, Wallace became presidential candidate of the Progressive Party, a newly organized third party with a pro-Soviet platform attacking the Marshall Plan and calling for disarmament. His motto, "This is the century of the common man," concisely expressed his focus on labor rights, civil rights, and international human rights.

Waller, Thomas "Fats" (1904–1943): A stride pianist and pipe organist, Waller's rollicking style and sense of humor made him a popular star. His best-known compositions were "Ain't Misbehavin'," "Honeysuckle Rose," "Black and Blue," and "Jitterbug Waltz."

Webb, "Chick" (1909–1939): William Henry "Chick" Webb was universally admired by drummers for his forceful sense of swing, accurate technique, control of dynamics, and imaginative breaks and fills. Although unable to read music, he committed to memory the arrangements played by the band and directed performances from a raised platform in the center of the ensemble, giving cues with his drumming.

Webster, Milton P. (1887–1965): Webster fought throughout his career to end racial discrimination in organized labor in general and within the defense industry in particular. In 1925 Webster was the first international vice president of the Brotherhood of Sleeping Car Porters. During World War II, Webster challenged the Roosevelt Administration by promoting worker racial integration in the defense industry.

Weltfish, Gene (1902–1980): Weltfish was a proponent of racial equality along with her Communist affiliations and viewpoints. She is best known for her studies of Pawnee Indian culture, art theory, and race and prejudice, and her book *The Lost Universe* received wide acclaim.

Wheatley, Phillis (1753?–1784): Kidnapped from the Senegal-Gambia region when she was about seven years old, Wheatley grew to be one of the most well-known poets in America during her day. In 1773 thirty-nine of her poems were published as *Poems on Various Subjects, Religious and Moral*, her only book, and the first volume of poetry to be published by an African American.

Wheeler, Burton Kendall (1882–1975): A Democrat and U.S. Senator from Montana (1923—1947), Wheeler generally supported Roosevelt's New Deal, but he opposed the proposed judiciary reorganization bill in 1937 and was one of the leaders of the isolationist movement in the years immediately preceding the entry of the United States into World War II.

White, Josh (1914–1969): A controversial blues, folk, and spirituals singer, White's association with the political Left and his recorded songs about being black in the U.S. brought him to the attention of Congressional oversight committees seeking to ferret out communist influence following the Second World War. Especially provocative were the songs of angry protest on his album *Southern Exposure* (1941), with liner notes written by Richard Wright.

White, Walter (1893–1955): White was assistant secretary and then secretary of the NAACP from 1918 until his death. Also a writer, he authored two novels and three books of nonfiction, his most famous being *Rope and Faggot* (1929). His blond hair, blue eyes, and fair skin color enabled him to pass easily for a white man. He used this to his advantage to investigate more than forty lynchings and eight race riots.

Whiteman, Paul (1890–1967): The Paul Whiteman Orchestra rarely played real jazz. It offered listeners dance music and semi-classical works. Despite its wide commercial appeal, jazz critics almost universally disliked his music, branding it saccharine and watered down.

Willkie, Wendell (1892–1944): Willkie was defeated by Roosevelt in the 1940 presidential election. As a special envoy for Roosevelt, he embarked on a worldwide goodwill trip in which he reassured foreign nations of a swift, secure end to the war. In his enormously popular book *One World* (1943), he predicted a postwar coalition that included China, Russia, and possibly the Middle Eastern nations.

Wilson, Teddy (1912–1986): Teddy Wilson rivaled Art Tatum and Earl Hines as one of the most important pianists of the Swing Era. He broke racial barriers when Benny Goodman hired him as an arranger and pianist.

WPA Writers' Project: One of the Works Progress Administration programs created by President Roosevelt to give unemployed writers work during the Depression.

Yergan, Max (1892–1975): When African American Max Yergan went to South Africa in 1921, his mission was to establish African YMCAs throughout the country. In three short years he established twenty-four YMCA associations with a membership of over 2,000 and by 1931, the number of YMCA associations had climbed to forty with 3,250 members, over 2,000 Bible study groups, and 500 groups in various types of social service.

Young, James Osborne "Trummy" (1912–1984): An underrated but influential trombonist, Young worked with several leading musicians including Earl Hines, Jimmie Lunceford, and Louis Armstrong.

Young, Lester (1909–1959): Lester Young was a major influence in creating the musical atmosphere in which bop could flourish, a distinctive and revolutionary approach to jazz.

Young, Vicki: Young recorded "All Shook Up" in 1956, a year before Elvis Presley did, but her version was overshadowed by his. "Affair with a Stranger," "Honey Love," and "Tweedle Dee" are some of her other notable hits.

INDEX